Limited Conservatorships

Protecting Adults Living With Developmental Disabilities: A How-to Guide

by
Barbara Holian Mejía
Attorney at Law

Barbara Holian Mejía
barbara@barbaramejia.com

ISBN: 978-0-9847512-2-8
Printed in the United States of America

What others are saying about Limited Conservatorships--Protecting Adults Living with Developmental Disabilities: a How-to Guide

"The decision to file for conservatorship is difficult for any parent. This book helps parents once they make that difficult decision. It takes parents through the legal process, demystifies the paperwork, and contains links to stay informed today and tomorrow."

--Tammy Nunez, parent of an autistic child

'Ms. Mejia's workbook provides the information needed to understand the process of limited conservatorship, and the legal tools to accomplish this feat semi-independently (without paying a small fortune in legal fees!)."

--Joaquin Gonzalez, parent of autistic children

"Ms. Mejía's empowering workbook is a '**must-have**' guide for every family/caregiver looking to protect the quality of life for an adult with intellectual disabilities (without paying a small fortune in legal fees!)."

--Jeni-Leah Bullock, parent of an autistic child

"Without Barbara Mejía's book, I would have found the limited conservatorship process impossible."

--Eamon Winston, parent of an autistic child

"As a California licensed fiduciary, I believe this workbook will be an essential tool to help guide families through the legal process of a limited conservatorship. This book is detailed but easy to understand and follow. **Love the visual presentation and space for notes**. Barbara, thank you for sharing your expertise."

--Saundra Randazzo, Private Fiduciary
and Professional Conservator

"A comprehensive yet practical guide for parents, with or without an attorney, to navigate the judicial process established to protect children with developmental disabilities during their transition to adulthood. The workbook is a clear, straightforward, and explanatory guide that takes the reader through each step in the petition process to successful completion. An indispensable tool for parents."

Ron DeHoff, Attorney at Law
Conservatorship Practice

"This book easily guides the parents of a young adult with developmental disabilities through the legal maze of obtaining a Limited Conservatorship. It is easy to read, understand, and the step-by-step instructions make it an indispensable resource. I highly recommend Ms. Mejía's book."

Suzette S. Perry, Attorney at Law
Conservatorship Practice

Need Help?

Services to assist you in this Workbook process can be found on our website at http://www.barbaramejia.com including blogs, customized pleadings, and legal updates.

Disclaimer. This Workbook provides information and general advice about the law. It does not create an attorney-client relationship between the author and the reader. Every situation has unique issues, and the law and procedures change frequently. The reader is advised to seek the expert advice of a licensed attorney experienced in the area of conservatorships at the conclusion of this Workbook and at any time during the process, as questions arise.

This workbook is dedicated to my dad
Darwin K. Holian
from whom I inherited my entrepreneurial spirit
with love in service to others.
May he rest in peace.

Table of Contents

Chapter 1
How To Use This Workbook

Step-by-step guide

This Workbook is designed for parents, teachers, or friends of children living with developmental disabilities who are turning the age of 18, although the reader is addressed as the parent and the child is identified as "your child", for ease of reading. It is a step-by-step guide in preparing the paperwork to initiate a Limited Conservatorship of a child's person. Throughout the Workbook, Ms. Mejía guides the reader with her wealth of experience and knowledge to make difficult forms understandable.

The Workbook includes every form you will need to present your case before a court in the State of California. Most counties will allow individuals to represent themselves without a lawyer in the conservatorship court. When you have completed this Workbook, you will have a clearer understanding of the legal process and what you must do to satisfy the legal requirements of the California Probate Code.

The California Probate Code dictates the rules for how conservatorships are initiated and managed by the court.

When you must use a lawyer

Some counties require that you be represented by a lawyer. In that case, after going through the Workbook, you will be able to better assist your counsel in drafting and preparing your case. That should result in a more reasonable cost to you, the client.

The process

You may move as quickly or slowly through this Workbook as is necessary to meet your objective. You may work through this Workbook alone, or in a group of similarly-minded persons, or with your individual family members. Remember to take notes of your questions for a later consultation with a conservatorship lawyer.

Goal of completion

The goal is for you to prepare the way so that before your child reaches the age of 18, you will have an *Order* from the court with the necessary protections in place for a seamless transition for your child into adulthood. The process will take approximately 45 days from the date all the paperwork is completed and submitted to the court, so it is important to plan far enough in advance to meet your child's needs.

You may not be able to stand alone in the court setting, but you can keep your costs to a minimum with the tips Ms. Mejía offers in this Workbook. You will learn how to utilize your attorney's time in the most productive way possible to establish the plan for your future and the future of your loved one.

Preparing legal forms

Throughout the course of this Workbook, you will be asked to locate and insert text on certain legal forms. Completed forms are found in Appendix A to assist you in preparing the same forms which are available to you from your Superior Court Clerk and/or on the Internet. If you have a printed copy of this Workbook, you may mark on the forms in Appendix A, so you are prepared to transfer the information to blank forms as you go through the Workbook exercises. If you have an electronic copy of this Workbook, you will want to print blank forms from the Internet as you proceed through the exercises.

Forms can be found on the Internet at the Judicial Council of California's website: www.courts.gov/forms.htm where you will request all forms for Guardianships and Conservatorships. Your county Superior Court's website will have all local court forms which are in addition to those on the Judicial Council's site. You can also find forms on Ms. Mejía's website: http://www.barbaramejia.com. Since all forms must be filed electronically, you will prepare the forms, print them, sign them, and then scan them as ".pdf" documents for submission to the court, retaining copies for yourself and the other attorneys and interested persons in your case. That will all be explained later in the Workbook.

County	Website
Alameda	http://www.alameda.courts.ca.gov/
Alpine	http://www.alpine.courts.ca.gov/
Amador	http://www.amadorcourt.org/
Butte	http://www.buttecourt.ca.gov/
Calaveras	http://www.calaveras.courts.ca.gov/
Contra Costa	http://www.cc-courts.org/
Del Norte	http://www.delnorte.courts.ca.gov/
El Dorado	http://www.eldoradocourt.org/
Fresno	http://www.fresno.courts.ca.gov/
Glenn	http://www.glenncourt.ca.gov/
Humboldt	http://www.humboldt.courts.ca.gov/
Imperial	http://www.imperial.courts.ca.gov/
Inyo	http://www.inyocourt.ca.gov/
Kern	http://www.kern.courts.ca.gov/
Kings	http://www.kings.courts.ca.gov/
Lake	http://www.lake.courts.ca.gov/
Lassen	http://www.lassencourt.ca.gov/

Los Angeles	http://www.lacourt.org/
Madera	http://madera.courts.ca.gov/
Marin	http://www.marincourt.org/
Mariposa	http://mariposacourt.org/
Mendocino	http://www.mendocino.courts.ca.gov/
Merced	http://www.mercedcourt.org/
Modoc	http://www.modocsuperiorcourt.ca.gov/
Mono	http://www.mono.courts.ca.gov/
Monterey	http://www.monterey.courts.ca.gov/
Napa	http://www.napa.courts.ca.gov/
Nevada	http://www.nccourt.net/
Orange	http://www.occourts.org/
Placer	http://www.placer.courts.ca.gov/
Plumas	http://www.plumascourt.ca.gov/
Sacramento	http://www.saccourt.ca.gov/
San Benito	http://www.sanbenito.courts.ca.gov/
San Bernardino	http://www.sb.court.org/
San Diego	http://www.sdcourt.ca.gov/
San Francisco	http://www.sfsuperiorcourt.org/
San Joaquin	http://www.sjcourts.org/
San Luis Obispo	http://slo.courts.ca.gov/
San Mateo	http://www.sanmateocourt.org/

Santa Barbara	http://www.sbcourts.org/
Santa Clara	http://www.scscourt.org/
Santa Cruz	http://www.santacruzcourt.org/
Shasta	http://www.shastacourts.com/
Sierra	http://www.sierra.courts.ca.gov/
Siskiyou	http://www.siskiyou.courts.ca.gov/
Solano	http://www.solano.courts.ca.gov/
Sonoma	http://sonoma.courts.ca.gov/
Stanislaus	http://www.stanct.org/
Sutter	http://www.suttercourts.com/
Tehama	http://tehamacourt.ca.gov/
Trinity	http://trinity.courts.ca.gov/
Tulare	http://www.tularesuperiorcourt.ca.gov/
Toulumne	http://www.tuolumne.courts.ca.gov/
Ventura	http://www.ventura.courts.ca.gov/
Yolo	http://www.yolo.courts.ca.gov/
Yuba	http://www.yubacourts.org/

Exercise #1

1. The "Caption"

Each form requires information about the petitioner, the conservator(s), and the conservatee in the caption found at the top of each page 1. On each form type or print the information requested, following the examples shown on the completed forms in Appendix A. The caption looks like this:

GC-020

ATTORNEY OR PARTY WITHOUT ATTORNEY *(Name, State Bar number, and address)*: Frank and Mary Doe 1234 Any Street Monterey, CA 93940 TELEPHONE NO.: (831) 123-4567 FAX NO. *(Optional)*: (831) 123-4568 E-MAIL ADDRESS *(Optional)*: 2does@yahoo.com ATTORNEY FOR *(Name)*: In pro per	*FOR COURT USE ONLY*
SUPERIOR COURT OF CALIFORNIA, COUNTY OF MONTEREY STREET ADDRESS: 1200 Aguajito Road MAILING ADDRESS: 1200 Aguajito Road CITY AND ZIP CODE: Monterey, CA 93940 BRANCH NAME: Monterey	
☐ GUARDIANSHIP ☒ CONSERVATORSHIP OF THE ☒ PERSON ☐ ESTATE OF *(Name)*: JOHN DOE ☐ MINOR ☒ (PROPOSED) CONSERVATEE	
NOTICE OF HEARING - GUARDIANSHIP OR CONSERVATORSHIP	CASE NUMBER:

This notice is required by law.
This notice does not require you to appear in court, but you may attend the hearing if you wish.

Read the following definitions for each person identified in the caption.

a. The "Petitioner"

Notice the parties in the case are in ALL CAPS. That includes the petitioner, the proposed conservator(s), and the proposed conservatee.

The "petitioner" is the person who is submitting the paperwork to the court. As that is you, type or print your name, your address, and your telephone number whenever you are asked to provide the petitioner's information on the forms. When you are not represented by an attorney, you are **In pro**

per. Where the forms ask "Attorney for____", type or print "In pro per".

b. The "Conservator(s)"

The "conservator" is the person who will be the one with authority over your child's personal decisions. You may decide whom you want to serve as conservator in the exercise following Chapter 4. However, if you already know you are the person or persons who want to be in that fiduciary role, type or print your full name(s) on the forms where that information is requested. If there are two persons requesting appointment, each name must be complete in itself. Rather than "Mr. and Mrs. Frank Doe", or "Frank and Jane Doe", indicate both individuals as "Frank Doe and Jane Doe".

IMPORTANT: **Whatever name you provide on the forms is the way each individual must sign the documents. The names must be consistent on every form.**

> If the individual uses a middle initial, every time the name appears on the forms, it must include the individual's middle initial.

c. The "Conservatee"

The "conservatee" is your child. Type or print your child's name wherever you are asked to provide the name of the conservatee on the forms.

<u>Page 1 of every form</u>
Provide your child's full name in the box on every page 1 of the forms.

<u>Page 2 and following of every form</u>
On the top of each page after page 1 is a box for you to type the full name of your child. Type or print the name of your child in the box at the top of each page as shown on the completed forms in Appendix A.

> The same rule about consistency in your name on every form applies to your child's name. The name is in ALL CAPS, and if you use a middle initial or middle name, that must appear every time you mention the name.

2. Caption Identifiers

On the first page of every form, check the boxes before ☐ Person and ☐ Limited Conservatorship, as shown on the completed forms in Appendix A.

3. Case Number

When you e-file the forms at court, you will be given a case number. For now, leave that box blank. For any forms you e-file after the initial filing, you will need to type the case number on every page of your paperwork.

When you have completed these form-preparation tasks, you are ready to go on to Chapter 2, Legal Considerations, in the Workbook.

Chapter 2
Legal Considerations

Parental control vs. Legal authority

An individual living with a developmental disability is a person with a disability that:

(1) originated before the age of 18,
(2) is expected to continue indefinitely, and
(3) constitutes a substantial handicap.

Common disabilities include autism, developmental language delays, cerebral palsy, and epilepsy. These conditions create a dependency on others in order to live independently and productively. While these individuals are under the age of 18, those in the role of parent, which includes grandparents, guardians, and foster parents, can make decisions for the best interests of the individuals.

> When a child becomes an adult at age 18, the law imposes on every citizen rights and responsibilities, including individuals with developmental disabilities.

However, when a child becomes an adult, at age 18, the person in the parent role no longer has legal standing to act on behalf of the individual without legal authority. The parent may know what is best for the child, but the law limits the right of the parent to create the environment needed for the child's healthy development.

Who is a conservator?

The conservator has powers limited to those areas of weakness for the individual with a developmental disability.

In order to continue care and protection of an adult living with a developmental disability in California, an individual is appointed by the local Superior Court to serve as his or her conservator. When that person is appointed by the court, he or she is granted only those powers that are needed to properly assist the individual with developmental disabilities in the areas of his or her unique weaknesses. As a conservator, the person is accountable to the court for the decisions he or she makes in those specific areas, and those decisions are reviewed by the court on a regular basis. The conservator is generally responsible to make choices that will lead to self-reliance and independence for the person who is conserved.

A conservator's duties

The Judicial Council of California has produced the Handbook for Conservators which can be purchased from a clerk at the reader's local Superior Court or acquired online. It is required reading for anyone seeking to become a conservator. Chapter 3 of the Handbook is on Limited Conservatorships. However, references are made to various parts of the book that will apply to circumstances which are general in nature, not specific to Limited Conservatorships. It is truly a helpful resource and guide to carrying out the duties of conservator.

The Internet location for the Handbook in English is:
http://www.courts.ca.gov/xbcr/cc/handbook.pdf

The Internet location for the Handbook in Spanish is:
http://www.courts.ca.gov/documents/manueldeltutor.pdf

Exercise #2

1. Purchase the Handbook for Conservators from your local Superior Court clerk, or locate it online, and read pages 19-25. (Cost is $20.)

2. Locate the completed form *Duties of Conservator and Acknowledgment of Receipt of Handbook* in Appendix A, and read at least Sections I, II, III, VI, and VIII.

3. Locate a blank form *Duties of Conservator and Acknowledgment of Receipt of Handbook*. Type your name on page 7 where indicated. Then, sign the form, and set it aside. You will date all forms at the time of filing.

When you have completed these tasks, go on to Chapter 3, Overview of Limited Conservatorships, in the Workbook.

Chapter 3
Overview of Limited Conservatorship

Limited Conservatorship process

The legal process granting authority to act on behalf of a person with developmental disabilities in his or her best interests is called "Limited Conservatorship". A Limited Conservatorship is ordered only as necessary to promote and protect the well-being of the conserved individual. Powers are granted by the court only to the extent the individual has proven substantial limitations. California Welfare and Institutions Code §4512(l) defines "substantial" as functional limitations in three or more of the following areas of major life activities, as determined by a Regional Center, and as appropriate to the person's age
:

Self-care

Receptive and expressive language

Learning

Mobility

Self-direction

Capacity for independent living

Economic self-sufficiency

Conservatorship of the Person and Conservatorship of the Estate

There are two types of conservatorships: conservatorship of the person and conservatorship of the estate. This Workbook deals only with the first type. If the proposed conservatee has an estate to manage, over and above his or her public benefits, it may be necessary to be appointed conservator of the estate of the individual as well. In that case, the reader is advised to seek the advice and counsel of a conservatorship attorney to discuss that aspect.

Individual competence

A limited conservatee is not presumed to be incompetent. A limited conservatee retains all legal and civil rights, except those a court order has designated as "legal disabilities" that have been specifically granted to the limited conservator. The intent of the California Legislature, as expressed in Section 4502 of the California Welfare and Institutions Code, is that citizens of California with developmental disabilities have rights including, but not limited to, the following:

(1) a right to services, supports, and living arrangements in the least restrictive conditions,

(2) a right to dignity, privacy, and humane care,

(3) a right to participate in an appropriate program of publicly supported education, regardless of degree of disability,

(4) a right to prompt medical care and treatment,

(5) a right to religious freedom and practice,

(6) a right to social interaction and participation in community activities,

(7) a right to physical exercise and recreational opportunities,

(8) a right to be free from harm, including unnecessary physical restraint, or isolation, excessive medication, abuse, or neglect,

(9) a right to be free from hazardous procedures, and

(10) a right to make choices in their own lives, including, but not limited to, where and with whom they live, their relationships with people in their community, the way they spend their time, including education, employment, and leisure, the pursuit of their personal future, and program planning and implementation.

Limited civil rights of limited conservatee

The primary purpose of the Limited Conservatorship is to provide what is needed for the limited conservatee to develop self-reliance and independence. The petitioner shall request only those powers limiting the civil rights of the limited conservatee that are absolutely necessary for the individual to grow and mature to his or her full capacity. Those rights are outlined in the California Probate Code at Section (§)2381.5(b):

(1) to fix the residence or specific dwelling of the limited conservatee,

(2) to access the confidential records and papers of the limited conservatee,

(3) to consent or withhold consent to the marriage of, or the entrance into a registered domestic partnership by, the limited conservatee,

(4) to limit the right of the limited conservatee to contract,

(5) to exercise the power of the limited conservatee to give or withhold medical consent,

(6) to limit the limited conservatee's right to control his or her own social and sexual contacts and relationships, and

(7) to make decisions concerning the education of the limited conservatee.

The court will not generally take from the limited conservatee the right to marry or enter into a registered domestic partnership. Nor will the court generally take from the limited conservatee the right to choose his or her own social and sexual contacts and relationships. The other civil rights listed in California Probate Code §2351.5(b) may be limited but for specific reasons that must be stated in an attachment to the *Petition for Appointment of Conservator*.

References made to the California Probate Code and the California Welfare and Institutions Code are to laws created by the California Legislature which serve to guide the legal structure of society. The Codes can be found on the Internet or at the reader's local library. However, the reader is not required to conduct further research in order to successfully complete the tasks in this Workbook.

Exercise #3

1. Gather your child's latest Individual Program Plan (IPP) or Individual Educational Plan (IEP).

2. Answer the following questions about your child:

   (a) What is the nature of your child's disability? ______________________

   ____

   (b) When did the disability begin? ______________________

   ____

   (c) Who is/are your child's treating physician(s)? ______________________

   ____

   (d) Where does your child receive his or her education? ______________________

   ____

   (e) How would you define your child's educational strengths and weaknesses?______________________

   ____

   ____

   (f) What activities does your child have difficulty doing alone? ____________

   ____

   ____

   (g) What activities does your child enjoy, and with whom does your child enjoy doing those activities?______________________

   ____

   ____

3. Locate the completed form in Appendix A titled *Petition for Appointment of Conservator*. Now find a blank form.

   At 5c(1) of the blank *Petition*, write your answers to 2(a), 2(b), and 2(f), above in a paragraph form, each answer to be a sentence in the paragraph.

   Add explanatory language, but keep this summary brief. See the completed form in Appendix A for an example.

4. Locate the completed form in Appendix A titled *Confidential Supplemental Information*. Now find a blank form.

   At the area numbered 2 on the form, write a descriptive paragraph incorporating all of your answers to 2(a)-(g) above for a clear picture of the strengths and weaknesses of your child, including the progress he or she is making toward short term and long term goals in his or her personal development plan. This form is strictly confidential, for the eyes of the judge and the conservatee's Attorney, not open to the general public.

5. You will want to encourage your child in his or her strengths and assist your child with his or her weaknesses. In order to be recognized as his or her approved assistant under the law, you will need powers that may limit his or her civil rights. To determine the powers appropriate to your appointment, please answer the following questions:

Is your child able to:	(Check response)
(a) understand and decide where to live?	Yes ____ No____
(b) understand and discuss rationally his or her personal confidential records?	Yes ____ No____
(c) understand and enter into contracts that benefit him or her?	Yes ____ No____

(d) understand and give medical consent? Yes ____ No____

(e) understand and make educational decisions for his or her own personal growth? Yes ____ No____

6. Locate the completed *Petition Attachments* in Appendix A, and review the reasons stated for each power requested. Now create the *Petition Attachments* or locate them on Ms. Mejía's website at http://www.barbaramejia.com/limited-conservatorship/. Make any changes necessary to address your child's needs.

When you have completed these tasks, go on to Chapter 4, Preliminary Decisions for the Family Process, in the Workbook.

Chapter 4
Preliminary Decisions for the Family Process

Commitment

The Limited Conservatorship process is really a family process. It is helpful if all family members are advised of this new development in your child's life and encouraged to participate as they can in making it a successful process. If possible, you can send copies of Chapter 3 in the Handbook for Conservators, so everyone has an opportunity to ask questions and feel like part of the process. The Handbook for Conservators can be found online at www.courts.ca.gov/xbcr/cc/handbook.pdf for the English version and www.courts.ca.gov/documents/manueldeltutor.pdf for the Spanish version.

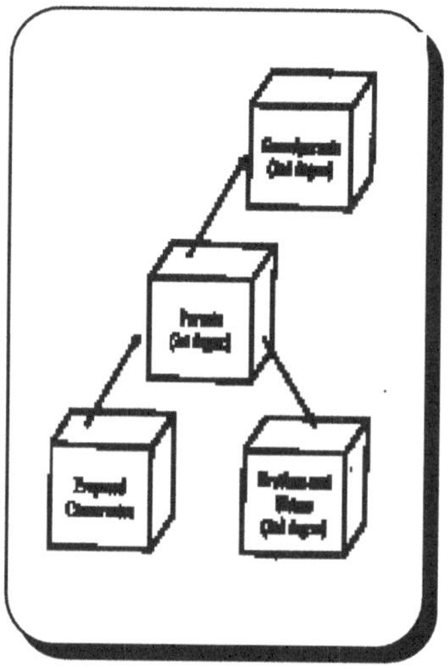

Notice of conservatorship to conservatee's relatives

Every first and second degree relative is required to be given notice of the conservatorship proceeding well in advance of the hearing date. This allows family members to stay involved, if they choose to, throughout the legal process.

First degree relatives of the proposed conservatee are your child's parents and children. Second degree relatives of your child are his or her grandparents and siblings. If any are deceased, those should be noted on the *Petition* at pages 6-7 where family members are listed. Identify whether the grandparents are maternal (mother's side) or paternal (father's side).

Petitioners are required to do their due diligence in locating all relatives to the second degree. If there are family members who are dangerous to the proposed conservatee, petitioner(s) should consult with an attorney at this stage to request a court *Order Dispensing With Notice*.

Public guardian vs. family members

The County Public Guardian is available to serve as conservator for persons without means and who have no family readily available to serve in that capacity. It is supposed that the readers of this Workbook are not considering that option. However, if the time comes where there is no one ready, willing, and able to carry out the duties of conservator in the conservatee's family, that agency may be asked by the court to take on the role, as needed.

Conservatorship is a family process, and siblings may be educated to carry on for a brother or sister when parents can no longer serve as conservators.

You can prepare for your incapacity by completing a "Nomination of Conservator" for your replacement. Keep this Nomination current by reviewing your choices on an annual basis, in the event a change is needed or an individual you have named can no longer carry out the duties for any reason, whatsoever.

Multiple conservators

When family members choose to petition the court for appointment as conservators, often parents will choose to serve as co-conservators.

If one of them becomes disabled or can no longer serve, the other can carry on, with notice to all interested persons and approval of the court to serve alone.

On occasion, when a parent is elderly or physically challenged, a child will serve as co-conservator, which will offer the same protection in the event the parent simply cannot continue.

The co-conservators are equally responsible, however, and not one can make independent decisions without the affirmation of the other. So it is not always the best policy to load up the position with a number of co-conservators.

It is a good idea to write a *Nomination of Conservator* in a form similar to the form shown below, so that if a vacancy occurs in the office of conservator, a petition can be submitted with the *Nomination* attached for the appointment of a replacement called a "successor conservator".

If you decide to serve as co-conservators, and you are concerned that either of you has authority to act on behalf of the other in an emergency situation, you may utilize a limited power of attorney in substantially the same form as that which appears below.

* * * * * * * * * *

Nomination of Conservator

I, (your name), am the parent of (name of your child), and the duly appointed conservator of his/her person in the (name of county) County Superior Court of California, Case No. (case number). In the event of a vacancy in the office of conservator, I nominate the following persons, in the order indicated, to serve in that position, or in combination if they agree to serve as co-conservators:

1. ____________________

2. ____________________

3. ____________________

Dated: ____________ (Signature)
Type or print your name below your signature.

* * * * * * * * * *

* * * * * * * * * * *

Limited Power of Attorney

I, (your name), am the parent of (name of your child), and a duly appointed co-conservator with my spouse, (your spouse's name), of his/her person in the (name of county) County Superior Court of California, Case No. (case number). I appoint my spouse as my agent to exercise any of the limited powers which we were granted by the court in the conservatorship proceeding, listed on the attachment to our Letters of Conservatorship dated (date) in the event I am not available for consent to any action concerning our son/daughter for his/her health, education, or welfare. I agree to indemnify any third party for claims that arise against the third party because of reliance on this power of attorney.

Dated: ________________ (Signature)______________________
Type or print your name below your signature.

(Sign your name in front of a Notary Public for an Acknowledgment that will be attached for legal effect.)

* * * * * * * * * * *

Legal Capacity

The court looks to the proposed limited conservatee's treating physician in determining the proposed conservatee's legal capacities.

Near the time your forms are complete for filing with the court, you, as the petitioner, will provide the *Capacity Declaration* form to your child's physician who will look at specific tasks that indicate whether your child can

(1) understand personal circumstances,

(2) deliberate concerning alternatives,

(3) make informed decisions, and

(4) communicate reasonable choices.

The court's primary concern in a conservatorship of the person of an individual is the individual's ability to provide for his or her own personal needs for physical health, food, clothing, or shelter and to resist fraud or undue influence. Your child's physician will assess your child's competence, to guide the court in its findings and orders concerning what powers are necessary to handle his or her personal matters.

<u>Qualification of proposed conservator</u>

Each proposed conservator must be screened by the Department of Justice to qualify as a fiduciary in California.

The court is concerned for the well-being of the proposed conservatee and will want to be assured the proposed conservator has no record of financial mismanagement, criminal activity, sex offense, or fiduciary removal in any other court case. The court will also want to know if anyone in the proposed conservator's household has any record of such behavior. The *Confidential Conservator Screening Form* is used for that purpose.

One reason for the time gap of 45 days between filing the paperwork and the court hearing of the case is to give sufficient time for law enforcement to run the necessary checks through its system.

Exercise #4

1. Prepare a *Nomination of Conservator* in substantially the same format as provided in this chapter, so your wishes are documented in the event you are unable to continue service as conservator(s). Keep this form with your other legal forms for this conservatorship process.

2. Decide, if you haven't already, who will be the petitioners and who will be the conservators.

   Petitioner(s):____

   Conservator(s):_______________________________________

   Generally, when parents will be co-conservators, they can petition for their appointment together as co-petitioners. Note, however, that they must <u>both</u> sign <u>all</u> documents submitted to the court. The completed forms in Appendix A are examples of that scenario. Make any revisions needed for your unique situation.

   If you have decided to serve as co-conservators, prepare a *Limited Power of Attorney* in substantially the same form as appears in this chapter or ask your local attorney to prepare one for you. Sign the document in front of a Notary Public <u>after you have been appointed by the court</u> so that you have a legal Acknowledgment of your decision. This can then be carried with you at all times together with your *Letters of Conservatorship*.

3. Discuss the commitment of your family members to this process for your child. Make copies of Chapter 3 of the <u>Handbook for Conservators</u> for brothers, sisters, and grandparents of the proposed conservatee. You may download the book from the Internet and send to others via email for further family discussions.

4. Locate and complete the following blank forms, using the completed forms in Appendix A to guide you:

   a. The *Capacity Declaration–Conservatorship* (with physician's name, office address, and telephone number) When delivering this form to your child's physician, remind him or her to:

      (1) date each page signed (far left of each signature line),

      (2) indicate on page 1 when your child was last seen, and

      (3) initial at item 7, if medical powers are necessary.

   b. The *Confidential Conservator Screening Form* (one for each proposed co-conservator) Remember to sign and date the form on the bottom of page 2. If any answers require explanation, add an 8½" x 11" page with your explanation(s) numbered the same as the question(s) on the form.

When you have completed these tasks, go on to Chapter 5, Establishing a Limited Conservatorship, in the Workbook.

Chapter 5
Establishing a Limited Conservatorship

Local rules of court

Every county has its own Local Rules of Court. They are posted on the Internet at the court's website. See the complete list of county websites in Chapter 1 of this Workbook for your county.

Every county has a unique set of rules for filing, setting dates, paying fees, and using court-specific forms. This Workbook is geared to Monterey County local rules. The reader is cautioned to check the Rules of Court specific to the county of the proposed conservatee's residence. That county has jurisdiction for granting the conservatorship.

Preparation for service

Most California counties require prospective conservators to purchase a Handbook for Conservators printed by the Judicial Council of California and to view a video at the courthouse entitled "With Heart– Understanding Conservatorships". Proposed conservators must arrange with the court to view the video before the hearing date on the *Petition for Appointment of Conservator*. In Monterey, that video is shown at 8:00 a.m. on the same Wednesday the court will hear the conservatorship *Petition for Appointment*, unless the party(ies) can arrange to see it before that date. In the alternative, it is also available online at www.youtube.com/watch?v=A-SX6YkFsP4.

In that case, you may sign Monterey County Clerk Form 134 or similar document for your county to affirm your having viewed the video. It is advised that parties see the video well in advance of the hearing date, in order to understand the complex nature of conservatorship and what the court will require of those who serve as conservators.

There may be a fee for viewing the video at the courthouse, if fees are not waived, so bring cash or your checkbook with you to the appointment.

IMPORTANT: The case number will be required before an appointment can be made, so the paperwork will have to be e-filed with the court before you can arrange to see the video.

Regional Centers are responsible for vocational and educational programs for adults with developmental disabilities in California.

Regional Center Report

The Regional Center, responsible to provide adult educational programs for those with developmental disabilities in your area, must e-file a report in advance of the hearing date on your *Petition*. While you are legal parents, you may request the report be prepared and submitted to the court. If your child is already 18 years of age, only he or she has the legal right to request that report. You may be required to e-file an *Ex Parte Application for Order Requiring Regional Center to Prepare an Assessment Report*. A suggested form is found in Appendix A in the event it is required, together with the *Ex Parte Order Requiring Regional Center to Prepare an Assessment Report* also found in Appendix A. Arrange well in advance of the hearing date to get this task on the calendar of the Regional Center. With budget cuts, the psychologists or psychiatrists who prepare the reports have limited work schedules within which to complete these reports, in addition to the other work required of them.

Blank line-numbered paper is available on Ms. Mejía's website barbaramejia.com for preparation of the Ex Parte Applications and Petitions proposed here.

Court-appointed Attorney for the proposed limited conservatee

In Limited Conservatorships, the proposed conservatee must be represented by an Attorney, primarily because his or her civil rights are being limited or assigned to the conservator. Because a limited conservatee does not usually have an estate to pay for those services, a pro bono Attorney is assigned by the court. Petitioners are required to prepare and submit with their initial paperwork an *Ex Parte Application for Appointment of Counsel for the Proposed Limited Conservatee*, together with an *Ex Parte Order Appointing Counsel for the Proposed Limited Conservatee*. Both forms can be found in Appendix A for captioning by petitioners consistent with the other paperwork submitted to the court, using pleading paper as required by the California Rules of Court.

Court Investigator's Report

The court has its own Court Investigator for conservatorships who will gather data for the judge and offer his or her recommendations in response to the *Petition for Appointment of Conservator*. In Monterey County, the investigation unit is notified of the conservatorship filing on receipt of the *Order Appointing Court Investigator* and *Referral to Court Investigator*. You should plan to give the Court Investigator at least 45 days from the date of filing the initial paperwork to review the documents e-filed, the screening results, and the proposed limited conservatee's living environment in preparation of the *Court Investigator's Report to the Court*. That report is not available until shortly before the hearing date. You will be visited at least once by the assigned Court Investigator who will meet with you and your child to get a sense of what needed powers are appropriate for the individual situation.

Court costs

The reader is advised to check the Local Court Rules and payment schedule for filing fees. In Monterey County, the following fees are presently charged and due on filing the initial paperwork with the court, unless they are waived:

Filing fee	$435.00
Court Investigator's fee	425.00

Ex Parte Order fees ($60 each x2) for	120.00
Court-appointed Attorney	
Regional Center report (if needed)	______
	$980.00

In addition, the following costs are assessed:

Viewing the Conservatorship video	$ 5.00
Handbook for Conservators	20.00
	$25.00

After the conservator is appointed, it is wise to have a certified copy of the official *Letters of Conservatorship* to show the Regional Center, treating physician, educational administrators, Social Security, and other agencies providing services and benefits to the limited conservatee. Each certified copy is $25 plus $.50 per page, or $26.50 each for conservator *Letters* (3 pages) as of this Workbook printing.

Waiver of Fees

You can see that fees will be substantial, as they are charged every time you need to e-file a petition for court approval during the Limited Conservatorship. When you e-file your documents electronically, you will be asked to complete a *Request to Waive Court Fees* based on your child's ability to afford those costs (not your checkbook). Do take advantage of that request, since your child receives public benefits, which will allow you to e-file documents, obtain uncertified and certified copies of court documents, and have court investigations throughout the years at no cost to you. Each time you e-file documents with the court, you will state that a Fee Waiver is in the court's record, so no costs are incurred by you. Completed forms for both the *Request to Waive Court Fees* and *Order on Court Fee Waiver* can be found in Appendix A. These Judicial Council forms can also be printed in Spanish, if that is helpful to you. The Spanish forms (FW-001-GC S and FW-003-GC S) are also included in Appendix A.

Exercise #5

1. Locate blank copies of the *Request to Waive Court Fees* and *Order on Court Fee Waiver* to compare with the completed forms in Apprendix A. You will e-file these documents together with all of the Limited Conservatorship documents, so filing fees, investigator fees, and copy costs will not be assessed.

2. Locate a blank copy of the *Petition for Appointment of Conservator--Limited Conservatorship* to compare with the completed form in Appendix A, and begin working through the many boxes required to be checked and explained in the *Attachments*.

   You have already completed the caption from Exercise #1. You have added a brief description of the nature of your child's disability from Exercise #3. And you have made changes to the *Attachments* from Exercise #3.

   Now, it is necessary to work through the balance of the form citing the unique limitations of your child and giving the reasons for your requests of the court in its *Order* approving your petition.

   Use the completed form in Appendix A as a guide. That scenario concerns an autistic child who cannot communicate his needs, so medical powers are requested and an allegation is made that he cannot understand or exercise his right to vote. You must think through the unique characteristics of your child as you compare the completed form to your own situation. If you have questions, you can make notes for consultation with a conservatorship attorney as will be discussed later in the Workbook.

3. Locate a blank copy of the *Confidential Supplemental Information* to compare with the completed form in Appendix A, and begin working through the statements which will be held in strict confidence by the court to protect the identity and

evaluative reports made in assessment of your child for his or her growth and development.

You have already completed the caption from Exercise #1. You have also added a paragraph at #2 of the form describing your child's disability, weaknesses, strengths, needs, and present goals.

To this form, you are encouraged to attach a recent report from your child's teacher, IPP, or IEP and any pertinent confidential documents that would assist the court in determining what powers are appropriate for your appointment as limited conservator(s).

4. Locate a blank copy of the *Ex Parte Application for Order Requiring Regional Center to Prepare an Assessment Report*, together with the *Ex Parte Order Requiring Regional Center to Prepare an Assessment Report* on Ms. Mejía's website to compare with the completed forms in Appendix A. Blank numbered pages are also available at the end of Appendix A for copying purposes to prepare these separate documents not found on the mandatory Judicial Council Forms.

5. Locate a blank copy of the *Order Appointing Court Investigator* to compare with the completed form in Appendix A. This form alerts the Court Investigator of his duties in preparing for your hearing and will be signed by the Judge and delivered to the Investigation Unit.

6. Locate a blank copy of the *Referral to Court Investigator* (required for Monterey County) to compare with the completed form in Appendix A. This form gives the Court Investigator confidential information, including the present location of the proposed conservatee, telephone numbers, names of the proposed conservator(s), attorneys of record (if any), addresses, telephone numbers, and relationships of all the parties, relatives, friends, and neighbors of the proposed conservatee. This is the document the Court Investigator may use to contact everyone who has any knowledge of the proposed conservatee and his/her present needs. Check your court's Local Rules of Court if there is another form

unique to your county which offers the same information for your Court Investigator.

7. When you are ready to e-file these documents (at the same time), you will sign and date them. For now, complete them, paperclip them together with their attached pages, and set them aside.

When you have completed these tasks, go on to Chapter 6, Temporary Conservatorships, in the Workbook.

Chapter 6
Temporary Conservatorships

Exigent circumstances

Occasionally, a temporary conservatorship is necessary to protect the limited conservatee from immediate harm. Possible scenarios may include protection from dangerous people or circumstances that will compromise the safety of the limited conservatee if the petitioner waits 45 days before he or she is appointed conservator. The petitioner should attach documents to substantiate the necessity of the temporary appointment. If those documents should be confidential for the court's review only, they should be attached to the *Confidential Supplemental Information* form and referenced in the *Petition for Temporary Conservatorship* at section #3 of the form.

> Immediate appointments are possible but not generally granted. There must be very serious circumstances warranting an appointment on a temporary basis while the court reviews the bulk of paperwork for permanent appointment.

Forms

In cases of emergency need for protection, the petitioner can e-file a *Petition for Temporary Conservatorship,* with its accompanying *Notice of Hearing, Order Appointing Temporary Conservator,* and *Letters of Temporary Conservatorship,* in addition to all the other paperwork required for a permanent conservatorship.

These Judicial Council forms are available online or on Ms. Mejía's website, and completed in Appendix A for a situation requiring appointment between the date the limited conservatee turns 18 and the hearing date. If the limited conservatee cannot attend the hearing, a declaration by a treating physician must be attached to the *Petition*. The Court-appointed Attorney must agree to the temporary appointment, or you will have to argue before the judge on the date of the hearing why the appointment is imperative, if the Court-appointed Attorney has not agreed with you.

To be appointed temporary conservator, you must submit all paperwork for both the temporary and the permanent conservatorship appointments at the same time.

When you submit these temporary appointment forms, you must also submit all of the permanent appointment forms. So go through the entire Workbook to prepare all of the forms, even if you want an emergency temporary conservatorship. The temporary forms will not be accepted alone.

Specificity of powers requested

If medical powers are needed on a temporary basis, the physician's completed *Capacity Declaration-Conservatorship* must be e-filed with the rest of the papers you have prepared to initiate the conservatorship action.

Hearing

You will be informed by your court's Local Rules of Court when the judge is available to hear your temporary *Petition*. Generally, five days before the hearing, you must have given a copy of the paperwork to your child, his or her Court-appointed Attorney, the Court Investigator, and all relatives of the proposed conservatee to the second degree: your child's parents, grandparents, children (though not likely), and siblings.

Order and *Letters*

When you submit the *Petition*, you must also submit a *Notice of Hearing*, an *Order*

Appointing Temporary Conservator, and *Letters of Temporary Conservatorship.* Note how the Attachment must list all necessary powers requested (in the *Petition*) and granted (in the *Order*) for the interim period.

Caution

Temporary conservatorships are not routinely ordered unless there are grave circumstances. You must submit your proof of service under penalty of perjury that you gave notice to all relatives to the second degree of the proposed limited conservatee in order to be heard by the Judge. See Chapter 7 for procedures on Proof of Service.

Exercise #6

1. If a temporary conservatorship is necessary and appropriate for your situation, complete the additional forms needed, as explained above:
   a. *Petition for Temporary Conservatorship*
   b. *Notice of Hearing*
   c. *Order Appointing Temporary Conservator*
   d. *Letters of Temporary Conservatorship*

   Remember to give copies of the *Petition* and *Notice of Hearing* to
   a. all relatives to the second degree of the proposed limited conservatee (parents, children, grandparents, siblings), and
   b. the Regional Center

   Copies of ALL documents you e-file with the court must be given to
   a. the Court Investigator, and
   b. the Court-appointed Attorney for the proposed limited conservatee.

   Prepare for a delay in receiving the *Order Appointing Counsel for the Proposed Limited Conservatee*, when determining the hearing date, as the Court-appointed Attorney is a key factor in your successfully securing the temporary appointment. Sometimes the documents are accepted and Orders are returned in 24 hours, but sometimes it takes 48-72 hours, so set the date out far enough that you can give appropriate notice to all required persons.

When you have prepared these documents (ONLY if you will seek temporary appointment), set them aside, and go on to Chapter 7, Filing and Serving Court Documents, in the Workbook.

Chapter 7
Filing and Serving Court Documents

Determine the date

Check your court's Local Court Rules for setting dates of hearing on your *Petition*. In Monterey County, Petitions in Probate Court are heard on the Law and Motion calendar, Wednesdays at 10:00 a.m. You may choose a date at least 45 days from the date you e-file the paperwork for your hearing date. Find out which Department (courtroom) Judge will hear your case, and at what time. Make a note of your date, time, and courtroom number that you will transfer to the forms in Exercise #7.

Mandatory Electronic Filing

When all the paperwork is completed, you must file the originals electronically with the court through an online service provider. Your documents must be in ".pdf" format when filing. You may run them through a scanner individually which will save them on your computer until you are ready to submit them all at one time through the system.

You will see a number of certified Electronic Filing Service Providers (EFSP's) on the county website at "E-Filing". When you are ready to e-file, I suggest you set up your case by going to "Odyssey eFile CA" at http://www.california.tylerhost.net/srl, to guide you through the process. Click on "Start Your Legal Process" followed by "Requesting a Limited Conservatorship" to begin the interview. At the end of the interview process, request a fee waiver, since your child does not have an estate to tap for the fees. That will eliminate your need to pay for copies or court investigations throughout the lifetime of your child under conservatorship.

You will upload all of your documents individually. Some will be designated "Confidential" and viewable only by the judge, while others will be "Public" and viewable by anyone. Be sure to make the correct designation as you enter each of the documents with the EFSP. Once they are all entered and you ask to submit them for review by the court clerk, you will receive an email that indicates they were received.

Within a day, you will receive notice of whether your documents were accepted by the court. If they were not accepted, you will be informed of the reason, so you can correct them. If they were accepted, conformed copies will be returned to you at your email address. You will then have an assigned case number for your Limited Conservatorship case and a file stamp on the first page of each document. Make copies of all of them for your records.

The court-stamped date on the documents conforms them to the originals in the court's file. That is why they are known as "conformed copies".

Proof of Service

Once you have a case number and your court date is approved, it is time to give copies to everyone required to know of the proceeding. This is one of the most challenging of all tasks in establishing a Limited Conservatorship. As noted before, the Court Investigator and the Court-appointed Attorney for your child must receive copies of all documents e-filed in the court. Your child and his or her relatives to the second degree (parents, children, siblings, and grandparents) are entitled to copies of the *Petition* and *Notice of Hearing* only. When service is complete, you prepare and e-file a *Proof of Service* with the court.

Making and serving copies

You must give one set of all documents to the Court Investigation Unit. You can insert all of them in an envelope and hand deliver them to the clerk to forward to the Court Investigator's office. You must also give one set of all documents to the Attorney appointed by the court to represent your child. When you receive the *Ex Parte Order Appointing Counsel for the Limited Conservatee*, you will know whom to give the second complete set of documents. If you have petitioned for temporary appointment as well, your temporary date will be delayed so your child's Attorney has the paperwork at least five days before the hearing date.

> "Ex Parte" means "without formal notice" (which is generally at least 15 days in advance), so matters of necessity can be heard by the judge on an emergency basis.

The same rule applies to your submission of the *Ex Parte Application for Order Requiring Regional Center to Prepare an Assessment Report*, and *Ex Parte Order Requiring Regional Center to Prepare an Assessment Report*, if required. You may send the Regional Center the *Petition* and *Notice of Hearing* together with the *Ex Parte Order* for its evaluation and report as soon as it is signed by the judge.

Notice of Hearing

You will then make copies of the *Petition* and *Notice of Hearing* for everyone on your "service list" who is a relative to the second degree. You will mail them the copies when you know the date of the temporary hearing. Finally, you will sign the back page of the *Notice of Hearing* and file it electronically with the court, showing that everyone who needed to have a copy was sent a copy by U.S. Mail and on what date.

Citation

Your child must also be given notice, but for notice, he or she receives a copy of the *Citation* you have prepared and submitted to the court with a copy of the *Petition*. The *Citation* you received from the court has an official seal of the court. That document must be returned to the court with the information completed on the back page showing when and where your child was hand delivered a copy of the *Citation* and a copy of the *Petition*. In the case of a temporary *Petition*, you must also e-file a *Proof of Service–Personal Service* showing your child received copies of the temporary *Petition* and *Notice of Hearing* for the temporary appointment, at least five days in advance of the hearing date, if that was requested.

You must assign a friend, relative, or neighbor with the responsibility of serving your child with a copy of the *Petition* and a copy of the *Citation*.

Electronically file all but one document

The only document you will not file electronically on the Odyssey website is the *Letters of Conservatorship*. The court requires the original signature on that document, so you must take that document to the courthouse for personal filing. You will have a case number to insert on that form after submitting all of the other documents.

Exercise #7

1. Locate and review the form *What is Proof of Service?* in Appendix A. This form is also available in Spanish (GC-510 S). A copy is included in Appendix A, to assist you in understanding the need and complexity of service.

2. Complete the following blank documents with your court date, time, and department number:

   a. *Petition for Appointment of Limited Conservator**
   b. *Capacity Declaration*
   c. *Confidential Conservator Screening Form*
   d. *Confidential Supplemental Information*
   e. *Notice of Hearing**
   f. *Citation*
   g. *Referral to Court Investigator*
   h. *Ex Parte Application for Order Requiring Regional Center to Prepare an Assessment Report* (court date only)
   i. *Ex Parte Application for Order Appointing Counsel for the Proposed Limited Conservatee* (court date only)

   and any other documents calling for the date, time, and department number in the caption.

3. If you have prepared for a temporary conservatorship as well, type the date, time, and department number on the following documents for the temporary hearing:

   a. *Petition for Temporary Limited Conservatorship**
   b. *Notice of Hearing**

c. *Proof of Service–Personal Service*

and prepare them the same as you did the documents for permanent appointment.

*** These documents will be addressed in Exercise #8 of Chapter 8, step 4g.**

When you have completed these tasks, go on to Chapter 8, Order and Letters of Conservatorship, in the Workbook.

Chapter 8
Order and Letters of Conservatorship

Letters are your authority

When you are appointed conservator(s), the *Letters* you sign will be stamped with the seal of the court. That is your proof of authority to act on behalf of your child, as the court has limited your powers (explained above in Chapter 5). You will attach a page to the *Letters* exactly like the page you attach to the *Order* showing the limited powers you have been granted.

Sign the *Letters* the day you submit the paperwork

The court will not accept the *Letters of Conservatorship* with a date earlier than the date your documents are e-filed with the court, so date those *Letters* the day you e-file the documents and take the *Letters* to the court.

Letters follow the *Order*

Before you can have *Letters* issued to you by the court, you must have the *Order* signed by the judge and e-filed with the court. Be sure the attached page to the *Order* is the same as the attached page to the *Letters*. They MUST MATCH exactly. The page attached to the *Letters* is called *Attachment 3g and 3i*, because it references the powers in items 3g and 3i of the *Letters* on the first page. The page attached to the *Order* is called *Attachment 31 and 33*, because it references the same powers but they appear in items 31 and 33 on page 3 of the *Order*.

Waiting on the *Letters* and *Order*

You will submit a number of *Orders* to the court. You will not serve any of those until they have been signed by the judge and returned to you by the court. Once they are sent to you by email, make copies and mail them to the Court Investigation Unit and the Court-appointed Attorney for your child.

When you receive the *Ex Parte Order Requiring Regional Center to Prepare an Assessment Report*, you will also send a copy with the *Petition* and *Notice of Hearing* to the Regional Center in your area.

Only after you have the *Order Appointing Limited Conservator* may you ask the court to issue to you the *Letters of Conservatorship–Limited Conservatorship* which are your authority to act on behalf of your child as an adult. Generally, they both can be picked up from the Clerk's Office after your court hearing.

Exercise #8

1. Complete the following documents with your court date, time, and department number:
   a. *Ex Parte Order Requiring Regional Center to Prepare an Assessment Report* (court date only)
   b. *Ex Parte Order Appointing Counsel for the Proposed Limited Conservatee* (court date only)
   c. *Order Appointing Limited Conservator*
   d. *Letters of Limited Conservatorship* (dated the same date you e-file everything)

2. If you have prepared for a temporary conservatorship as well, type the date, time, and department number on the following documents for the temporary hearing:
   a. *Order Appointing Temporary Limited Conservator*
   b. *Letters of Temporary Conservatorship–Limited Conservatorship* (dated the same date you e-file everything)

3. You may want to move to Chapter 9 at this time to check your paperwork before filing or to see if you have missed any important distinction. If not, proceed to step 4 below.

4. Complete Proof of Service tasks:
   a. Scan all signed documents into your computer as ".pdf" documents.
   b. E-file all ".pdf" documents with an EFSP online.
   c. Take the original *Letters of Conservatorship* to the courthouse for submission with your other case documents with the new case number showing in the caption. Make sure the *Letters* are dated the same date as you e-filed all of the case documents.

d. Prepare a 9" x 12" manilla envelope in which you will insert one of each conformed copy you receive back from the court clerk for service on the Court Investigation Unit, with a copy of the non-conformed *Order Appointing Court Investigator* on top. Take it to the court clerk for delivery to the Investigation Unit, or mail it to the Court Investigator. Check the address for the Court Investigator on your court's website.

e. Prepare another similar envelope of all court documents for the Attorney appointed for your child. As soon as you receive the *Ex Parte Order Appointing Counsel for the Proposed Limited Conservatee* back from the court, you must send him or her the envelope of documents.

f. From the copies you will keep in your records, make copies for your child's relatives to the second degree of the documents starred (*) in 2 and 3 of Exercise #7 in this Workbook: the *Petition(s)* and *Notice(s) of Hearing*. Send them by U.S. Mail first class.

g. Finally, complete the *Proof of Service* on the back of your *Notice(s) of Hearing*, stating what day you sent everyone the documents and how. If you hand delivered the set to the Court Investigator, you can use the *Proof of Service* on pleading paper (numbered paper) to inform the court, and e-file the original maintaining the conformed copy you receive from the court by email for your records. See Appendix A for this alternate form.

When you have completed these tasks, go on to Chapter 9, Using an Attorney in a Limited Conservatorship, in the Workbook.

Chapter 9
Using an Attorney in a Limited Conservatorship

Unusual needs

Every situation requiring a Limited Conservatorship is unique. You may think your situation has no unusual elements to consider. However, to be on the safe side, it is best to make an appointment with an attorney licensed in your state and experienced in Limited Conservatorships for a consultation. When you call to make the appointment, you can inform the attorney's office that you have completed the forms necessary for a Limited Conservatorship, and that you want a consultation to review the paperwork, to be sure you have covered everything that may arise in the court proceeding.

Protecting an inheritance

If your child has an estate to protect or is anticipating an inheritance, it is extremely important that you see an experienced attorney. A limited conservatee is receiving public benefits, because he or she is not considered capable of earning a living to meet his or her financial needs. An estate or an anticipated inheritance could disqualify your child from continuing public benefits. An attorney experienced in Limited Conservatorships can advise you on whether a Special Needs Trust is advisable, which you may need to petition the court to establish for your child. Certainly, anyone in your family who is considering leaving funds to your child by inheritance should establish a personal Special Needs Trust in his or her estate plan or add the inheritance to an already established Special Needs Trust to further protect your child's entitlement to public benefits.

Substituted judgment

The procedure you use to establish a Special Needs Trust is called Substituted Judgment. If someone in the family failed to establish a Special Needs Trust and instead willed assets (money or property) to your child, you must petition the court to use its powers to re-make the estate plan of the deceased family member so that a Special Needs Trust can be established after death. If your child takes any benefit before a Special Needs Trust is established, you will have jeopardized his or her rights to continuing benefits. Do not delay in consulting with an experienced attorney if this scenario arises.

Frame your questions

Throughout this Workbook, you have taken the time to jot down your questions. Go back through your notes now, and check off any questions you were able to answer as you proceeded. For those questions or concerns you did not check, please make a point to consult with an experienced attorney to get the clarification you need to proceed to the hearing date.

Exercise #9

1. Make a list of the questions you have not checked as having been answered while you worked through the Workbook exercises.

2. Make an appointment with an attorney licensed in your state and experienced in your county in Limited Conservatorship law for a consultation.

    a. When making the appointment, inform the receptionist that you want the attorney to look over your paperwork for anything you may have missed in filing for Limited Conservatorship.

    b. If any issues listed in Chapter 9 are pertinent to your child's life or estate, i.e. estate expectations or trust issues, be ready to give the facts for a speedy and efficient use of the attorney's time while reviewing your paperwork. You may need his or her assistance in the future. You want to develop a professional relationship for legal advice from time to time, if that is acceptable to the attorney.

3. After your consultation, return to Exercise 8 at the end of Chapter 8, and complete the Proof of Service tasks outlined in step 4.

When you have completed these tasks, you are ready to go on to Chapter 10, Before the Hearing, in the Workbook.

Chapter 10
Before the Hearing

Check documents

Look over your documents. Be sure each form has been stamped by the court clerk. Be sure the court's date-stamp on each form was stamped well enough in advance to satisfy your court's local rules (in Monterey County, 45 days before the permanent hearing and 5 days before the temporary hearing). Use the list at the beginning of Appendix A as your guideline of necessary documents to have e-filed. The *Order Appointing Limited Conservator* and the *Letters of Conservatorship–Limited Conservatorship* should have been submitted to the court at least two weeks in advance of the hearing date, if not with your original paperwork. You will receive those the date of the hearing or soon after. Arrange to have the signature of the Attorney appointed for your child on the last page of the *Order Appointing Limited Conservator* which may be required before the judge will sign it, so get that and e-file it well in advance of the hearing date. You cannot get *Letters* without the court's signed and e-filed *Order*. See an example of the *Order* in Appendix A as instructive in preparing the same for your hearing, as explained above.

Check service

Be sure your *Notice of Hearing* on the *Petition for Appointment of Limited Conservator* was served on every relative to the second degree, the Court Investigator, and the

Attorney appointed for your child. The *Notice of Hearing* should be signed and date-stamped at least 15 days before the date of the hearing on the *Petition*.

E-file the *Citation*

Check that the original *Citation* (with the original blue court stamp at the bottom left of the first page) was signed and dated by the person who served your child. Check to see that it was submitted to the court well in advance of the hearing date, and that you have a court date-stamped (conformed) copy of it in your file.

E-file the *Capacity Declaration–Conservatorship*

Check to be sure the *Capacity Declaration* completed by your child's treating physician was signed and dated on pages 1 and 3, the date your child was last seen is noted on page 1, and that the physician initialed #7 on page 3 if medical powers are needed. Check that the original was e-filed with the court well in advance of the hearing date, that a copy was served on the Court Investigator and the Attorney appointed for your child, and that you have a court date-stamped (conformed) copy of the document in your file.

If the *Capacity Declaration* was received from the doctor after the case number was assigned (on filing the conservatorship documents), be sure to add the case number assigned by the court before serving and filing it.

E-file the *Regional Center Report*

Finally, be sure you have a copy of the Regional Center's report to the court, that the original was e-filed with the court, that it was served on the Court Investigator and the Attorney appointed for your child, and that you have a court date-stamped (conformed) copy of the document in your file.

Exercise #10

Put your conformed copies (court date-stamped copies) in the following order, and take them to court with you for reference if any of them is questioned or requested by the judge:

- ☐ a. *Request to Waive Court Fees*
- ☐ b. *Order on Court Fee Waiver*
- ☐ c. *Petition for Appointment of Limited Conservator*
- ☐ d. *Notice of Hearing*
- ☐ e. *Capacity Declaration*
- ☐ f. *Confidential Supplemental Information*
- ☐ g. *Confidential Conservator Screening Form* (one for each petitioner)
- ☐ h. *Duties of Conservator*
- ☐ i. *Ex Parte Application for Order Requiring Regional Center to Prepare an Assessment Report* (if it was necessary)
- ☐ j. *Ex Parte Order Requiring Regional Center to Prepare an Assessment Report* (if it was necessary)
- ☐ k. *Ex Parte Application for Order Appointing Counsel for the Proposed Limited Conservatee*
- ☐ l. *Ex Parte Order Appointing Counsel for the Proposed Limited Conservatee*
- ☐ m. *Order Appointing Court Investigator*
- ☐ n. *Referral to Court Investigator* (or your county-specific form)
- ☐ o. *Citation*

When you have completed these tasks, you are ready to go on to Chapter 11, At the Court Hearing on Appointment, in the Workbook.

Chapter 11
At the Court Hearing on Appointment

Law and Motion calendar

The hearing on your *Petition for Appointment of Limited Conservator* will be held on the Probate Law and Motion calendar. Arrive 15 minutes early to locate the courtroom and to be seated in the courtroom after the doors open.

The court proceeding is recorded stenographically by the court reporter, so speak clearly and audibly.

Conservatee in attendance

Your child should be in attendance if your child's treating physician stated on the *Capacity Declaration* that he or she could attend the hearing. If the physician did not, your child does not need to attend the hearing. Every proposed conservator must be in attendance. When the case is called, which will be at any time during the Law and Motion Calendar, the proposed conservator(s) and your child will walk up to the front table and state your name(s) for the court record.

Necessary and appropriate

If all of your paperwork is in order, the judge will ask if anyone has anything to add. If not, the judge will make a finding that the Limited Conservatorship is necessary and appropriate and that the proposed conservator(s) is(are) the best suited person(s) for the position. The court may release the Attorney appointed for your child at the first hearing date or at some review hearing date in the future. Until that person is released by the court, you must serve him or her with every document you e-file with the court in the case.

Date of review hearing

At the first hearing, the judge will set a Review Hearing for six months later. In advance of that date, the Court Investigator will evaluate whether the plan in place is working well for your child. You will receive a copy of the six-month review by the Court Investigator in advance of the next hearing date. If everything appears fine to him or her, there may be no need to attend the Review Hearing date. The judge will just receive the report into the court record and set the next Review Hearing for six months later.

Process *Order* and *Letters*

Most courts will have the *Order Appointing Limited Conservator* and *Letters of Conservatorship–Limited Conservatorship* ready for pick up by you. If so, you will be able to collect them at the court clerk's window after the hearing. You will receive a copy of each document. At that time, it is a good idea to ask for a certified copy of the *Letters*. You can present the certified copy to each of your child's physicians, school teachers, administrators, and Regional Center for them to copy for their records. Always maintain an original (with blue stamp) in your file.

Exercise #11

1. Review the process that will take place on your appearance at the hearing on your appointment petition as follows:
   a. Arrive 15 minutes early.
   b. Walk up to the counsel table when your case is called, with your child if possible.
   c. State your name clearly for the court reporter's record, and state the name of everyone standing with you for the court reporter's record:

   "Good morning, your Honor. My name is _____________, and I am the mother/father of _____________, who is also present with me."

   or if your child cannot be present, say:

   "Good morning, your Honor. My name is _____________, and I am the mother/father of _____________, who could not be here today, for medical reasons stated in his/her doctor's *Capacity Declaration*."

   d. If the Judge grants your petition, make a note of the next hearing date, time, and courtroom, if you will need to appear.
   e. If you have not been informed, you may ask the judge, "May I pick up the *Order* and *Letters* from the court clerk today?"

2. Review the process after court
   a. If you were given the *Letters* and *Order* from the court clerk's processing window, ask for a certified copy of the *Letters of Conservatorship–Limited Conservatorship*.
   b. If you did not receive the *Order* that day, you will receive it by email. If it arrives with copies of the *Letters*, go back to the court for a certified copy of the *Letters*. The certified *Letters* are free if you were granted a Fee Waiver.

When you have completed these tasks, you are ready to go on to Chapter 12, After Appointment, in the The Workbook.

Chapter 12
After Appointment

Notice of Conservatee's Rights

You are required to complete and send the *Notice of Conservatee's Rights* to every relative of your child to the second degree, the Court Investigator, and the Attorney appointed for your child. To the *Notice of Conservatee's Rights*, you must attach a copy of the *Order Appointing Limited Conservator*. NOTICE: You now have a Case Number for subsequent documents you e-file with the court. Remember to insert the case number on all new documents, including this new *Notice of Conservatee's Rights*. This form is also available in Spanish (GC-341 S). A copy is included in Appendix A, if you would like to include that form with notice tp relatives whose primary language is Spanish.

Determination of Conservatee's Appropriate Level of Care

You are required to complete and e-file a *Determination of Conservatee's Appropriate Level of Care* with the court within 60 days of your appointment, with service on the Court Investigator and the Attorney appointed for your child, if he or she has not been released from the case. In the *Determination of Conservatee's Appropriate Level of Care*, you want to inform the court where your child resides and whether you believe it is the best (least restrictive) place for him or her. Address any issues raised by the Court Investigator in his or her initial report to the court and any issues raised by the Attorney appointed for your child. If they approve of your child's placement, it is a good idea to remind the court by adding pertinent language in the *Determination of Conservatee's Appropriate Level of Care* from their Report(s). See the completed *Determination of Conservatee's Appropriate Level of Care* form in Appendix A for an example to follow.

Six-month review

At the initial hearing date, you were given the date the court will review the *Court Investigator's Six-month Review Report* to the court. You will receive a copy of the *Report* in advance of the hearing date. If the *Report* states everything is proceeding well, you will not need to attend the court hearing. It is just a time for the court to put on its record that the review was made, the conservatorship is necessary and appropriate, and the limited conservator(s) is(are) acting in the best interests of the limited conservatee.

Annual Reviews

The same process as the six-month review occurs at the one-year anniversary of your appointment. If your court has "probate notes" on its website, you can look there to see if an appearance is necessary. If no appearance is necessary, receive and review the *Annual Report*, and keep it with your complete legal file of documents.

Public benefits

Work with your Regional Center to ensure your child is getting the educational opportunities advisable for him or her. The goal is for your child to continue his or her development toward further personal growth and independence. There are likely active parent groups in your community with whom you can network and gain support. If not, you may want to initiate such a group with other parents in your community.

Changes of addresses and phone numbers

All changes of address and phone number for you and for your child must be given to the court on the *Referral to Court Investigator* form or other form unique to your county. Make the changes on the form, and check the box as to why you are filing it. This document must be served on the Court Investigator, the Attorney appointed for your child, and all persons who have requested special notice. Once it has been completed, signed, and mailed to everyone necessary, e-file the original (with signed *Proof of Service*) and when it is received back by email, keep the conformed copy in your file.

Exercise #12

1. Locate a blank copy of the *Notice of Conservatee's Rights* to compare with the completed form in Appendix A. This form is also available in Spanish (GC-341 S). A copy is included in Appendix A.

   a. Use the *Attachment to Notice of Conservatee's Rights* to add names of all relatives required to receive a copy, as well as your child's Court-appointed Attorney and the Court Investigator, who must receive every copy of the court's e-filed documents. Remember to add the court case on all pages of the *Notice of Conservatee's Rights* before making copies.

   b. Make copies of the *Order Appointing Limited Conservator*, and attach a copy to each *Notice of Conservatee's Rights* to send out by U.S. Mail.

   c. Make envelopes for everyone who must get a copy, and mail a copy of the *Notice of Conservatee's Rights* with an attached conformed copy of the *Order Appointing Limited Conservator* in each envelope. Include a copy of the Spanish form if you have relatives whose primary language is Spanish.

   d. Sign the *Proof of Service* on the *Notice of Conservatee's Rights* when you have mailed copies to everyone, and make a copy of the document with your signature. Then, e-file the original through the EFSP system. You will receive a conformed copy back by email from the court clerk for your records. DO NOT attach the *Order Appointing Limited Conservator* to the *Notice of Conservatee's Rights* that you e-file with the court.

2. Locate a blank copy of the *Determination of Conservatee's Appropriate Level of Care* to compare with the completed form in Appendix A.

a. Refer to the *Court Investigator's* [first] *Report to Court* and the *Regional Center Report* for language to insert if they were favorable to your child's present placement. If not, address the issues raised by them in your *Determination of Conservatee's Appropriate Level of Care*. Sign and date the *Determination of Conservatee's Appropriate Level of Care*.

b. Add the Court Investigator and the Attorney appointed for your child with their addresses to the *Proof of Service*.

c. Make two (2) copies of the completed *Determination of Conservatee's Appropriate Level of Care* with the *Proof of Service* attached to it (one for the Court Investigator, and one for the Court-appointed Attorney for the limited conservatee).

d. Make envelopes for the Court Investigator and the Attorney appointed for your child, and mail each a copy of the *Determination of Conservatee's Appropriate Level of Care* with attached *Proof of Service*.

e. Sign the *Proof of Service* attached to the *Determination of Conservatee's Appropriate Level of Care* when you have mailed copies to the Court Investigator and Attorney appointed for your child, and e-file the original (with your signature) through the EFSP system. You will receive a conformed copy back by email for your records.

3. Put the six-month hearing date on your calendar, and check with the Court Investigator if you do not receive a copy of his or her *Court Investigator's Report* a week in advance of the next court date. The court will review all new documents e-filed at the Six-month Review Hearing, including your *Notice of Conservatee's Rights* and *Determination of Conservatee's Appropriate Level of Care*. If there are outstanding issues, you may be asked to appear and explain why you have or have not remedied the concerns by that date.

Congratulations! You have completed the tasks for establishing a Limited Conservatorship! One final chapter remains. Read that now to understand the closure process.

Chapter 13
Terminating a Limited Conservatorship

Conservatee dies

When your child dies, the conservatorship terminates. At that time, you are required to notify the court by filing a *Notice of Conservatee's Death* (Judicial Council Form GC-399) found in Appendix A, and serving everyone who received the *Notice of Hearing* on the initial hearing. Look back at that document in your legal file. If anyone who was first notified of the conservatorship has died, your *Proof of Service* should note that status.

Conservatee achieves full independence

When your child achieves full independence, you can petition to terminate the conservatorship. A *Petition to Terminate Conservatorship** must be e-filed with a *Notice of Hearing* showing proper proof of service and an *Order to Terminate Conservatorship** for the Judge's signature. It must state grounds sufficient for the court to order that the "Limited Conservatorship is no longer necessary". The petitioner should attach proof of independence from the local Regional Center or the conservatee's treating physician or both.

Conservatee requires general conservatorship

If powers other than the limited powers authorized by California Probate Code §2381.5(b) are needed to protect the conservatee, a general conservatorship may be necessary. That process is beyond the scope of this Workbook. The reader is advised to seek the assistance of a licensed attorney experienced in conservatorship law under those circumstances.

Conservator dies

When the conservator dies, if there is no co-conservator, the deceased conservator's nominated person will petition for appointment just as the deceased conservator did, initially. He or she will attach the *Nomination of Conservator* to the *Petition for Appointment of Limited Conservator* and proceed as the nominated successor.

If there is a co-conservator, the co-conservator will notify the court of the co-conservator's death. The surviving co-conservator will request the court issue new *Letters of Conservatorship* showing the survivor as the sole conservator, by e-filing an *Application for Appointment of Co-conservator as Sole Conservator and Issuance of New Letters of Conservatorship** together with an *Order for Appointment of Limited Conservator* and new *Letters of Limited Conservatorship* signed by the surviving conservator. The survivor may also petition for another individual to serve as a co-conservator. In that case, the petitioner will use the same paperwork as in the beginning to become appointed with the survivor. Each prospective conservator or co-conservator must be screened for approval by the court in the same way any former conservator was, when the conservatorship was initiated.

Conservator chooses to resign

If the conservator chooses to resign, he or she must find someone to take his or her place. If no individual will take the responsibility, the conservator may contact the county Public Guardian to discuss taking over the case. The parties may then determine who will petition for appointment of the Public Guardian to serve as limited conservator. There must be written *Consent** by the Public Guardian to act.

Court must discharge conservator

In a Limited Conservatorship of the person only, the *Notice of Conservatee's Death* is sufficient to terminate the conservatorship action. If a conservator chooses to resign, only the court may discharge that conservator upon review of his or her actions while serving. The *Petition for Appointment of Successor Limited Conservator* must include an *Order** for discharge of the former conservator.

* These subsequent forms are beyond the scope of this Workbook. Please contact an attorney licensed in your state and experienced in Limited Conservatorship law to advise you on how to proceed.

Glossary of Terms

Appointment	A court's action on a petition for establishing a Limited Conservatorship, whereby an individual or individuals are given authority to act on behalf of an adult with developmental disabilities.
Attachment	An extra sheet of paper attached to a document filed in a court proceeding that provides explanations corresponding to the numbered items on the court document.
Autism	A disorder of neural development occurring before a child is three years old characterized by impaired social interaction and communication and by restricted and repetitive behavior.
California Probate Code	One of California's 29 legal subject areas compiling legislative laws dealing with wills, trusts, estates, and fiduciary roles concerning such matters.
California Rules of Court	General rules of practice in California courts applicable to all subject areas.
California Welfare and Institutions Code	One of California's 29 legal subject areas compiling legislative laws having to deal with State institutions established for the benefit of its citizenry and the rights of persons so affected.
Capacity	The ability or aptitude of an individual to understand personal circumstances, deliberate concerning alternatives, make informed decisions, and communicate reasonable choices.

Caption	The heading of a Judicial Council form, or pleading on line-numbered paper, which indicates the person filing the document, the case name, the case number, and often the hearing date, time, and location for the court's review and decision.
Case Number	The chronological number assigned to a court case which must appear on each page of a document submitted to the court for inclusion in the case file and served on all persons affected by the case.
Cerebral Palsy	A condition occurring for a child in the first two years of life, sometimes thought of as a group of disorders, that can involve brain and nervous system functions such as movement, learning, hearing, seeing, and thinking.
Certified Copy	A copy of a document filed with the court which contains an original stamp by the court as a statement certifying that it is a true and correct copy of the original in the court's case file.
Competency	The quality of being sufficient or adequate to satisfy the needs and wants of life, to provide for one's physical health, food, clothing, or shelter and to resist fraud or undue influence.
Conformed Copy	A copy of a document filed with the court which contains a stamp in the upper right corner showing the date the document was submitted to the court for its case file.
Conservatee	The person for whom a conservatorship is established by a court of law to protect the individual in matters relating to his or her person and estate, or either.

General Conservatee	A protected person in a conservatorship who requires assistance by someone appointed by the court to manage his or her person and estate, or either.
Limited Conservatee	A person living with developmental disabilities in a Limited Conservatorship who requires assistance by someone appointed by the court to make decisions as limited by the court for the person's protection in one or more specific areas of weakness.
Proposed Conservatee	A person who is being considered by a court for conservatorship protection upon petition by a person or entity requesting fiduciary authority.
Conservator	The person appointed by a court to make decisions for a conservatee in matters concerning his or her personal care and finances, or either.
General Conservator	A person appointed by a court to protect an adult who is unable to properly provide for his or her own personal or financial needs.
Limited Conservator	A person appointed by a court to make decisions for an adult living with developmental disabilities to provide what is needed for him or her to develop self-reliance and independence.
Proposed Conservator	A person who is being considered by a court for appointment as a conservator upon a petition to a court requesting specific authority.
Conservatorship	The legal procedure for protection of adults who require assistance in areas of weakness, either mental or physical or both.
Conservatorship of the Estate	The legal procedure for protection of an adult's finances.

Conservatorship of the Person	The legal procedure for protection of an adult's personal care.
General Conservatorship	The legal procedure for protection of a adult who does not have the capacity to make legally informed decisions for him or herself.
Limited Conservatorship	The legal procedure for protection of an adult living with developmental disabilities with regard to certain specific areas of weaknesses.
Court-appointed Attorney	The Attorney assigned by a court to represent a proposed conservatee at the hearing for appointment of a conservator requesting authority to exercise certain civil rights of the individual, and who may continue throughout the case as requested by the court.
Court Clerk	An employee of the court who receives e-filed court documents, manages court case files, and issues Letters of Conservatorship and certified copies of court documents as requested.
Court Investigator	An independent attorney employed by the court to assist the judge in reviewing conservatorship cases. This person meets with the proposed conservatee initially, and if the conservatorship is established, then periodically, to determine the appropriateness of the care and needs of the individual.
Department of Justice	The governmental agency under the office of the Attorney General tasked with the duty to collect, hold, and manage personal information for the protection of children, seniors, and dependent adults.

Developmental Language Delays	A failure to develop language abilities on the usual developmental timetable, demonstrating deficits in the underlying knowledge of language, distinct from speech delay.
Developmental Disability	A condition that begins before the age of 18, continues indefinitely, and causes a substantial handicap; for example, mental retardation, cerebral palsy, epilepsy, and autism.
Epilepsy	A chronic neurological disorder characterized by seizures which are symptoms of abnormal, excessive, or synchronous neuronal activity in the brain.
Ex Parte	Communication with the court without regular notice prescribed by statute for hearing by a judge, usually due to the emergency nature of a request.
Fiduciary	One who stands in the shoes of another to make specific decisions as allowed by law or ordered by a court with authority to grant such powers.
Handbook for Conservators	A publication produced by the Judicial Council of California, to advise and instruct readers in making sense of conservatorships and the duties attendant thereto.
In Pro Per	Standing of an individual who is not represented by an attorney in a court case and who is an interested party.
Individual Educational Plan (IEP)	The plan designed to meet the unique educational needs of a child who may have a disability as defined by Federal Regulations, mandated by the Individuals with Disabilities Education Act (IDEA), which sets specific goals and objectives and target dates for achieving them.

Individual Program Plan (IPP)	Person-centered planning to assist persons with developmental disabilities and their families to build their capacities and capabilities, including a preferred place to live, favored people with whom to socialize, and preferred types of daily activities, by a team consisting of the person, his or her family, regional center representatives, and others.
Judicial Council Forms	Official practice forms created by the Judicial Council of California, which are mandatory for use in California courts.
Judicial Council of California	A state governmental body chaired by the Chief Justice of the California Supreme Court, charged with improving the administration of justice in California's courts by performing a number of tasks.
Jurisdiction	The subject matter authority of a court to deal with and make decisions on legal matters within a defined area of responsibility. In conservatorship law, the California Superior Court, in the county of the proposed conservatee's residence, is the court with jurisdiction to hear and administer justice accordingly.
Law and Motion Calendar	The prescribed date and time for hearing short cause matters, including uncontested petitions for appointment of conservators. Conservatorship petitions are heard on the Probate Law and Motion Calendar in the county of the proposed conservatee's residence.
Letters of Conservatorship	The document issued by the court after the Order Appointing Conservator is signed and e-filed in the court case, giving the appointed conservator the fiduciary authority determined by the court to be appropriate for the protection of the conservatee.

Local Rules of Court	Rules of practice unique to each county in the State of California, found on the court website of each county.
Notice	The length of time required between the date of filing and serving court documents and the date of the court hearing. Notice is prescribed by the California Probate Code for various petitions, but notice may be extended by local rules of court.
Order	The document signed by a judge in determining the issues of a petition. In conservatorships, the Order must be signed and e-filed before Letters of Conservatorship may be issued by the court clerk.
Penalty of Perjury	A statement under oath that allegations of the declarant in a document are true and correct or that the allegations on the declarant's information and belief are true and correct. It serves to offer the allegations as legal evidence on which a court may act in making its orders. The statement reads as follows: "I declare under penalty of perjury under the laws of the State of California that the foregoing is true and correct, except as to those matters stated on my information and belief, and as to those matters, I believe them to be true."
Petition	A request of the court setting forth allegations under penalty of perjury and a prayer for relief in the manner requested.
Petitioner	The person who requests an order of the court.
Pleading Paper	Plain white paper with numbered double-spaced lines down the left margin for non-judicial council forms of court filings.

Powers	Authority granted by a court to exercise in the best interests of the limited conservatee, powers that limit the civil rights of the limited conservatee to do what he or she otherwise has the legal right to do.
Prayer	The requested Orders sought by a petition e-filed in a court case. It follows the allegations and starts with: "WHEREFORE, petitioner requests an order that:"
Pro Bono Attorney	An attorney who serves his or her client without compensation. In a Limited Conservatorship, a proposed limited conservatee does not likely have an estate from which his or her attorney may seek compensation for representation. Therefore, court-appointed attorneys for limited conservatees generally serve pro bono.
Probate	The area of law that deals with an individual's fiduciary power over the personal and financial affairs of another individual.
Probate Court	The court having jurisdiction over matters of probate law in the State of California.
Proof of Service	A statement showing proof that certain individuals were served with copies of documents e-filed with the court on a given date and at a given place. A Proof of Service for personal service will show who delivered the documents, and where and when the person was given the documents, signed by the server under penalty of perjury. A Proof of Service for mailed service will show who mailed the documents, what date they were mailed, and what post office was given the mailings for delivery.

Public Guardian	The governmental agency under the County Health Department charged with the physical and financial safety of county residents who are unable to do so on their own and have no family or other persons involved in their lives to assist them.
Regional Center	A nonprofit agency that contracts with the State of California to provide or find services for people with developmental disabilities. These services include assessment, case management, advocacy for disabled persons' rights, job training, counseling, recreation, and personal care. There are 21 regional centers throughout the state.
Relatives to the Second Degree	Those relatives who are grandparents, parents, siblings, children, and grandchildren of the proposed conservatee, for notice of matters in the Limited Conservatorship proceeding.
Seal of the Court	Seal of the State of California and County of the Superior Court stamped on the Citation of Conservatorship that is served on the proposed limited conservatee and also stamped on the Letters of Conservatorship and every certified copy of documents in the court file when requested.
Service List	The list of people who must be noticed in the Limited Conservatorship proceeding, including all relatives to the second degree, the Court-appointed Attorney for the proposed limited conservatee, and the Court Investigator.
Service of Process	The manner in which delivery was made to those on the Service List, whether by personal service, or by mailing, to name the most common by "In pro per" petitioners.

Special Needs Trust	A Trust specially designed for persons with developmental disabilities that protects their rights to receive public benefits if they inherit assets, which otherwise may be seized by providing agencies in recovery of funds expended while the individuals had no estates from which to pay for their services.
Substantial Limitations	When An individual living with developmental disabilities has functional limitations in three or more of the following areas of major life activities, determined by a Regional Center for application of services, pursuant to the California Welfare and Institutions Code §4512(l): a. Self-care b. Receptive and expressive language c. Learning d. Mobility e. Self-direction f. Capacity for independent living g. Economic self-sufficiency
Substituted Judgment	The legal procedure for establishing a Special Needs Trust in the event a limited conservatee acquires an inheritance that could jeopardize his or her right to receive public benefits.
Temporary Conservatorship	The emergency proceeding for appointment of a temporary limited conservator when there exists a danger to the conservatee to wait the regular noticed time period (up to 45 days) for the hearing on appointment of the limited conservator.

"With Heart – Understanding Conservatorships"	A video produced by the Judicial Council of California for use in all Superior Courts of the counties in California to prepare proposed conservators for their duties and responsibilities as fiduciaries for their conservatees. The video is generally geared to conservatorships for elders and physically impaired adults but may be adapted for Limited Conservatorships, and may be required viewing before the court will entertain a petition for appointment in the Limited Conservatorship proceeding.

Appendix A

Completed Forms for Limited Conservatorships

1. *Request to Waive Court Fees* (followed by Spanish form for translation only)

2. *Order on Court Fee Waiver* (followed by Spanish form for translation only)

3. *Duties of Conservator and Acknowledgment of Receipt of Handbook* (followed by Spanish form for translation only)

4. *Petition for Appointment of Probate Conservator of the ☐ Person ☐ Limited Conservatorship* (with Attachments 1c, 1h, 1j, 3f1, 3f2, and 5f)

5. *Confidential Supplemental Information*

6. *Capacity Declaration–Conservatorship* (for treating physician)

7. *Confidential Conservator Screening Form* (one for each proposed co-conservator)

8. *Ex Parte Application for Order Requiring Regional Center to Prepare an Assessment Report*

9. *Ex Parte Order Requiring Regional Center to Prepare an Assessment Report*

10. *Ex Parte Application for Order Appointing Counsel for the Proposed Limited Conservatee*

11. *Ex Parte Order Appointing Counsel for the Proposed Limited Conservatee*

12. *Order Appointing Court Investigator*

13. *Referral to Court Investigator*

14. *Conservator Viewing Receipt* (Video online - one for each proposed co-conservator)

15. *Petition for Appointment of Temporary Conservator*

16. *Notice of Hearing on Temporary Conservatorship*

17. *Proof of Service–Personal Service* (for attachment to #16 above)

18. *Order Appointing Temporary Conservator*

19. *Letters of Temporary Conservatorship*

20. *What is Proof of Service?* (followed by Spanish form for translation)

21. *Proof of Service* (pleading form prepared for San Andreas Regional Center)

22. *Notice of Hearing* (for limited conservatorship)

23. *Citation–Conservatorship*

24. *Order Appointing Limited Conservator*

25. *Letters of Conservatorship–Limited Conservatorship*

26. *Notice of Conservatee's Rights* (followed by Spanish form for translation)

27. *Determination of Conservatee's Appropriate Level of Care*

FW-001-GC Request to Waive Court Fees (Ward or Conservatee)

CONFIDENTIAL

Clerk stamps date here when form is filed.

Fill in court name and street address:

Superior Court of California, County of
MONTEREY
1200 Aguajito Road
Monterey, CA 93940

Fill in case number and name:

Case Number:

Case Name:
Limited Conservatorship of JOHN DOE

This form must be used by a guardian or conservator, or by a petitioner for the appointment of a guardian or conservator, to request a waiver of court fees in the guardianship or conservatorship court proceeding or in any other civil action in which the guardian or conservator represents the interests of the ward or conservatee as a plaintiff or defendant.

If the ward or conservatee (including a proposed ward or conservatee if a petition for appointment of a guardian or conservator has been filed but has not yet been decided by the court) directly receives public benefits or is supported by public benefits received by another for his or her support, is a low-income person, or does not have enough income to pay for his or her household's basic needs and the court fees, you may use this form to ask the court to waive the court fees. The court may order you to answer questions about the finances of the ward or conservatee. If the court waives the fees, the ward or conservatee, his or her estate, or someone with a duty to support the ward or conservatee, may still have to pay later if:

- You cannot give the court proof of the ward's or conservatee's eligibility,
- The ward's or conservatee's financial situation improves during this case, or
- You settle the civil case on behalf of the ward or conservatee for **$10,000** or more. The trial court that waives fees will have a lien on any such settlement in the amount of the waived fees and costs. The court may also charge the ward or conservatee, or his or her estate, any collection costs.

1. **Your Information** *(guardian or conservator, or person asking the court to appoint a guardian or conservator):*
   Name: Frank and Mary Doe Phone: (831) 123-4567
   Street or mailing address: 1234 Any Street
   City: Monterey State: CA Zip: 93940

2. **Your Lawyer** *(if you have one):* Name: ____
   Firm or Affiliation: ____ State Bar No.: ____
   Address: ____ Phone: (___) ___-____
   City: ____ State: ____ Zip: ____ E-mail: ____

   a. The lawyer has agreed to advance all or a portion of court fees or costs *(check one):* Yes ☐ No ☐
   b. *(If yes, your lawyer must sign here.)* Lawyer's signature: ____
   If your lawyer is not providing legal-aid type services based on your or the ward's or conservatee's low income, you may have to go to a hearing to explain why you are asking the court to waive the fees.

3. **Ward's or Conservatee's Information** *(file a separate* Request *for each ward in a multiward case):*
   Name: John Doe Age and date of birth *(ward only):* ____
   Street or mailing address: 1234 Any Street
   City: Monterey State: CA Zip: 93940
   Phone: (831) 123-4567

4. **Ward's or Conservatee's Lawyer**, if any: Name: Deputy Public Defender
   Firm or Affiliation: Monterey County Public Defender State Bar No.: ____
   Address: 168 West Alisal Street Phone: (831) 755-5058
   City: Salinas State: CA Zip: 93901 E-mail: ____

5. **Ward or Conservatee's Job** *(job title; if not employed, so state):* **unemployed**
   Name of employer: ____
   Employer's address: ____ State: ____ Zip: ____

Name of (Proposed) Ward or Conservatee: ______________________ | **Case Number:**

6 **What court's fees or costs are you asking to be waived?**

☒ Superior Court (See *Information Sheet on Waiver of Superior Court Fees and Costs* (form FW-001-INFO).)
☐ Supreme Court, Court of Appeal, or Appellate Division of Superior Court (See *Information Sheet on Waiver of Appellate Court Fees* (form APP-015/FW-015-INFO).)

7 ☐ Check here if you asked the court to waive court fees for this case in the last six months. *(If your previous request is reasonably available, please attach it to this form and check here):* ☐

8 **Why are you asking the court to waive the ward's or conservatee's court fees?**

a. ☒ The ward or one or both of the ward's parents, or the conservatee or the conservatee's spouse or registered domestic partner, receive *(check all that apply):*

☐ Supplemental Security Income (SSI) ☐ State Supplemental Payment (SSP) ☐ SNAP (Food Stamps)
☐ IHSS (In-Home Supportive Services) ☐ CalWORKS or Tribal TANF ☒ Medi-Cal
☐ County Relief/General Assistance ☐ CAPI (Cash Assistance Program for Aged, Blind, and Disabled)

(Names and relationships to ward or conservatee of persons who receive the public benefits listed above):

____

____

b. ☐ The gross monthly income of the ward's or conservatee's household (before deductions for taxes) is less than the amount listed below. *(If you check 8b, you **must** fill out items 14, 15, and 16 on page 4 of this form.)**

Family Size	Family Income	Family Size	Family Income	Family Size	Family Income	*If more than 6 people at home, add $450.00 for each extra person.*
1	$1,264.59	3	$2,164.59	5	$3,064.59	
2	$1,714.59	4	$2,614.59	6	$3,514.59	

c. ☐ The ward's or conservatee's household does not have enough income to pay for its basic needs *and* the court fees. I ask the court to *(check one, and you **must** fill out items 14, 15, 16, 17, and 18 on page 4):**

(i) ☐ Waive all court fees and costs. (ii) ☐ Waive some court fees and costs.

(iii) ☐ Let the (proposed) guardian or conservator, on behalf of the (proposed) ward or conservatee, make payments over time.

* *(Do not include income of guardian or conservator living in the household in 8b or 8c or count him or her in family size in 8b, unless he or she is a parent of the ward or the spouse or registered domestic partner of the conservatee.)*

Guardians or petitioners for their appointment must complete items 9 and 10.

9 **Ward's Estate:** ☒ Person only, no estate. ☐ Inventory or petition estimated value:

Source *(e.g., gift, inheritance, settlement, judgment, insurance):* Est. collection date:

10 **Ward's Parents' Information:**

a. Name of ward's father: Frank Doe ☐ Deceased *(date of death):* ________
Street or mailing address: 1234 Any Street
City: Monterey State: CA Zip: 93940
Phone: (831) 123-4567

b. Name of ward's mother: Mary Doe ☐ Deceased *(date of death):* ________
Street or mailing address: 1234 Any Street
City: Monterey State: CA Zip: 93940
Phone: (831) 123-4567

c. Ward's parents are *(check all that apply):* ☒ married ☒ living together ☐ separated ☐ divorced

Support order for ward? ☒ No ☐ Yes Payable to *(name):* ________

Payor *(name):* ________

Court: ________ Case Number: ________

Date of order *(if multiple, date of latest):* ________ Monthly amount: ________

Name of (Proposed) Ward or Conservatee: ____________________

Case Number:

Conservators or petitioners for their appointment must complete items 11–13.

(11) Conservatee's Estate: ☒ Person only, no estate.

☐ Inventory or petition estimated value: Est. collection date:

(12) Conservatee's Spouse's or Registered Domestic Partner's Information:

Name of conservatee's spouse or registered domestic partner: None ☐ Spouse ☐ Partner

Date of marriage or partnership: ________ ☐ Deceased *(date of death):* ________

Street or mailing address: ________ Phone: (___) ___-____

City: ________ State: ___ Zip: ________

Name of employer *(if none, so state):* ________

Employer's address: ________ State: ___ Zip: ________

The conservatee's spouse or partner ☐ is ☐ is not managing, or following appointment of a conservator is planning to manage, some or all of the couple's community property outside the conservatorship estate.

If you selected "is" above: The income, money, and property shown on page 4 ☐ includes ☐ does not include the income and property managed, or expected to be managed, by the spouse/partner outside the estate.

☐ Divorced *(date of final judgment or decree):* ________

Court: ________

Case Number: ________ Support order for conservatee? ☐ No ☐ Yes

Date of support order *(if multiple, date of latest):* ________ Monthly amount: ________

(13) The Conservatee and Trusts:

The conservatee:

a. ☐ Is ☒ Is not a trustor or settlor of a trust.

b. ☐ Is ☒ Is not a beneficiary of a trust.

If you selected "Is" to complete any of the above statements, identify and provide, in an attachment to this *Request*, the current address and telephone number of the current trustee(s) of each trust, describe the general terms of and value of each trust and the nature and value of the conservatee's interest in each trust, and the amount(s) and frequency of any distributions to or for the benefit of the conservatee prior to your appointment as conservator of which you are aware. *(You may use Judicial Council form MC-025 for this purpose.)*

All applicants who checked item 8b or item 8c on page 2 must continue to and follow the instructions for completion of items 14–16 or items 14–18 on page 4, before signing below.

The information I have provided on this form and all attachments about the (proposed) ward or conservatee is true and correct to the best of my information and belief. The information I have provided on this form and all attachments concerning myself is true and correct. I declare under penalty of perjury under the laws of the State of California that the foregoing is true and correct.

Date: [Insert filing date]

FRANK DOE and MARY DOE ▶ ____________________

Print your name here *Sign here*

Name of (Proposed) Ward or Conservatee: ______________________

Case Number:

*If you checked 8a on page 2, do not fill out below. If you checked 8b, you **must** answer questions 14–16. If you checked 8c, you **must** answer questions 14–18. If you need more space, attach form MC-025 or attach a sheet of paper, and write "Financial Information" and the ward's or conservatee's name and case number at the top.*

(14) ☐ Check here if the ward's or conservatee's income changes a lot from month to month. If it does, complete the form based on his or her average income for the past 12 months.

(15) Ward's or Conservatee's Gross Monthly Income

a. List the source and amount of ***any*** income the ward or conservatee gets each month, including: wages or other income from work before deductions, spousal/child support, retirement, social security, disability, unemployment, military basic allowance for quarters (BAQ), veterans payments, dividends, interest, trust income, annuities, net business or rental income, reimbursement for job-related expenses, gambling or lottery winnings, etc.

(1) ______________ $______
(2) ______________ $______
(3) ______________ $______
(4) ______________ $______
(5) ______________ $______

b. **Total monthly income**: $______

(16) Ward's or Conservatee's Household's Income

a. List the income of all other persons living in the ward's or conservatee's home who depend in whole or in part on him or her for support, or on whom he or she depends in whole or in part for support.

	Name	Age	Relationship	Gross Monthly Income
(1)				$
(2)				$
(3)				$
(4)				$
(5)				$
(6)				$
(7)				$
(8)				$
(9)				$
(10)				$

b. **Total monthly income of persons above:** $______

Total monthly income *and* household income *(15b plus 16b)*: $______

To list any other facts you want the court to know, such as the (proposed) ward's or conservatee's unusual medical expenses, etc, attach form MC-025 or attach a sheet of paper and write "Financial Information" and the (proposed) ward's or conservatee's name and case number at the top.

Check here if you attach another page. ☐

Important! **If the ward's or conservatee's financial situation or ability to pay court fees improves, you must notify the court within five days on form FW-010-GC.**

Do not include income of guardian or conservator living in the household in item 16, his or her money and property in item 17, or his or her deductions and expenses in item 18 unless he or she is a parent of the ward or the spouse or registered domestic partner of the conservatee.

(17) Ward's or Conservatee's Household's Money and Property

a. Cash $______

b. All financial accounts *(list bank name and amount)*:

(1) ______________ $______
(2) ______________ $______
(3) ______________ $______

c. Cars, boats, and other vehicles

	Make / Year	Fair Market Value	How Much You Still Owe
(1)		$	$
(2)		$	$
(3)		$	$

d. Real estate

	Address	Fair Market Value	How Much You Still Owe
(1)		$	$
(2)		$	$

e. Other personal property (jewelry, furniture, furs, stocks, bonds, etc.):

	Describe	Fair Market Value	How Much You Still Owe
(1)		$	$
(2)		$	$

(18) Ward's or Conservatee's Household's Monthly Deductions and Expenses

a. List any payroll deductions and the monthly amount below:

(1) ______________ $______
(2) ______________ $______
(3) ______________ $______
(4) ______________ $______

b. Rent or house payment and maintenance $______
c. Food and household supplies $______
d. Utilities and telephone $______
e. Clothing $______
f. Laundry and cleaning $______
g. Medical and dental expenses $______
h. Insurance (life, health, accident, etc.) $______
i. School, child care $______
j. Child, spousal support (another marriage) $______
k. Transportation, gas, auto repair and insurance $______
l. Installment payments *(list each below)*:

Paid to:

(1) ______________ $______
(2) ______________ $______
(3) ______________ $______

m. Wages/earnings withheld by court order $______

n. Any other monthly expenses *(list each below)*.

Paid to: How Much?

(1) ______________ $______
(2) ______________ $______
(3) ______________ $______

Total monthly expenses *(add 18a –18n above)*: $______

FW-001-GC S Solicitud de exención de cuotas de la corte (Dependiente o pupilo)

CONFIDENCIAL

El secretario pone un sello con la fecha aquí cuando se presenta el formulario.

Solo para información

No entregue a la corte

Ponga el nombre y dirección de la corte:

Corte Superior de California, Condado de

Ponga el número y nombre del caso:

Número de caso:
Solo para información

Nombre del caso:

Este formulario tiene que ser utilizado por el tutor de un menor o un adulto, o por la persona que solicita ser nombrada tutor, para pedir una exención de las cuotas de la corte en un proceso de tutela o cualquier otra acción civil en la cual el tutor represente los intereses del dependiente o pupilo como demandante o demandado. Si el dependiente o pupilo (o un dependiente o pupilo propuesto, si se presentó una petición para nombrar a un tutor pero la corte aún no tomó la decisión) recibe beneficios públicos, u otra persona recibe beneficios para su manutención, tiene bajos ingresos o no tiene los ingresos suficientes para pagar por las necesidades básicas de su hogar y además las cuotas de la corte, puede usar este formulario para pedir a la corte que lo exima del pago de las cuotas. La corte le puede ordenar que responda a preguntas sobre las finanzas del dependiente o pupilo. Si la corte otorga la exención de cuotas, es posible que el dependiente o pupilo, o su patrimonio, o alguien que tenga el deber de mantener al dependiente o pupilo, tenga que pagarlas más adelante si:

- No puede proporcionar a la corte una prueba de la elegibilidad del dependiente o pupilo;
- Se mejora la situación económica del dependiente o pupilo durante este caso; o
- Resuelve el caso civil en nombre del dependiente o pupilo con un fallo por **$10,000** o más. La corte de primera instancia que exima sus cuotas impondrá un derecho de retención sobre dicho fallo por el monto de las cuotas eximidas. La corte también puede cobrar todos los gastos de cobranza al dependiente, pupilo o a su patrimonio.

① **Su información** *(tutor de un menor o un adulto, o persona que le pide a la corte que nombre un tutor):*
Nombre: ***Solo para información*** Teléfono: ____________
Domicilio o dirección postal: ____________
Ciudad: ____________ Estado: ________ Cód. postal: ________

② **Su abogado** *(si tiene uno):* Nombre: ____________
Firma o afiliación: ____________ Núm. del Colegio de Abogados del Estado: ________
Domicilio: ____________ Teléfono: ____________
Ciudad: ____________ Estado: ________ Cód. postal: ________ Email: ____________

a. ¿Aceptó el abogado adelantar el monto total o una parte de las cuotas y costos? *(Marque una):* Sí ☐ No ☐

b. *(Si responde "sí," su abogado tiene que firmar aquí).* Firma del abogado: ____________
Si su abogado no le cobra por los servicios legales con base en los ingresos del dependiente o pupilo, es posible que tenga que explicar al juez por qué solicita una exención de cuotas.

③ **Información sobre el dependiente o pupilo** *(en un caso con múltiples dependientes, presente una* Solicitud *por separado para cada dependiente):*
Nombre: ____________
Domicilio o dirección postal: ____________
Ciudad: ____________ Estado: ________ Cód. postal: ________
Teléfono: ____________
Edad y fecha de nacimiento *(dependiente solamente):* ____________

④ **Abogado del dependiente o pupilo,** si tiene uno: Nombre: ____________
Firma o afiliación: ____________ Núm. del Colegio de Abogados del Estado: ________
Domicilio: ____________ Teléfono: ____________
Ciudad: ____________ Estado: ________ Cód. postal: ________ Email: ____________

⑤ **Trabajo del dependiente o pupilo** *(puesto en el trabajo; si no está empleado, indíquelo):* ____________
Nombre del empleador: ____________
Dirección del empleador: ____________

(6) ¿Para cuáles cuotas o costos de la corte solicita una exención?

☐ Cuotas de la Corte Superior (Vea la *Hoja informativa sobre la exención de cuotas y costos de la Corte Superior* (formulario FW-001-INFO)).

☐ Cuotas de la Corte Suprema, Corte de Apelación o División de Apelaciones de la Corte Superior (Vea la *Hoja informativa sobre la exención de cuotas y costos de una corte de apelación* (formulario APP-015/FW-015-INFO)).

(7) ☐ Marque aquí si pidió a la corte que lo eximiera del pago de las cuotas de este caso en los últimos seis meses. *(Si tiene la solicitud anterior o la puede conseguir razonablemente, adjúntela a este formulario y marque aquí):* ☐

(8) ☐ **¿Por qué le pide a la corte que le dé una exención de cuotas del dependiente o pupilo?**

a. ☐ El dependiente o uno o ambos padres del dependiente, o el pupilo o el cónyuge o pareja de hecho registrada del pupilo, reciben *(marque todo lo que corresponda):*

☐ SSI ☐ SSP ☐ SNAP (cupones de alimentos)
☐ IHSS ☐ CalWORKS o TANF Tribal ☐ Medi-Cal
☐ Ayuda general ☐ CAPI

(Nombre de las personas que reciben los beneficios públicos indicados más arriba, y su relación con el dependiente o pupilo):

b. ☐ Los ingresos mensuales brutos del hogar del dependiente o pupilo (antes de deducir impuestos) son menores al monto indicado a continuación. *(Si marcó 8b, **tiene que** llenar los puntos 14, 15 y 16 en la página 4 de este formulario).**

Tamaño de familia	Ingresos familiares	Tamaño de familia	Ingresos familiares	Tamaño de familia	Ingresos familiares
1	$1,226.05	3	$2,092.71	5	$2,959.38
2	$1,659.38	4	$2,526.05	6	$3,392.71

Si hay más de 6 personas en el hogar, agregue $433.34 por cada persona adicional.

c. ☐ El hogar del dependiente o pupilo no tiene ingresos suficientes para pagar por sus necesidades básicas y también las cuotas de la corte. Le pido a la corte que *(marque una, y **tiene que** llenar los puntos 14, 15, 16, 17 y 18 en la página 4):**

(i) ☐ me exima de pagar todas las cuotas de la corte. (ii) ☐ me exima de pagar algunas cuotas y costos de la corte.
(iii) ☐ le permita al tutor (propuesto) que pague las cuotas a plazos en nombre del dependiente o pupilo (propuesto).

**(No incluya los ingresos de un tutor que viva en el hogar en 8b. o 8c. ni lo cuente para calcular el tamaño de familia en 8b. a menos que sea el padre o madre del dependiente o el cónyuge o pareja de hecho del pupilo).*

Los tutores de menores, o aquellos que piden su nombramiento como tutor, tienen que llenar los puntos 9 y 10.

(9) Patrimonio del dependiente: ☐ De la persona solamente, no del patrimonio. ☐ Valor estimado indicado en el inventario o petición:

Fuente *(por ej., regalo, herencia, liquidación, fallo, seguro):* Fecha estimada de cobranza:

(10) Información sobre los padres del dependiente:

a. Nombre del padre del dependiente: ____________ ☐ Difunto *(fecha de defunción):* ________
Domicilio o dirección postal: ____________
Ciudad: ________ Estado: ______ Cód. postal: ______
Teléfono: ____________

b. Nombre de la madre del dependiente: ____________ ☐ Difunto *(fecha de defunción):* ________
Domicilio o dirección postal: ____________
Ciudad: ________ Estado: ______ Cód. postal: ______
Teléfono: ____________

c. Los padres del dependiente están *(marque todo lo que corresponda):* ☐casados ☐ viven juntos ☐ separados ☐divorciados

¿Orden de manutención para el dependiente? ☐ No ☐ Sí Pagadera a *(nombre):* ____________
Pagador *(nombre):* ____________
Corte: ____________ Número de caso: ________
Fecha de la orden *(si hay múltiples órdenes, fecha de la más reciente):* ______ Monto mensual: ______

Los tutores de adultos, o aquellos que piden su nombramiento como tutor, tienen que llenar los puntos 11 a 13.

(11) **Patrimonio del pupilo:** ☐ De la persona solamente, no del patrimonio.

☐ Valor estimado indicado en el inventario o petición: Fecha estimada de cobranza:

(12) **Información sobre el cónyuge o pareja de hecho registrada del pupilo:**

Nombre del cónyuge o pareja de hecho registrada del pupilo: ____________ ☐ Cónyuge ☐ Pareja de hecho

Fecha de matrimonio o registro de la pareja de hecho: ________ ☐ Difunto *(fecha de defunción):* ________

Domicilio o dirección postal: ____________ Teléfono: ________

Ciudad: ________ Estado: ________ Cód. postal: ________

Nombre del empleador *(si no tiene un empleador, indíquelo):* ________

Dirección del empleador: ____________ Estado: ________ Cód. postal: ________

El cónyuge o pareja de hecho del pupilo ☐ está ☐ no está administrando parte o todos los bienes comunitarios de la pareja fuera de la tutela del patrimonio, o piensa hacerlo después del nombramiento del tutor.

Si seleccionó "está" más arriba: Los ingresos, dinero y bienes indicados en la página 4 ☐ incluyen ☐ no incluyen los ingresos y bienes administrados por el cónyuge/pareja de hecho fuera de la tutela del patrimonio, o que el cónyuge/pareja de hecho piensa administrar fuera de la tutela del patrimonio.

☐ Divorciado *(fecha del fallo o decreto final):* ________

Corte: ________

Número de caso: ________ ¿Orden de manutención para el pupilo? ☐ No ☐ Sí

Fecha de la orden *(si hay múltiples órdenes, fecha de la más reciente):* ________ Monto mensual: ________

(13) **El pupilo y fideicomisos:**

El pupilo:

a. ☐ Es ☐ No es un fiduciante o liquidador de un fideicomiso.

b. ☐ Es ☐ No es el beneficiario de un fideicomiso.

Si seleccionó "Es" en alguno de los puntos anteriores, identifique y ponga, en un adjunto a esta *Solicitud*, la dirección y número de teléfono actual del/de los fiduciario(s) actuales de cada fideicomiso, describa los términos generales y el valor de cada fideicomiso, y la naturaleza y el interés del pupilo en cada fideicomiso, y la(s) cantidad(es) y frecuencia de cualquier distribución recibida por el pupilo, o dada en beneficio del mismo, antes del nombramiento de un tutor, de las que usted esté enterado. *(Para ese fin puede usar el formulario MC-025 del Consejo Judicial).*

Todos los solicitantes que marcaron el punto 8b o 8c de la página 2 tienen que pasar a los puntos 14 a 16 o los puntos 14 a 18 al principio de la página 4, y seguir las instrucciones correspondientes para completarlos, antes de firmar a continuación.

La información que proporcioné en este formulario y en todos los adjuntos sobre el dependiente o pupilo (propuesto) es verdadera y correcta según mi leal saber y entender. La información que he proporcionado sobre mí en este formulario y en todos los adjuntos es verdadera y correcta. Declaro bajo pena de perjurio conforme a las leyes del estado de California que lo anterior es verdadero y correcto.

Fecha: ________

________ **Solo para información**

Su nombre en letra de molde *Firme aquí*

Si marcó el punto 8a en la página 2, no tiene que llenar esta página. Si marcó el punto 8b, conteste las preguntas 14 a 16. Si marcó el punto 8c, ***tiene que*** *llenar toda esta página. Si necesita más espacio, adjunte el formulario MC-025 o una hoja separada, y escriba* "Financial Information", *y el nombre y número de caso del dependiente o pupilo en la parte superior de la hoja.*

14 ☐ Marque aquí si los ingresos del dependiente o pupilo cambian mucho de un mes para otro, y llene este formulario usando el promedio de sus ingresos durante los últimos 12 meses.

15 Ingresos brutos mensuales del dependiente o pupilo

a. Indique el origen y monto de ***cualquier*** otro ingreso que reciba el dependiente o pupilo por mes, como por ejemplo: sueldo u otro ingreso del trabajo (antes de deducir los impuestos), manutención del cónyuge/hijo, jubilación, seguro social, discapacidad, desempleo, asignación militar básica para vivienda (BAQ), pagos a veteranos de guerra, dividendos, intereses, ingresos de fideicomisos, anualidades, ingresos netos de negocio o renta, reembolsos de gastos relacionados con el trabajo, ganancias de juegos de apuestas o lotería, etc.

(1) ____________ $________
(2) ____________ $________
(3) ____________ $________
(4) ____________ $________
(5) ____________ $________

b. **Sus ingresos mensuales totales:** $________

16 Ingresos del hogar del dependiente o pupilo

a. Indique los ingresos de todas las otras personas que viven en el hogar del dependiente o pupilo y que dependen de él/ella para mantenerse, por completo o en parte, o de quienes dependa él/ella para mantenerse, ya sea por completo o en parte.

	Nombre	Edad	Relación	Ingresos mensuales brutos
(1)				$
(2)				$
(3)				$
(4)				$
(5)				$
(6)				$
(7)				$
(8)				$
(9)				$
(10)				$

b. **Ingresos mensuales totales de las personas arriba indicadas:** $________

Ingresos mensuales totales *más* ingresos del hogar *(15b más 16b)*: $________

Si desea poner otros datos que la corte deba conocer, como por ejemplo gastos médicos inusuales del dependiente o pupilo (propuesto), etc., adjunte el formulario MC-025 o adjunte una hoja separada, y escriba "Financial Information", y el nombre y número de caso del dependiente o pupilo (propuesto) en la parte superior de la hoja.

Si adjunta otra hoja, marque aquí. ☐

¡Importante! **Si se mejora la situación económica o la capacidad de pagar las cuotas de la corte del dependiente o pupilo, tiene que notificar a la corte dentro de cinco días utilizando el formulario FW-010-GC.**

No incluya los ingresos de un tutor que vive en el hogar en el punto 16 ni su dinero o bienes en el punto 17, ni sus deducciones y gastos en el punto 18, a menos que sea el padre o madre del dependiente o el cónyuge o pareja de hecho registrada del pupilo.

17 Dinero y bienes del hogar del dependiente o pupilo

a. Efectivo $________

b. Todas sus cuentas financieras *(Indique el nombre del banco y el monto)*:
(1) ____________ $________
(2) ____________ $________
(3) ____________ $________

c. Carros, lanchas y otros vehículos

	Marca / Año	Valor justo de mercado	Cuánto debe todavía
(1)		$	$
(2)		$	$
(3)		$	$

d. Bienes raíces

	Dirección	Valor justo de mercado	Cuánto debe todavía
(1)		$	$
(2)		$	$

e. Otros bienes personales (joyas, muebles, pieles, acciones, bonos, etc.)

	Descripción	Valor justo de mercado	Cuánto debe todavía
(1)		$	$
(2)		$	$

18 Deducciones y gastos mensuales del dependiente o pupilo

a. Indique cada deducción de nómina y el monto mensual a continuación:
(1) ____________ $________
(2) ____________ $________
(3) ____________ $________
(4) ____________ $________

b. Pago de su casa o alquiler, más mantenimiento $________
c. Comida e insumos del hogar $________
d. Servicios públicos y teléfono $________
e. Ropa $________
f. Lavandería y limpieza $________
g. Gastos médicos y dentales $________
h. Seguro (de vida, de salud, contra accidentes, etc.) $________
i. Escuela, cuidado de niños $________
j. Manutención de hijos, del cónyuge (otro matrimonio) $________
k. Transporte, gasolina, reparación y seguro de automóviles $________
l. Pagos a plazos *(indique todos a continuación)*:
Pagado a:
(1) ____________ $________
(2) ____________ $________
(3) ____________ $________
m. Sueldos/Ingresos retenidos por orden de la corte $________
n. Cualquier otro gasto mensual *(indique todos a continuación)*. $________
Pagado a: ¿Cuánto?
(1) ____________ $________
(2) ____________ $________
(3) ____________ $________

Gastos mensuales totales *(sume 18a a 18n de arriba)*: $________

FW-003-GC **Order on Court Fee Waiver (Superior Court) (Ward or Conservatee)**

Clerk stamps date here when form is filed.

1. **(Proposed) guardian or conservator who asked the court to waive court fees for (proposed) ward or conservatee:**
   Name: Frank and Mary Doe
   Street or mailing address: 1234 Any Street
   City: Monterey State: CA Zip: 93940
   Telephone: (831) 123-4567

2. **Lawyer, if person in (1) has one:**
   Name: ______ State Bar No: ______
   Firm or Affiliation: ______
   Street or mailing address: ______
   City: ______ State: ___ Zip: ______
   E-mail: ______ Telephone: ______

3. **(Proposed) ward or conservatee:**
   Name: John Doe
   Street or mailing address: 1234 Any Street
   City: Monterey State: CA Zip: 93940
   Telephone: ______

4. **Lawyer for (proposed) ward or conservatee, if any:**
   Name: Deputy Public Defender State Bar No: ______
   Firm or Affiliation: Monterey County Public Defender
   Street or mailing address: 168 West Alisal Street
   City: Salinas State: CA Zip: 93901
   E-mail: ______ Telephone: (831) 755-5058

5. A request to waive court fees was filed on *(date)*: [Insert filing date]
   ☐ The court made a previous fee waiver order in this case on *(date)*:

Fill in court name and street address:

Superior Court of California, County of
MONTEREY
1200 Aguajito Road
Monterey, CA 93940

Fill in case number and name:

Case Number:

Case Name:
Ltd Conservatorship of JOHN DOE

Read this form carefully. All checked boxes ☒ are court orders.

Notice: The court may order you to answer questions about the ward's or conservatee's finances after granting a waiver and may later order payment of the waived fees from his or her estate. If this happens and the fees are not paid, the court can also charge collection fees. The court may also direct you to make efforts to collect money to pay back waived fees from persons who owe a duty to support the ward or conservatee. If there is a change in the ward's or conservatee's financial circumstances during this case that increases his or her ability to pay fees and costs, you must notify the trial court within five days. (Use form FW-010-GC.)

If this case is an action against another party and you win the case on behalf of the ward or conservatee, the trial court may order the other side to pay some or all of the waived fees. If you settle the matter for **$10,000** or more, the trial court will have a lien on the settlement in the amount of the waived fees. The trial court may not dismiss the case until the lien is paid.

The court may also have a lien against the ward's or conservatee's estate that must be paid before the estate is distributed, the guardianship or conservatorship proceeding is concluded, and you are discharged as guardian or conservator.

6. After reviewing your: ☒ *Request to Waive Court Fees* ☐ *Request to Waive Additional Court Fees* ***the court makes the following orders:***

   a. ☒ The court **grants** your request concerning the ward's or conservatee's court fees and costs, as follows:

      (1) ☒ **Fee Waiver.** The court grants your request and waives the fees and costs listed below. *(Cal. Rules of Court, rules 3.55 and 8.818.)* You do not have to pay the court fees for the following:
      - Filing papers in Superior Court
      - Making copies and certifying copies
      - Sheriff's fee to give notice
      - Court fee for phone hearing
      - Giving notice and certificates
      - Sending papers to another court department
      - Court-appointed interpreter in small claims court

      (List continued on next page.)

6 a. (1)
- Reporter's fee for attendance at hearing or trial, if reporter provided by the court
- Assessment for court investigations under Probate Code section 1513, 1826, or 1851
- Preparing, certifying, copying, and sending the clerk's transcript on appeal
- Holding in trust the deposit for a reporter's transcript on appeal under rule 8.130 or 8.834
- Making a transcript or copy of an official electronic recording under rule 8.835

(2) ☐ **Additional Fee Waiver.** The court grants your request and waives the additional superior court fees and costs that are checked below. *(Cal. Rules of Court, rule 3.56.)* You do not have to pay for the checked items.

☐ Jury fees and expenses
☐ Fees for court-appointed experts
☐ Other*(specify)*: ______________________
☐ Fees for a peace officer to testify in court
☐ Court-appointed interpreter fees for a witness

b. ☐ The court **denies** your fee waiver request, as follows:

Warning! If you miss the deadline below, the court cannot process your request for hearing or the court papers you filed with your original request. If the papers were a notice of appeal, the appeal may be dismissed.

(1) ☐ The court **denies** your request because it is incomplete. You have **10 days** after the clerk gives notice of this order (see date of service on next page) to:
- Pay the ward's or conservatee's fees and costs, or
- File a new revised request that includes the items listed below *(specify incomplete items)*:

____
____
____

(2) ☐ The court **denies** your request because the information you provided on the request shows that the ward or conservatee is not eligible for the fee waiver you requested *(specify reasons)*:

____
____
____
____

The court has enclosed a blank *Request for Hearing About Court Fee Waiver Order (Ward or Conservatee)(Superior Court)*, form FW-006-GC.You have **10 days** after the clerk gives notice of this order (see date of service on next page) to:
- Pay the fees and costs in full or the amount listed in c below, or
- Ask for a hearing in order to show the court more information. *(Use form FW-006-GC to request hearing.)*

c. ☐ The court needs more information to decide whether to grant your request. You must go to court on the date below. The hearing will be about *(specify questions regarding eligibility)*:

____
____
____
____

☐ Bring the following proof to support your request if reasonably available:

____
____
____
____

Name of (Proposed) Ward or Conservatee: ______

Case Number:

Warning! If item c is checked, and you do not go to court on your hearing date, the judge will deny your request to waive court fees, and you will have 10 days to pay the ward's or conservatee's fees. If you miss that deadline, the court cannot process the court papers you filed with your request. If the papers were a notice of appeal, the appeal may be dismissed.

NOTE TO GUARDIAN or CONSERVATOR: If there are unpaid court fees after a denial of a request for a fee waiver, your case—including the guardianship or conservatorship proceeding if the waiver is requested in that matter—might not go forward. After a denial, you may choose to advance the court costs yourself to ensure that the case proceeds. If you or another person is appointed as guardian or conservator, you would have an opportunity to be reimbursed for such advances from the assets of the guardianship or conservatorship estate, if any, as allowable expenses of administration. You might also have the right to reimbursement for advanced court costs from persons with an obligation to support the ward or conservatee from assets not part of his or her estate, such as a parent of the ward, the spouse or registered domestic partner of the conservatee who is managing the couple's community property outside the conservatorship estate, or the trustee of a trust of which the conservatee is a beneficiary.

Hearing Date Date: ______ Time: ______
Dept.: ______ Room: ______

Name and address of court if different from above:
______

Date: ______ ▶ ______
Signature of (check one): ☐ *Judicial Officer* ☐ *Clerk, Deputy*

Request for Accommodations. Assistive listening systems, computer-assisted real-time captioning, or sign language interpreter services are available if you ask at least 5 days before your hearing. Contact the clerk's office for *Request for Accommodation,* Form MC-410. (Civil Code, § 54.8.)

Clerk's Certificate of Service

I certify that I am not involved in this case and *(check one):* ☐ A certificate of mailing is attached.

☐ I handed a copy of this order to the party and attorney, if any, listed in ①, ②, and ④ at the court, on the date below.

☐ This order was mailed first class, postage paid, to the party and attorney, if any, at the addresses listed in ①, ②, and ④, from *(city):* ______, California on the date below.

Date: ______ Clerk, by ______, Deputy

This is a Court Order.

FW-003-GC S Orden sobre la exención de cuotas de la corte (Corte Superior) (Dependiente o pupilo)

El secretario pone un sello con la fecha aquí cuando se presenta el formulario.

Solo para información
No entregue a la corte

① **Tutor (propuesto) que pidió a la corte la exención de cuotas para el dependiente o pupilo (propuesto):**
Nombre: *Solo para información*
Domicilio o dirección postal: ______
Ciudad: ______ Estado: ______ Cód. postal: ______
Teléfono: ______

② **Abogado, si la persona en ① tiene uno:**
Nombre: ______ Núm. del Colegio de Abogados del Estado: ______
Firma o afiliación: ______
Domicilio o dirección postal: ______
Ciudad: ______ Estado: ______ Cód. postal: ______
Email: ______ Teléfono: ______

Ponga el nombre y dirección de la corte:
Corte Superior de California, Condado de

③ **Dependiente o pupilo (propuesto):**
Nombre: ______
Domicilio o dirección postal: ______
Ciudad: ______ Estado: ______ Cód. postal: ______
Teléfono: ______

Ponga el número y nombre del caso:
Número de caso:
Solo para información
Nombre del caso:

④ **Abogado del dependiente o pupilo (propuesto), si tiene uno:**
Nombre: ______ Núm. del Colegio de Abogados del Estado: ______
Firma o afiliación: ______
Domicilio o dirección postal: ______
Ciudad: ______ Estado: ______ Cód. postal: ______
Email: ______ Teléfono: ______

⑤ Se presentó una solicitud de exención de cuotas de la corte el *(fecha):* ______
☐ La corte dictó una orden anterior de exención de cuotas en este caso el *(fecha):*

Lea este formulario con atención. Todas las casillas marcadas así ☒ son órdenes de la corte.

Aviso: La corte le puede ordenar que responda a preguntas sobre las finanzas del dependiente o pupilo después de otorgar una exención, y puede ordenar más tarde el pago de las cuotas eximidas, con fondos de su patrimonio. Si llega a ocurrir esto y no paga las cuotas, la corte también le puede cobrar los gastos de cobranza. La corte también le puede instruir que se esfuerce por conseguir dinero para pagar las cuotas eximidas de las personas que tienen el deber de mantener al dependiente o pupilo. Si cambian las circunstancias económicas del dependiente o pupilo durante el caso y se mejora su capacidad de pagar las cuotas y costos, tiene que notificar a la corte de primera instancia dentro de cinco días. (Use el formulario FW-010-GC).

Si este caso es una acción civil contra otra parte y usted gana el caso en nombre del dependiente o pupilo, la corte de primera instancia puede ordenar a la otra parte que pague las cuotas. Si resuelve su caso por **$10,000** o más, la corte de primera instancia impondrá un derecho de retención sobre el monto del acuerdo por el valor de las cuotas eximidas. La corte puede negarse a despedir el caso hasta que el derecho de retención quede saldado.

La corte también podrá imponer un derecho de retención contra el patrimonio del dependiente o pupilo, que se tendrá que pagar antes de que se distribuya el patrimonio, se concluya el proceso de la tutela y le den de alta como tutor.

⑥ ***La corte dicta las siguientes órdenes*** después de revisar su: ☐ *Solicitud de exención de cuotas de la corte*
☐ *Solicitud de exención de cuotas adicionales de la corte*

a. ☐ La corte **otorga** su solicitud sobre las cuotas y costos de la corte del dependiente o pupilo, tal como sigue:

(1) ☐ **Exención de cuotas.** La corte aprueba su solicitud y exime las cuotas y costos de la corte indicados a continuación. *(Reglas de la Corte de Cal., reglas 3.55 y 8.818).* No tendrá que pagar cuotas de la corte por lo siguiente:

- Presentar documentos a la corte superior
- Hacer y certificar copias
- Cuota del alguacil para dar aviso
- Cuota de la corte por audiencia telefónica
- Entregar avisos y certificados
- Enviar documentos a otro departamento judicial
- Intérprete nombrado por la corte en la corte de reclamos menores

(La lista continúa en la página siguiente).

(6) a. (1)
- Cuota de taquígrafo por asistir a la audiencia o juicio, si la corte proporciona el taquígrafo
- Costo de investigaciones de la corte conforme al Código Testamentario, sección 1513, 1826 o 1851
- Preparar, certificar, fotocopiar y enviar el acta oficial del secretario en una apelación
- Mantener en fideicomiso el depósito para el acta del taquígrafo en una apelación conforme a la regla 8.130 u 8.834
- Preparar el acta oficial o la copia de una grabación electrónica oficial conforme a la regla 8.835

(2) ☐ **Exención de cuotas adicionales.** La corte aprueba su solicitud y exime las cuotas y costos adicionales de la corte superior que están marcados a continuación. *(Reglas de la Corte de Cal., regla 3.56)* No tiene que pagar por las cuotas y costos marcados a continuación.

☐ Cuotas y gastos de jurado ☐ Cuota para que un oficial del orden público testifique ante la corte
☐ Cuotas de expertos nombrados por la corte ☐ Cuota de intérprete nombrado por la corte para un testigo
☐ Otro *(especificar)*: ______

b. ☐ La corte **rechaza** su solicitud, de la siguiente manera:

> **¡Alerta!** Si deja pasar la fecha límite indicada a continuación, la corte no podrá procesar su solicitud de audiencia ni los documentos de la corte que presentó junto con su solicitud original. Si los documentos eran un aviso de apelación, es posible que la apelación se despida.

(1) ☐ La corte **rechaza** su solicitud porque está incompleta. Tiene **10 días** a partir de la fecha en que el secretario le dé aviso de esta orden (vea la fecha a continuación) para:
- Pagar las cuotas y costos del dependiente o pupilo; o
- Presentar una solicitud corregida que incluya los elementos indicados a continuación *(especificar los elementos incompletos)*:

______
______

(2) ☐ La corte **rechaza** su solicitud porque la información provista en la solicitud demuestra que el dependiente o pupilo no es elegible para recibir la exención de cuotas que solicitó *(especificar las razones)*:

______
______
______

La corte ha incluido una copia en blanco de la *Solicitud de audiencia sobre la orden de exención de cuotas de la corte (Dependiente o pupilo) (Corte Superior)*, formulario FW-006-GC. Tiene **10 días** a partir de la fecha en que el secretario le dé aviso de esta orden (ver la fecha de entrega legal en la siguiente página) para:
- Pagar las cuotas y costos por completo o el monto indicado en c. a continuación; o
- Solicitar una audiencia para presentar más información a la corte. *(Para solicitar la audiencia, use el formulario FW-006-GC).*

c. ☐ La corte necesita más información para decidir si aprueba su solicitud. Tiene que ir a la corte en la fecha indicada a continuación. La audiencia considerará lo siguiente *(especificar las preguntas sobre la elegibilidad)*:

______
______
______
______

☐ Lleve las siguientes pruebas para respaldar su solicitud, si están razonablemente disponibles.

______
______
______

Nombre del dependiente o pupilo (propuesto):
Solo para información

Número de caso:
No entregue a la corte

¡Alerta! Si está marcado el punto c. y no se presenta en la corte en la fecha de su audiencia, el juez rechazará su solicitud de exención de cuotas de la corte y tendrá que pagar las cuotas del dependiente o el pupilo dentro de 10 días. Si no paga para la fecha límite, la corte no podrá tramitar sus documentos. Si los documentos son para un aviso de apelación, es posible que la apelación se despida.

AVISO AL TUTOR: Si hay cuotas de la corte impagas después del rechazo de una solicitud de exención de cuotas, es posible que su caso – incluyendo los procesos de tutela, si pidió la exención en ese caso – no avance. Después de un rechazo, puede optar por adelantar los costos de la corte de su propio bolsillo para asegurar que el caso prosiga. Si usted u otra persona es nombrada como tutor, tendrá la oportunidad de recibir un reembolso por dichos adelantos de los fondos del patrimonio de la tutela, si corresponde, como gastos permitidos de administración. Es posible que tenga el derecho a recibir un reembolso de los costos de la corte adelantados por personas que tienen la obligación de mantener al dependiente o pupilo, de fondos que no forman parte de su patrimonio, como de un padre del dependiente, o del cónyuge o pareja de hecho registrada del pupilo, que está administrando los bienes comunitarios de la pareja fuera de la tutela del patrimonio, o del fiduciario de un fideicomiso cuyo beneficiario es el pupilo.

Fecha de audiencia → Fecha: ____________ Hora: ____________
Depto.: ____________ Sala: ____________

Nombre y dirección de la corte si es distinto a lo anterior:
____
____
____
____
____

Fecha: ____________________

▶ ______________________________
Firma del (marcar una): ☐ *Funcionario judicial* ☐ *Secretario, Asistente*

Solicitud de modificaciones. Hay a su disposición: sistemas para ayudarle a escuchar, sistemas computarizados que generan subtítulos en tiempo real, o la ayuda de un intérprete del lenguaje de señas si lo solicita al menos 5 días antes de su audiencia. Comuníquese con el secretario de la corte para conseguir una *Solicitud de modificaciones*, formulario MC-410. (Código Civil, sección 54.8).

Certificado del secretario de entrega legal

Certifico que no estoy involucrado en este caso y *(marque una):* ☐ Se adjunta un certificado de envío por correo.

☐ Entregué en persona en la corte una copia de esta orden a la parte y abogado, si corresponde, indicados en ①, ② y ④, en la fecha indicada a continuación.

☐ Esta orden fue enviada por correo de primera clase con porte pagado a la parte y abogado, si corresponde, a las direcciones indicadas en ①, ② y ④, desde *(ciudad):* ____________________, California, en la fecha indicada a continuación.

Fecha: ____________________ Secretario, por ____________________________, Asistente

Esta es una orden de la corte.

ATTORNEY OR PARTY WITHOUT ATTORNEY *(Name, State Bar number, and address):*
Frank and Mary Doe
1234 Any Street
Monterey, CA 93940

TELEPHONE NO.: (831) 123-4567 FAX NO. *(Optional):*
E-MAIL ADDRESS *(Optional):* 2does@yahoo.com
ATTORNEY FOR *(Name):* In pro per

FOR COURT USE ONLY

SUPERIOR COURT OF CALIFORNIA, COUNTY OF MONTEREY
STREET ADDRESS: 1200 Aguajito Road
MAILING ADDRESS: 1200 Aguajito Road
CITY AND ZIP CODE: Monterey, CA 93940
BRANCH NAME: Monterey

CONSERVATORSHIP OF THE ☑ PERSON ☐ ESTATE OF
(Name): JOHN DOE
CONSERVATEE

DUTIES OF CONSERVATOR
and Acknowledgment of Receipt of *Handbook for Conservators*

CASE NUMBER:

DUTIES OF CONSERVATOR

When you are appointed by the court as a conservator, you become responsible to the court and assume certain duties and obligations. All of your actions as conservator are subject to review by the court. You should clearly understand the information on this form. You will find additional information in the Judicial Council's *Handbook for Conservators,* receipt of which, in addition to a copy of this form, you are required by law to acknowledge.

I. THE CONSERVATEE'S RIGHTS

Conservatees do not lose all rights or all voice in important decisions affecting their lives. All conservatees have the right to be treated with understanding and respect, the right to have their wishes considered, and the right to be well cared for by their conservators. Conservatees generally keep the right to (1) control their own wages or salary from employment, (2) make or change a will, (3) marry, (4) receive personal mail, (5) be represented by a lawyer, (6) ask a judge to change conservators, (7) ask a judge to end the conservatorship, (8) vote, unless a judge decides they are not capable of exercising this right, (9) control personal spending money if a judge has authorized an allowance, and (10) make their own medical decisions, unless a judge has taken away that right and given it exclusively to their conservators.

II. CONSULT WITH YOUR ATTORNEY

Your attorney will advise you on your duties, the limits of your authority, the conservatee's rights, your dealings with the court, all other topics discussed in this form, and many other matters. He or she will tell you when you must ask for prior court approval to take an action, when you may do so (and why it might be a good idea), and when prior court approval is not required. All legal questions should be discussed with your attorney, not the court staff, which is not permitted to give legal advice.

Your attorney will also help prepare your inventories, accountings, petitions, and all other documents to be filed with the court; and will see that the persons entitled to be notified of your actions are given proper notice. He or she will also advise you about legal limits on estate investments, leases and sales of estate assets, loans, lawsuits against others involving the conservatee or his or her property, and many other matters, and can prepare or review documents needed in these matters. You should communicate frequently and cooperate fully with your attorney at all times. **When in doubt, contact your attorney.**

Other questions may be answered by calling on local community resources. (To find these resources, see the *Handbook for Conservators* and the local supplement distributed by the court.)

III. CONSERVATOR OF THE PERSON

If the court appoints you as conservator of the person, you are responsible for the conservatee's care and protection. You must decide, within certain limits, where the conservatee will live; and you must arrange for the conservatee's health care, meals, clothing, personal care, housekeeping, transportation, and recreation.

A. DETERMINE THE APPROPRIATE LEVEL OF CARE FOR THE CONSERVATEE

You must determine the conservatee's appropriate level of care. Your determination must be in writing, signed under penalty of perjury, must be filed with the court within 60 days of the date of the court's order appointing you as conservator, and must include:

CONSERVATORSHIP OF *(Name)*: JOHN DOE CONSERVATEE	CASE NUMBER:

III. A. 1. An evaluation of the level of care existing when the petition for your appointment as a conservator was filed and the measures that would be necessary to keep the conservatee in his or her **personal residence.**

(Note: The conservatee's ***personal residence*** *is the residence the conservatee understood or believed to be his or her permanent residence on (1) the date the petition for appointment of a conservator was filed in this matter, or (2) on the last earlier date the conservatee could form or communicate an understanding or belief about a permanent residence, whether or not he or she was living there when the appointment petition was filed. See Cal. Rules of Court, rule 7.1063(b).)*

2. A plan to return the conservatee to his or her **personal residence** or an explanation of the limitations or restrictions on a return of the conservatee to that residence in the foreseeable future if the conservatee was not living there when the petition for appointment of a conservator was filed.

3. A reevaluation after a material (important) change in circumstances affecting the conservatee's needs for placement and care after your initial determination.

4. If the conservatee is a limited conservatee who is developmentally disabled, special rules may apply to the determination of his or her level of care and residential placement. See item **VI** below.

B. DECIDE WHERE THE CONSERVATEE WILL LIVE

1. You must decide where the conservatee will live. You may choose a residence in California without prior approval of the court, but you must choose the least restrictive appropriate residence that is available and necessary to meet the conservatee's needs and that is in his or her best interests.

2. You must file a written notice of any change of the conservatee's residence with the court within 30 days of the move, and you must mail copies of the notice to the conservatee's attorney, the conservatee's spouse or registered domestic partner, and the conservatee's relatives who were mailed copies of the petition for your appointment as conservator, unless the court excuses you from the mailing to prevent harm to the conservatee. (There is a court form you must use for this notice and another form you may use to prove that you have mailed it. The forms are the *Post-Move Notice of Change of Residence of Conservatee or Ward* (form GC-080) and the *Attachment to Post-Move Notice, etc.* (form GC-080(MA). These forms refer to a "post-move notice" because the notice may be filed and mailed after the date of the move.)

3. The law presumes that the conservatee's **personal residence** (see item **IIIA**) is the conservatee's least restrictive appropriate residence. There must be a reason supported by sufficient evidence to justify a change of residence from the conservatee's personal residence (including a move from a care facility or other temporary placement to a residence that is not the conservatee's personal residence).

4. If you want to move the conservatee from his or her **personal residence,** in addition to the post-move notice described in item 2, you must mail a notice of your intent to change the conservatee's residence to the conservatee, the conservatee's attorney, if any, and to each other person or entity entitled to notice of the hearing on the petition for your appointment as conservator; and then you must file with the court proof that the notice was mailed. Unless there is an emergency requiring a shorter period of notice, this notice must be mailed at least 15 days before the date of the proposed move. (There is a court form you must use for this notice and another form you may use to prove that you have mailed it. The forms are the *Pre-Move Notice of Proposed Change of Personal Residence of Conservatee or Ward* (form GC-079) and the *Attachment to Pre-Move Notice, etc.* (form GC-079(MA). These forms refer to a "pre-move notice" because the notice must be mailed before the move.)

5. If you want to establish the conservatee's residence outside California, you must petition the court for permission before the move. Notice of the court hearing on this petition, together with a copy of the petition, must be mailed to the conservatee and the other persons and entities that were entitled to notice of the hearing on the petition for your appointment as conservator. There is a court form for this petition, the *Petition to Fix Residence Outside the State of California* (form GC-085). Notice of the hearing and proof of its mailing is given on another court form, the *Notice of Hearing—Guardianship or Conservatorship* (form GC-020).

6. You may not place the conservatee involuntarily in a mental health treatment facility unless he or she has been determined to be gravely disabled as the result of a mental disorder or impairment by chronic alcoholism, you have been appointed as conservator under the Lanterman-Petris-Short Act (Welf. & Inst. Code, § 5350 et seq.), and then only if the court has authorized the placement. If the court has authorized you to place the conservatee in a secured-perimeter residential care facility or a locked and secured nursing facility because he or she suffers from dementia, you must be sure that the placement is the least restrictive placement appropriate to the conservatee's needs.

CONSERVATORSHIP OF (Name): JOHN DOE CONSERVATEE	CASE NUMBER:

III. C. PROVIDE MEDICAL CARE FOR THE CONSERVATEE

You are responsible for making sure that the conservatee's health care needs are met. But there are special rules you must follow to meet these needs. Two of the most important rules are as follows:

1. Unless the court has given you exclusive authority to consent to the conservatee's medical treatment because the court has determined that the conservatee has lost the capacity to make sound medical decisions, your consent or refusal to consent to such treatment is not sufficient if the conservatee disagrees (except in certain emergency situations). If you do have exclusive medical consent authority, you should be sure that all medical treatment and medications are appropriate.
2. If the conservatee has dementia and has lost the capacity to give an informed consent to the administration of medications for its treatment and care, you must be given specific authority by the court to consent to the administration of these medications. If you do have this authority, you should be sure that the medications are appropriate.

D. WORK WITH THE PERSON(S) RESPONSIBLE FOR MANAGING THE CONSERVATEE'S PROPERTY

If other persons are handling the conservatee's property, such as his or her estate conservator, the conservatee's spouse or registered domestic partner in possession of the couple's marital or partnership property, or the trustee of a trust created for the management of the conservatee's property and for his or her support, you must work together to be sure that the conservatee can afford the care you arrange. Purchases you make for the conservatee must be approved by the person(s) responsible for managing the conservatee's assets or you may not be reimbursed or your reimbursement may be delayed.

IV. CONSERVATOR OF THE ESTATE

The conservatee's property or assets and income are known as the conservatee's "estate." If the court appoints you as conservator of the estate, you will manage the conservatee's finances, protect the conservatee's income and property or assets, make an inventory of the conservatee's property or assets, make sure the conservatee's bills are paid, invest the conservatee's money, see that the conservatee receives all the income and benefits to which he or she is entitled, ensure that the conservatee's tax returns are filed on time and all taxes paid, keep accurate financial records, and regularly report the conservatee's financial condition to the court. *(Note: Property or assets and income in a trust for the conservatee's support and maintenance are usually not considered as part of the conservatee's estate, particularly if the trust was created and funded before the appointment of a conservator. Unless the conservatee's spouse or registered domestic partner consents to its inclusion in the conservatee's estate, the community property of the conservatee and his or her spouse or registered domestic partner under the management and control of the spouse or partner is also not part of the conservatee's estate.)*

A. MANAGING THE ESTATE

1. **Prudent management for the benefit of the conservatee; prudent investments**

   You must manage the estate's property or assets and income for the benefit of the conservatee and with the care of a prudent person dealing with someone else's property. You must not make unreasonably risky investments of money or property of the estate.

2. **Prior court approval required for fees, borrowing, loans, and gifts**

   You must ask and receive the court's permission, after full disclosure of all relevant facts, before you may pay from the conservatee's estate fees to yourself for your services as conservator and to your attorney for his or her services to you; borrow money for or loan money from the conservatee's estate (to yourself or anyone else); or make gifts of estate assets or property.

3. **Keep estate money and property separate from your or anyone else's money or property**

   You must keep the money and property of the conservatee's estate separate from your money or property or from the money or property of any other person. Never deposit estate funds in your personal bank account or otherwise mix them with your or anyone else's funds, even for brief periods. Title to individual stocks, bonds, or other securities; securities broker accounts; mutual funds; and accounts with banks and other financial institutions must show that these assets are property of the conservatorship estate and not your or anyone else's property.

4. **Interest-bearing accounts and other investments**

   Except for a checking account intended for payment of ordinary expenses, estate bank accounts must earn interest. You may deposit estate funds in one or more insured accounts in financial institutions, but you should not put more than the FDIC insurance limit, currently $250,000, in any single institution. You have authority to make some investments without court approval. Other investments may be made only after court approval has been obtained. Consult with an attorney before making any investments, even those you have authority to make without court approval.

CONSERVATORSHIP OF (Name): JOHN DOE CONSERVATEE	CASE NUMBER:

IV. A. 5. **Claims against others on behalf of the conservatee**

Pursue claims against others on behalf of the conservatee's estate when it is in the best interests of the conservatee or his or her estate to do so. The court may require you to be represented by a lawyer to proceed with litigation on behalf of the conservatee's estate. Consider requesting prior court authority to pursue or compromise large or complex claims, particularly those that might require litigation and the assistance of legal counsel and those that might result in an award of attorney fees for the other party against the conservatee's estate if you are unsuccessful. You may sign a contingent fee agreement with legal counsel on behalf of the conservatee's estate if such agreements are customary for the type of case involved, but the court must approve the agreement before it is enforceable. You may ask for court approval of a contingent fee agreement before signing it and before legal counsel performs any services under it.

6. **Defend against claims against the conservatee's estate**

Defend against actions or claims against the conservatee or his or her estate when it is in the best interest of the conservatee or the estate to do so. The court may require you to be represented by a lawyer for your defense of a lawsuit against the conservatee's estate. You may request court approval or instructions concerning the defense or compromise of such a lawsuit.

7. **Public and insurance benefits**

You must learn about and collect all public and insurance benefits for which the conservatee is eligible.

8. **Evaluate the conservatee's ability to manage cash and other assets**

You should evaluate the conservatee's ability to manage cash or other assets and take appropriate action, including asking for prior court approval when necessary or appropriate, to enable the conservatee to do so to the level of his or her ability.

9. **Locate the conservatee's estate planning documents**

You should undertake, as soon as possible after your appointment and qualification as conservator, to locate and take reasonable steps to ensure the safety of the conservatee's estate planning documents, including wills and codicils, living trusts, powers of attorney for health care and finances, life insurance policies, and pension records.

10. **Preserve property mentioned in the conservatee's estate planning documents**

Make reasonable efforts to identify, locate, and preserve property mentioned in the conservatee's estate planning documents.

11. **Guard against inappropriate disclosure of the conservatee's financial information**

Subject to your duty of full disclosure to the court and persons entitled under the law to receive it, you must closely guard against unnecessary or inappropriate disclosure of the conservatee's financial information.

12. **Conservatee's tangible personal property**

If you plan to dispose of any of the conservatee's tangible personal property, inform the conservatee's family members in advance and give them an opportunity to acquire the property, with approval or confirmation of the court.

13. **Factors to consider when deciding whether to dispose of any of the conservatee's property**

In deciding whether it is in the best interest of the conservatee to dispose of property of his or her estate, consider the following factors, among others, as appropriate in the circumstances:

(A) The likely benefit or improvement of the conservatee's life that disposing of the property would bring;

(B) The likelihood that the conservatee would need or benefit from the property in the future;

(C) The previously expressed or current desires of the conservatee concerning the property, unless accommodating those desires would violate your fiduciary duty to the conservatee or impose an unreasonable expense on the estate;

(D) The provisions of the conservatee's estate plan concerning the property;

(E) The tax consequences of disposing of the property;

(F) The impact of disposition on the conservatee's eligibility for public benefits;

(G) The condition of the entire estate;

(H) The likelihood that the property will deteriorate or be subject to waste if kept in the estate; and

(I) The benefit versus the cost or liability of maintaining the property in the estate.

CONSERVATORSHIP OF *(Name)*: JOHN DOE CONSERVATEE	CASE NUMBER:

IV. A. 14. Property, casualty, and liability insurance

Determine the appropriate kinds and adequate levels of property, casualty, and liability insurance covering the property, assets, risks, and potential liabilities of the conservatee and his or her estate. Maintain the insurance in force during the entire period of the administration (except for assets after they are sold).

15. Communicate with conservator of the person and trustee

You should communicate as necessary and appropriate with the conservator of the conservatee's person, if any, and with the trustee of any trust of which the conservatee is a beneficiary.

16. Other limitations or restrictions

There are many limitations or restrictions on your authority to deal with estate assets not mentioned here. If you do not obtain the court's permission when it is required before taking an action, you may be removed as conservator or you may be required to reimburse the estate from your own personal funds, or both.

B. INVENTORY OF ESTATE PROPERTY

1. Locate and take possession of the estate's property and prepare an inventory

You must identify, locate, take possession of, and protect all the conservatee's property, assets, and income that will be or become part of the conservatorship estate. You must change the record title or ownership of most property and assets of the estate to reflect the conservatorship. You must record a copy of your *Letters of Conservatorship* (form GC-350) with the county recorder in each county where the conservatee owns real property. You must then prepare an inventory, or a list, of all of the real and personal property of the estate. There are court forms that must be used for the inventory. These consist of a two-page cover sheet, *Inventory and Appraisal* (form DE-160/GC-040) and one or more pages to be attached to the cover sheet containing the list of property, *Inventory and Appraisal Attachment* (form DE-161/GC-041). The property is separated into two categories, cash and cash-equivalent items, listed on Attachment 1; and all other types of real and personal property, listed on Attachment 2.

2. Determine the value of the estate's property

You must arrange to have a **probate referee** appointed by the court appraise, or determine the fair market value of, the noncash property of the estate shown in Attachment 2 of your inventory unless the referee's appointment is waived by the court. You, rather than the referee, may appraise the value of the cash and cash-equivalent items of property listed in Attachment 1, such as bank accounts.

3. File and mail copies of the inventory and appraisal and notice of how to object

Within 90 days after your appointment as conservator, unless the court gives you more time, you must file with the court your inventory containing the appraisals of estate property, signed by you and, if the probate referee has appraised assets, by the referee. You must also mail copies of the completed inventory and appraisal to the conservatee, the conservatee's attorney, if any, and the conservatee's spouse or registered domestic partner, parents, and children, and must give them written notice of how to file an objection to the inventory and appraisal. There is a court form that must be used for this notice, the *Notice of Filing of Inventory and Appraisal and How to Object to the Inventory or the Appraised Value of Property* (form GC-042).

C. RECORD KEEPING AND ACCOUNTING

1. Keep records and prepare accountings

You must keep complete and accurate records of each financial transaction affecting the estate, including all receipts of income, changes in assets or property held in the estate, and expenditures. The checkbook for the conservatorship checking account is your indispensable tool for keeping records of income and expenditures. You should also save original bills or invoices paid, records of property sale transactions, receipts for money spent, and bank or other institutions' statements showing income received and money spent. You must prepare periodic accountings of all money and property you have received, what you have spent, the date of each transaction, and its purpose. Your accountings must describe in detail what you have left after you pay the estate's expenses. There are court forms you may, or in some situations must, use for your accountings. You will have to file original statements from banks and other institutions with your accountings.

CONSERVATORSHIP OF *(Name)*: JOHN DOE CONSERVATEE	CASE NUMBER:

IV. C. 2. Court review of your accountings and records

You must file with the court a report with each of your accountings that shows the current circumstances of the conservatee and the estate, along with a petition requesting that the court review and approve the accounting. Your first accounting is due one year after your appointment, and later accountings must be filed at least every two years after that. The court may order you to file more frequent accountings. You must save your receipts and other original records because the court may ask to review them. If you do not file your accountings as required, the court will order you to do so. You may be removed as conservator if you fail to properly prepare and file your accountings or comply with the court's orders.

V. DUTY TO DISCLOSE CHANGES IN MARITAL OR DOMESTIC PARTNERSHIP STATUS

If you are the spouse of the conservatee, you must disclose to the court, and give notice to interested persons under the Probate Code, of the filing of any action or proceeding against the conservatee for (1) legal separation, (2) dissolution of marriage, or (3) adjudication of nullity of the marriage. If you are or were the registered domestic partner of the conservatee, you must disclose to the court any termination of the domestic partnership. The disclosure must be made within 10 days of the initial filing of the action or proceeding or termination of the partnership by filing a notice with the court. If you are not the spouse or registered domestic partner or former partner of the conservatee and one of these events occurs, the conservatee's spouse or former registered domestic partner must disclose the event to you within the same 10-day period.

VI. LIMITED CONSERVATOR (for the developmentally disabled only)

A. AUTHORITY SPECIFIED IN YOUR *LETTERS OF CONSERVATORSHIP* AND APPOINTMENT ORDER

If the court appoints you as limited conservator, you will have authority to take care of **only** those aspects of the conservatee's life and financial affairs specified in your *Letters of Conservatorship* and the court's order appointing you. The conservatee retains all other legal and civil rights. Although most of the information provided in this form also applies to limited conservatorships (especially the duties of the conservator of the person), you should clarify with your attorney exactly which information applies in your case.

B. DUTY TO HELP LIMITED CONSERVATEE DEVELOP SELF-RELIANCE

You must secure treatment, services, and opportunities that will assist the limited conservatee to develop maximum self-reliance and independence. This assistance may include training, education, medical and psychological services, social opportunities, vocational opportunities, and other appropriate help.

C. DETERMINATION OF LEVEL OF CARE FOR CERTAIN LIMITED CONSERVATEES

The level of care determination described in item **IIIA** does not apply to a limited conservatee who receives services from a regional center for the developmentally disabled and for whom the Director of Developmental Services or the regional center is acting as conservator. Determination of the services provided for and residential placement of these limited conservatees are to be identified, delivered, and evaluated consistent with the individual program plan process described in Welfare and Institutions Code sections 4640–4659. *(See Prob. Code, § 2352.5(e).)*

VII. TEMPORARY CONSERVATOR

If the court appoints you as temporary conservator, you will generally have the same duties and authority as general conservators, **except** the conservatorship will end on the date specified in your *Letters of Temporary Conservatorship*. Most of the information in this form also applies to temporary conservatorships, but you must consult your attorney about which duties you will **not** perform because of the short duration of the temporary conservatorship appointment. A temporary conservator should avoid making long-term decisions or changes that could safely wait until a general conservator is appointed. As temporary conservator, you may not move a conservatee from his or her home, unless there is an emergency, or sell or give away the conservatee's home or any other assets without prior court approval.

Sign the *Acknowledgment of Receipt* on page 7.

CONSERVATORSHIP OF (Name): JOHN DOE CONSERVATEE	CASE NUMBER:

VIII. JUDICIAL COUNCIL FORMS

This form identifies a number of Judicial Council forms used for court filings in conservatorship proceedings. This form, the petition for your appointment as conservator, and the order that appoints you as conservator are examples of Judicial Council forms. Judicial Council forms are either mandatory or optional. If a mandatory form applies to a situation or proposed action, it must be used. Optional forms may be used, at the option of the person preparing and filing the form or, in some situations, at the option of the court. Each form is identified on the bottom left side of its first page as optional or mandatory. Judicial Council forms are not available for every situation where a document may or must be filed with the court, but the forms address the most common and important matters that occur during a conservatorship. The *Handbook for Conservators* has additional information about Judicial Council conservatorship forms.

Your attorney will select and prepare the appropriate Judicial Council forms. However, if you do not have an attorney, you can prepare them yourself. All Judicial Council forms are posted on the California courts' public website, *www.courts.ca.gov*. Select "Forms" at the top of the site's home page, then select the form group in the drop-down menu in the middle of the page. All conservatorship forms are collected in the Probate—Guardianships and Conservatorships form group. They are designated with the prefix "GC," followed by a three-digit number. Forms shown in the drop-down list with an asterisk are mandatory forms.

The forms are posted on the website in both unfillable and fillable versions, as PDF files. The unfillable versions are designed to be completed by typewriter or, in some cases, by hand. Fillable forms may be filled out online, then printed out ready for signing and filing with the court, and they may also be saved to your computer and completed in more than one sitting. Go to the "Forms and Information" page at the Web site's Self-Help Center for more information on accessing the forms.

ACKNOWLEDGMENT OF RECEIPT
of *Duties of Conservator* and *Handbook for Conservators*
(Probate Code, § 1834)

I acknowledge that I have received this statement of the duties and liabilities of the office of conservator, the *Duties of Conservator* (form GC-348), and the *Handbook for Conservators* adopted by the Judicial Council.

I declare under penalty of perjury under the laws of the State of California that the foregoing is true and correct.

Date: [Insert filing date]

FRANK DOE
(TYPE OR PRINT NAME) ▶ (SIGNATURE OF (PROPOSED) CONSERVATOR)

Date: [Insert filing date]

MARY DOE
(TYPE OR PRINT NAME) ▶ (SIGNATURE OF (PROPOSED) CONSERVATOR)

Date:

(TYPE OR PRINT NAME) ▶ (SIGNATURE OF (PROPOSED) CONSERVATOR)

NOTICE

This statement of duties and liabilities is a summary and is not a complete statement of the law. Your conduct as a conservator is governed by the law itself and not by this summary or by the Judicial Council's *Handbook for Conservators.* When in doubt, consult your attorney.

ABOGADO o PARTE SIN ABOGADO: *(Nombre, Núm. del colegio de abogados estatal y dirección):* TELÉFONO: FAX: EMAIL: ABOGADO DE (nombre):	SOLO PARA USO DE LA CORTE **Solo para Información** **No entregue a la corte**
CORTE SUPERIOR DE CALIFORNIA, CONDADO DE DIRECCIÓN (calle y número): DIRECCIÓN POSTAL: CIUDAD Y CÓDIGO POSTAL: NOMBRE DE LA SUCURSAL:	
TUTELA DE ADULTO ☐ DE LA PERSONA ☐ DEL PATRIMONIO DE *(Nombre):* PUPILO	
RESPONSABILIDADES DEL TUTOR y acuse de recibo del *Manual del Tutor*	NÚMERO DE CASO:

RESPONSABILIDADES DEL TUTOR

Cuando la corte lo nombra como tutor, usted pasa a ser responsable ante la corte y asume ciertas responsabilidades y obligaciones. Todas sus acciones como tutor están sujetas a la revisión de la corte. Usted debería entender claramente la información de este formulario. Encontrará más información en el *Manual del tutor* del Consejo Judicial. La ley requiere que confirma el recibo del *Manual del tutor*, además de una copia de este formulario.

I. DERECHOS DEL PUPILO

El pupilo no pierde todos sus derechos ni toda su participación en las decisiones importantes que afectan su vida. Todos los pupilos tienen derecho a ser tratados con comprensión y respeto, y a que se tengan en cuenta sus deseos, así como derecho a un buen cuidado por parte del tutor. El pupilo, en general, seguirá teniendo los siguientes derechos: (1) controlar directamente su propio salario que proviene de su empleo, (2) hacer o cambiar su testamento, (3) casarse, (4) recibir correspondencia, (5) tener un abogado, (6) pedirle al juez que cambie al tutor, (7) pedirle al juez que dé por terminada la tutela, (8) votar, a menos que el juez diga que no puede ejercer este derecho, (9) controlar su dinero para gastos personales, si el juez permite que se le pague una asignación al pupilo directamente, y (10) tomar sus propias decisiones sobre atención de la salud, a menos que el juez le transfiera esos derechos al tutor exclusivamente.

II. CONSULTAR CON SU ABOGADO

Su abogado lo asesorará sobre sus responsabilidades, los límites de sus poderes, los derechos del pupilo, sus trámites en la corte, todos los otros temas tratados en este formulario y muchos otros asuntos. Su abogado le dirá cuándo tiene que pedir aprobación previa de la corte para actuar, cuándo puede pedirla (y por qué es recomendable que lo haga) y cuándo no es necesaria la aprobación previa de la corte. Usted debería hacer todas las preguntas sobre temas legales a su abogado, y no al personal de la corte, que no tiene permitido dar asesoramiento legal.

Su abogado también lo ayudará a preparar sus inventarios, registros contables, solicitudes y todos los otros documentos que hay que presentar en la corte; también controlará que las personas con derecho a recibir un aviso de sus acciones reciban el aviso adecuado. Además, lo asesorará sobre los límites legales con relación a las inversiones del patrimonio, alquileres y ventas de bienes del patrimonio, préstamos, demandas contra otras personas que involucren al pupilo o sus bienes, y muchos otros asuntos, y puede preparar o revisar los documentos necesarios para esas cuestiones. Usted debería comunicarse con frecuencia y colaborar plenamente con su abogado en todo momento. **Cuando tenga una duda, hable con su abogado.**

Otras preguntas pueden resolverse llamando a los recursos comunitarios locales. (Para acceder a estos recursos, vea el *Manual del tutor* y el suplemento local distribuido por la corte.)

III. TUTOR DE LA PERSONA

Si la corte lo nombra tutor de la persona, usted es responsable de cuidar y proteger al pupilo. Tiene que decidir, dentro de ciertos límites, dónde vivirá el pupilo; y tiene que ocuparse de la atención de la salud, las comidas, la vestimenta, el cuidado personal, el mantenimiento de la casa, el transporte y la recreación del pupilo.

A. DETERMINAR EL NIVEL DE CUIDADOS ADECUADOS PARA EL PUPILO

Usted tiene que determinar el nivel de cuidados adecuados para el pupilo. Su decisión tiene que estar por escrito, firmada bajo pena de perjurio, tiene que ser presentada en la corte dentro de los 60 días siguientes a la fecha de la orden de la corte que lo nombra a usted como tutor y tiene que incluir lo siguiente:

III. A. 1. Una evaluación del nivel de cuidados existente cuando se presentó la solicitud de su nombramiento como tutor y las medidas que serían necesarias para mantener al pupilo en su domicilio personal.

*(Nota: El **domicilio personal** del pupilo es la residencia que el pupilo consideraba o creía que era su residencia permanente (1) en la fecha en la que se presentó la solicitud de nombramiento de un tutor en este caso, o (2) en la última fecha anterior en la que el pupilo pudo saber o comunicar cuál era o cuál creía que era su domicilio permanente, ya sea que viviera allí o no cuando se presentó la solicitud de nombramiento. Ver regla 7.1063(b) de las Reglas de la Corte de California.)*

2. Un plan para regresar al pupilo a su **residencia personal** o una explicación de los límites o restricciones para que el pupilo regrese a esa residencia en el futuro cercano si el pupilo no estuviera viviendo allí cuando se presentó la solicitud de nombramiento del tutor.
3. Una reevaluación después de un cambio importante en las circunstancias que afectan las necesidades del pupilo de vivienda y cuidados después de su decisión inicial.
4. Si el pupilo es un pupilo limitado con una discapacidad del desarrollo, podrían aplicarse reglas especiales a la decisión sobre su nivel de cuidados y vivienda. Ver el punto **VI** siguiente.

B. DECICIDIR DÓNDE VIVIRÁ EL PUPILO

1. Usted tiene que decidir dónde vivirá el pupilo. Usted puede elegir una residencia en California sin aprobación previa de la corte, pero tiene que elegir una residencia apropiada que sea la menos restrictiva entre las que haya disponibles, que permita cubrir las necesidades del pupilo y que responda de la mejor manera a los intereses del pupilo.
2. Tiene que presentar en la corte un aviso por escrito de cualquier cambio en la residencia del pupilo dentro de los 30 días siguientes al cambio y tiene que enviar por correo copias del aviso al abogado del pupilo, al cónyuge o pareja de hecho registrada del pupilo y a los familiares del pupilo a los que se les hayan enviado copias de la solicitud de su nombramiento como tutor, a menos que la corte indique que no hay que hacer el envío por correo para evitar un daño al pupilo. (Hay un formulario de la corte que tiene que usar para este aviso y otro formulario que puede usar para probar que lo envió por correo. Los formularios son el *Aviso de cambio de domicilio* (formulario GC-080) y el *Adjunto al aviso de cambio de domicilio* (formulario GC-080(MA)). Estos formularios hacen referencia a un "aviso posterior a la mudanza" porque el aviso puede ser presentado y enviado por correo después de la fecha de la mudanza.)
3. La ley presume que el **domicilio personal** del pupilo (ver el punto **IIIA**) es la residencia apropiada y menos restrictiva para el pupilo. Tiene que haber un motivo respaldado por suficientes pruebas para justificar un cambio en el domicilio personal del pupilo (incluida una mudanza de un hogar de cuidado u otro lugar temporal a una residencia que no sea el domicilio personal del pupilo).
4. Si desea mudar al pupilo de su **domicilio personal**, además del aviso posterior a la mudanza indicada en el punto 2, tiene que enviar por correo un aviso de su intención de cambiar el domicilio del pupilo al pupilo, al abogado del pupilo, si corresponde, y a cada una de las otras personas o entidades con derecho a recibir aviso de la audiencia sobre la solicitud de su nombramiento como tutor; después, tiene que presentar en la corte prueba de que se envió por correo el aviso. A menos que haya una emergencia que requiera un periodo de aviso más breve, este aviso tiene que ser enviado al menos 15 días antes de la fecha de la mudanza propuesta. (Hay un formulario de la corte que tiene que usar para este aviso y otro formulario que puede usar para mostrar que lo envió por correo. Los formularios son el *Aviso de cambio de domicilio personal propuesto de un pupilo o dependiente previo a la mudanza* (formulario GC-079) y el *Adjunto al aviso previo a la mudanza, etc.* (formulario GC-079(MA)). Los formularios hacen referencia a "aviso previo a la mudanza" porque el aviso tiene que ser enviado antes de la mudanza.)
5. Si usted desea establecer la residencia del pupilo fuera de California, tiene que pedir permiso a la corte antes de la mudanza. Tiene que enviar por correo un aviso de la audiencia de la corte sobre esta solicitud, junto con una copia de la solicitud, al pupilo y a las otras personas y entidades que tenían derecho a recibir un aviso de la audiencia sobre la solicitud de su nombramiento como tutor. Hay un formulario de la corte para esta solicitud, la *Solicitud de fijar residencia fuera del estado de California* (formulario GC-085). El aviso de la audiencia y la prueba de su envío por correo se hacen con otro formulario de la corte, el *Aviso de audiencia de tutela de menor o tutela de adulto* (formulario GC-020).
6. Usted no puede internar al pupilo en una clínica para el tratamiento de trastornos mentales en contra de su voluntad a menos que se haya determinado que el pupilo tiene una discapacidad grave como resultado de una enfermedad o discapacidades del desarrollo por alcoholismo crónico, o a menos que usted haya sido nombrado tutor de conformidad con la Ley Lanterman-Petris-Short (§ 5350 y siguientes del Código de Bienestar e Instituciones), y solo si el tribunal aprueba la internación. Si la corte lo ha autorizado a internar al pupilo en un hogar de cuidado médico con seguridad perimetral o en un hogar de atención cerrado y con seguridad porque sufre demencia, tiene que estar seguro de que la internación es la medida adecuada y menos restrictiva según las necesidades del pupilo.

TUTELA DE *(Nombre)*: ***Solo para información*** PUPILO	NÚMERO DE CASO: ***No entregue a la corte***

III. C. GESTIONAR LA ATENCIÓN MÉDICA PARA EL PUPILO

Usted está a cargo de garantizar que se satisfagan las necesidades de atención médica del pupilo. Pero hay reglas especiales que tiene que seguir para satisfacer dichas necesidades. Dos de las reglas más importantes son las siguientes:

1. A menos que la corte le haya dado facultades exclusivas para dar consentimiento para el tratamiento médico del pupilo porque la corte determinó que el pupilo perdió la capacidad de tomar decisiones médicas sensatas, su consentimiento o negativa de consentimiento para el tratamiento no es suficiente si el pupilo no está de acuerdo (excepto en ciertas situaciones de emergencia). Si usted cuenta con la autoridad exclusiva para dar consentimiento con relación a las cuestiones médicas, tiene que estar seguro de que los medicamentos sean adecuados.
2. Si el pupilo tiene demencia y perdió la capacidad de dar su consentimiento informado para la administración de medicamentos para su tratamiento y atención, usted tiene que recibir facultades específicas de la corte para dar consentimiento para la administración de los medicamentos. Si usted tiene estas facultades, tiene que asegurarse de que los medicamentos sean adecuados.

D. COLABORAR CON LA/S PERSONA/S A CARGO DE ADMINISTRAR LOS BIENES DEL PUPILO

Si otras personas están manejando los bienes del pupilo, tales como su tutor del patrimonio, el cónyuge o pareja de hecho registrada del pupilo en poder de los bienes del matrimonio o de la pareja de hecho, o el fideicomisario de un fideicomiso establecido para la administración de los bienes del pupilo y para su manutención, usted tiene que trabajar en conjunto con estas personas para asegurarse de que el pupilo pueda cubrir los gastos de los cuidados que usted le gestione. Las compras que usted haga para el pupilo tienen que ser aprobadas por la/s persona/s a cargo de administrar los bienes del pupilo o no se le reembolsarán o se demorará su reembolso.

IV. TUTOR DEL PATRIMONIO

Los bienes o activos e ingresos del pupilo son conocidos como el "patrimonio" del pupilo. Si la corte lo nombra tutor del patrimonio, usted administrará las finanzas del pupilo, protegerá los ingresos y los bienes o activos del pupilo, hará un inventario de los bienes o activos del pupilo, se asegurará de que se paguen las cuentas del pupilo, invertirá el dinero del pupilo, controlará que el pupilo reciba todos los ingresos y beneficios a los que tenga derecho, se asegurará de que las declaraciones de impuestos del pupilo se presenten a tiempo y de que se paguen todos los impuestos, llevará registros financieros precisos e informará regularmente la situación financiera del pupilo a la corte. *(Nota: Los bienes o activos e ingresos que estén en un fideicomiso para la manutención del pupilo no suelen considerarse parte del patrimonio del pupilo, en particular si el fideicomiso se creó y financió antes del nombramiento del tutor. A menos que el cónyuge o la pareja de hecho registrada del pupilo dé su consentimiento para su inclusión en el patrimonio del pupilo, los bienes comunitarios del pupilo y de su cónyuge o a la unión del pupilo y su pareja de hecho registrada que estén bajo la administración y el control del cónyuge o de la pareja de hecho tampoco serán parte del patrimonio del pupilo.)*

A. ADMINISTRACIÓN DEL PATRIMONIO

1. **Administración prudente en beneficio del pupilo; inversiones prudentes**
Usted tiene que administrar los bienes o activos e ingresos del patrimonio en beneficio del pupilo y con los cuidados de una persona prudente que maneja los bienes de otra persona. Usted no puede hacer inversiones riesgosas de dinero o bienes del patrimonio fuera de lo razonable.
2. **Se requiere la aprobación previa de la corte de honorarios, préstamos y donaciones**
Usted tiene que pedir y recibir el permiso de la corte, después de dar a conocer todos los hechos pertinentes, para poder usar el dinero del patrimonio del pupilo para cobrar sus servicios como tutor y pagar a su abogado por los servicios que le preste a usted; tomar dinero prestado a favor del patrimonio del pupilo o tomar dinero prestado del patrimonio del pupilo (para usted o para otra persona); o hacer donaciones de activos o bienes del patrimonio.
3. **Separación del dinero y los bienes del patrimonio del dinero y los bienes suyos o de otras personas**
Usted tiene que mantener el dinero y los bienes del patrimonio del pupilo separados de su dinero y bienes y de los bienes y el dinero de otras personas. Nunca deposite los fondos del patrimonio en su cuenta bancaria personal ni los mezcle de otra forma con sus fondos o los de otras personas, incluso por periodos cortos. La propiedad de acciones, bonos u otros títulos valores individuales; las cuentas con agentes de bolsa; los fondos mutuos; y las cuentas en bancos y otras instituciones financieras tienen que mostrar que estos activos son de propiedad del patrimonio de la tutela y no bienes suyos o de otra persona.
4. **Cuentas que generan intereses y otras inversiones**
Excepto las cuentas corrientes destinadas al pago de gastos ordinarios, las cuentas bancarias del patrimonio tienen que generar intereses. Usted puede depositar los fondos del patrimonio en una o más cuentas con seguro en instituciones financieras, pero no debería poner más que el límite del seguro del FDIC, actualmente $250,000, en una misma institución. Usted tiene facultades para hacer algunas inversiones sin aprobación de la corte. Otras inversiones solo pueden hacerse después de haber obtenido aprobación de la corte. Consulte con un abogado antes de hacer inversiones, incluso las que tiene facultades para hacer sin aprobación de la corte.

IV. A. 5 **Reclamos contra otros en representación del pupilo**

Haga reclamos contra otros en representación del patrimonio del pupilo cuando hacerlo sea para el mejor interés del pupilo o de su patrimonio. El tribunal puede exigirle que esté representado por un abogado para litigar en representación del patrimonio del pupilo. Considere pedir autorización previa de la corte para plantear o perseguir reclamos importantes o complejos, en particular los que podrían requerir un litigio y el asesoramiento de un abogado y los que podrían tener como resultado una determinación de honorarios para los abogados de la otra parte contra el patrimonio del pupilo si usted no gana el reclamo. Puede firmar un pacto de cuota litis con el abogado en representación del patrimonio del pupilo si este tipo de acuerdo es habitual para el tipo de caso en cuestión, pero el tribunal tiene que aprobar el acuerdo antes de que sea ejecutable. Puede pedir la aprobación de la corte de un pacto de cuota litis antes de firmarlo y antes de que el abogado preste cualquier servicio conforme a dicho pacto.

6. **Defensa de reclamos contra el patrimonio del pupilo**

Usted tiene que ejercer la defensa en las acciones o los reclamos contra el pupilo o su patrimonio cuando hacerlo sea en el mejor interés del pupilo o de su patrimonio. El tribunal puede exigirle que esté representado por un abogado para ejercer la defensa en un juicio contra el patrimonio del pupilo. Usted puede pedir aprobación o instrucciones a la corte sobre la defensa o los acuerdos en este tipo de juicios.

7. **Beneficios públicos y de seguros**

Usted tiene que saber sobre todos los beneficios públicos y de seguros a los que tenga derecho el pupilo y tiene que cobrarlos.

8. **Evaluar la capacidad del pupilo de administrar efectivo y otros activos**

Usted debe evaluar la capacidad del pupilo de administrar dinero en efectivo u otros activos y tomar las medidas apropiadas, incluso pedir aprobación previa de la corte cuando sea necesaria o apropiada, para permitir al pupilo que lo haga en la medida de su capacidad.

9. **Localizar los documentos de planificación del patrimonio del pupilo**

Tan pronto como sea posible después de su nombramiento y habilitación como tutor, usted debe ubicar y tomar las medidas razonables para garantizar la seguridad de los documentos de planificación del patrimonio del pupilo, incluidos los testamentos y codicilos, declaraciones de última voluntad, poderes para atención médica y finanzas, pólizas de seguros de vida y registros de pensiones.

10. **Preservar los bienes mencionados en los documentos de planificación del patrimonio del pupilo**

Usted tiene que hacer lo posible, dentro de lo razonable, para identificar, ubicar y proteger los bienes mencionados en los documentos de planificación del patrimonio del pupilo.

11. **Proteger contra la divulgación inapropiada de la información financiera del pupilo**

Sujeto a su responsabilidad de divulgación total a la corte y a las personas con derecho conforme a la ley a recibirla, usted tiene que cuidar bien que no haya divulgaciones innecesarias o inapropiadas de la información financiera del pupilo.

12. **Bienes muebles tangibles del pupilo**

Si usted planea deshacerse de alguno de los bienes muebles del pupilo, informe a los integrantes de la familia del pupilo con anterioridad y deles la oportunidad de comprar los bienes, con la aprobación o confirmación de la corte.

13. **Factores para tener en cuenta al decidir si vender alguno de los bienes del pupilo**

Al decidir si vender bienes de su patrimonio es para el mejor interés del pupilo, tenga en cuenta los siguientes factores, entre otros, según corresponda conforme a las circunstancias:

(A) El beneficio o la mejora probables en la vida del pupilo que generaría la venta del bien;

(B) La probabilidad de que el pupilo necesite o se beneficie del bien en el futuro;

(C) Los deseos expresados anteriormente o actualmente por el pupilo con relación al bien, a menos que hacer caso a esos deseos violara su responsabilidad fiduciaria para con el pupilo o impusiera un gasto irrazonable sobre el patrimonio;

(D) Las disposiciones del plan del patrimonio del pupilo con relación al bien;

(E) Las consecuencias impositivas de vender el bien;

(F) Los efectos de la venta sobre la elegibilidad del pupilo para acceder a beneficios públicos;

(G) La situación de todo el patrimonio;

(H) La probabilidad de que el bien se deteriore o quede sujeto a destrucción si se mantiene en el patrimonio; y

(I) El beneficio frente al costo o la responsabilidad de mantener el bien en el patrimonio.

TUTELA DE *(Nombre)*: ***Solo para información*** PUPILO	NÚMERO DE CASO: ***No entregue a la corte***

IV. A. **14. Seguros de bienes, daños y responsabilidad**

Determine los tipos correctos y los niveles adecuados de seguros de bienes, daños y responsabilidad que cubran los bienes, los activos, los riesgos y la posible responsabilidad del pupilo y su patrimonio. Mantenga el seguro vigente durante todo el periodo de la administración (con excepción de los de bienes después de su venta).

15. Comunicación con el tutor de la persona y el fideicomisario

Usted tiene que comunicarse según sea necesario y apropiado con el tutor de la persona del pupilo, si lo hubiera, y con el fideicomisario de todo fideicomisos en el que el pupilo sea beneficiario.

16. Otras limitaciones o restricciones

Hay muchas limitaciones o restricciones a su facultad de administrar los bienes del patrimonio que no están mencionadas aquí. Si no obtiene el permiso de la corte cuando es necesario antes de actuar, pueden destituirlo como tutor o le pueden pedir que devuelva el dinero al patrimonio de sus fondos personales, o ambas cosas.

B. INVENTARIO DE BIENES DEL PATRIMONIO

1. Localizar y tomar posesión de los bienes del patrimonio y preparar un inventario

Usted tiene que identificar, localizar, tomar posesión y proteger todos los bienes, activos e ingresos del pupilo que serán o se convertirán en parte del patrimonio de la tutela. Tiene que cambiar la titularidad registrada o propiedad de la mayoría de los bienes y activos del patrimonio para reflejar la tutela de adulto. Tiene que registrar una copia de sus *Cartas de tutela* (formulario GC-350) con el secretario del condado en cada condado en que el pupilo tenga bienes inmuebles. Después tiene que preparar un inventario o una lista de todos los bienes muebles e inmuebles del patrimonio. Hay formularios de la corte que tienen que usarse para el inventario. Estos formularios están compuestos por dos páginas de carátula, *Inventario y tasación* (formulario DE-160/GC-040) y una o más páginas que hay que adjuntar a la carátula que contienen el listado de bienes, *Adjunto de inventario y tasación* (formulario DE-161/GC-041). Los bienes se dividen en dos categorías, dinero en efectivo y equivalentes de efectivo, indicados en el Adjunto 1; y todos los demás tipos de bienes muebles e inmuebles, indicados en el Adjunto 2.

2. Determinar el valor de los bienes del patrimonio

Tiene que hacer que un **perito tasador** nombrado por la corte tase o determine el valor justo de mercado de los bienes que no sean dinero en efectivo del patrimonio que se indican en el Adjunto 2 de su inventario, a menos que la corte determine que no es necesario el nombramiento de un perito. Usted, en vez del perito, puede tasar el dinero en efectivo y los equivalentes de efectivo incluidos en el Adjunto 1, tales como las cuentas bancarias.

3. Presentar y enviar por correo copias del inventario y de la tasación y notificación sobre cómo objetar

Dentro de los 90 días siguientes a su nombramiento como tutor, a menos que la corte le dé más tiempo, tiene que presentar en la corte su inventario con las tasaciones de los bienes del patrimonio, firmadas por usted y, si el perito tasó bienes, por el perito. También tiene que enviar por correo copias del inventario y de la tasación realizados al pupilo, al abogado del pupilo, si lo hubiera, y al cónyuge o pareja de hecho registrada, padres e hijos del pupilo, y tiene que enviarles un aviso por escrito sobre cómo presentar una objeción al inventario y la tasación. Hay un formulario de la corte que debe usarse para este aviso, el *Aviso de presentación de inventario y tasación y sobre cómo objetar el inventario o el valor tasado de los bienes* (formulario GC-042).

C. REGISTROS Y CONTABILIDAD

1. Mantener registros y preparar los estados contables

Tiene que mantener registros precisos y completos de todas las operaciones financieras que afecten el patrimonio, incluidos todos los recibos de ingresos, cambios en bienes o activos mantenidos en el patrimonio y gastos. La chequera de la cuenta corriente de la tutela es su herramienta indispensable para mantener los registros de ingresos y gastos. También debería guardar los recibos o facturas originales que haya pagado, registros de operaciones de venta de bienes, recibos de dinero gastado y estados de cuenta bancarios o de otras instituciones en los que consten los ingresos recibidos y el dinero gastado. Tiene que preparar estados contables periódicos de todo el dinero y los bienes que recibió, lo que gastó, la fecha de cada operación y su finalidad. Su estado contable tiene que describir en detalle lo que le queda después de pagar los gastos del patrimonio. Hay formularios de la corte que puede o a veces tiene que utilizar para el estado contable. Tendrá que presentar estados de cuenta originales de bancos y otras instituciones con su estado contable.

TUTELA DE *(Nombre)*: ***Solo para información*** PUPILO	NÚMERO DE CASO: ***No entregue a la corte***

IV. C. 2. Revisión de la corte de estados contables y registros

Usted tiene que presentar en la corte un informe con cada uno de sus registros contables que muestre las circunstancias actuales del pupilo y del patrimonio, junto con una solicitud para que la corte revise y apruebe el estado contable. Tiene que presentar su primer registro contable un año después de su nombramiento, y los registros contables posteriores tienen que presentarse al menos cada dos años después de esa fecha. Puede suceder que la corte le ordene presentar registros contables con mayor frecuencia. Tiene que guardar los recibos y los registros originales porque la corte puede pedir revisarlos. Si no presenta sus registros contables como se exige, la corte le ordenará hacerlo. Puede ser destituido de su cargo de tutor si no logra preparar y presentar correctamente sus registros contables o cumplir las órdenes de la corte.

V. RESPONSABILIDAD DE INFORMAR CAMBIOS EN LA SITUACIÓN MATRIMONIAL O DE PAREJA DE HECHO

Si usted es el cónyuge del pupilo, tiene que informar a la corte y avisar a las partes interesadas conforme al Código Testamentario sobre la presentación de toda acción o proceso contra el pupilo por (1) separación legal, (2) disolución del matrimonio, o (3) anulación del matrimonio. Si es o era pareja de hecho registrada del pupilo, tiene que informar a la corte sobre la finalización de la pareja de hecho. Ello tiene que ser informado dentro de los 10 días siguientes a la presentación inicial de la acción o proceso o a la finalización de la pareja de hecho mediante la presentación de un aviso en la corte. Si usted no es el cónyuge o la pareja o ex pareja de hecho registrada del pupilo y ocurre alguno de los acontecimientos mencionados, el cónyuge o la ex pareja de hecho registrada del pupilo tiene que comunicarle el acontecimiento a usted dentro del mismo periodo de 10 días.

VI. TUTOR LIMITADO (solo para personas con discapacidades del desarrollo)

A. PODERES INCLUIDOS EN SUS *CARTAS DE TUTELA* Y ORDEN DE NOMBRAMIENTO

Si la corte lo nombra tutor limitado, tendrá poderes para encargarse **solo** de aquellos aspectos de la vida y asuntos económicos del pupilo especificados en sus *Cartas de tutela* y en la orden de nombramiento de la corte. El pupilo conserva todos los demás derechos civiles y jurídicos. Aunque la mayor parte de la información incluida en este formulario también se aplica a las tutelas limitadas (en particular las responsabilidades del tutor de la persona), usted debería aclarar con su abogado exactamente qué información se aplica en su caso.

B. RESPONSABILIDAD DE AYUDAR AL PUPILO LIMITADO A QUE SEA AUTOSUFICIENTE

Usted tiene que gestionar los tratamientos, servicios y oportunidades que ayuden al pupilo limitado a desarrollar la máxima autosuficiencia e independencia. Esta ayuda puede incluir capacitación, educación, servicios médicos y psicológicos, oportunidades sociales, oportunidades vocacionales y otro asesoramiento apropiado.

C. DETERMINACIÓN DEL NIVEL DE CUIDADOS PARA CIERTOS PUPILOS LIMITADOS

La determinación del nivel de cuidados descrita en el punto **IIIA** no se aplica al pupilo limitado que recibe servicios de un centro regional para personas con discapacidades del desarrollo y tiene como tutor el director de Servicios de Desarrollo o el centro regional. La determinación de los servicios provistos y el lugar de vivienda de estos pupilos limitados se identificarán, entregarán y evaluarán de acuerdo con el proceso del plan de programa individual descrito en las secciones 4640–4659 del Código de Bienestar e Instituciones. *(Ver § 2352.5(e) del Código Testamentario.)*

VII. TUTOR TEMPORAL

Si la corte lo nombra tutor temporal, en general tendrá las mismas responsabilidades y facultades que los tutores generales, con la **excepción** de que la tutela de adulto finalizará en la fecha especificada en sus *Cartas de tutela temporal de un menor o adulto.* La mayor parte de la información de este formulario también se aplica a las tutelas temporales, pero tiene que consultar a su abogado sobre los deberes que **no** cumplirá debido a la corta duración del nombramiento de la tutela temporal. El tutor temporal debe evitar tomar decisiones a largo plazo o hacer cambios que puedan esperar sin peligro hasta que se nombre a un tutor general. Como tutor temporal, no puede mudar al pupilo de su casa, a menos que haya una emergencia, ni vender ni donar la casa del pupilo ni ninguno de sus bienes sin la aprobación previa de la corte.

Firme el *Acuse de recibo* de la página 7.

TUTELA DE *(Nombre)*: ***Solo para información*** PUPILO	NÚMERO DE CASO: ***No entregue a la corte***

VIII. FORMULARIOS DEL CONSEJO JUDICIAL

Este formulario menciona una serie de formularios del Consejo Judicial usados para presentaciones en la corte en procesos de tutela de adulto. Este formulario, la solicitud de su nombramiento como tutor y la orden que lo nombra como tutor son ejemplos de formularios del Consejo Judicial. Los formularios del Consejo Judicial son obligatorios u opcionales. Si un formulario obligatorio se aplica a una situación o acción propuesta, tiene que ser usado. Los formularios opcionales pueden usarse a opción de la persona que prepara y presenta el formulario o, en algunas situaciones, a opción de la corte. Cada formulario se identifica en el lado izquierdo de abajo de su primera página como opcional u obligatorio. No hay formularios del Consejo Judicial disponibles para todas las situaciones en las que se puede o se tiene que presentar un documento en la corte, pero los formularios tratan la mayoría de los asuntos más comunes e importantes que ocurren durante una tutela de adulto. El *Manual del tutor* tiene más información sobre los formularios de tutela de adulto del Consejo Judicial.

Su abogado seleccionará y preparará los formularios adecuados del Consejo Judicial. Pero si usted no tiene un abogado, puede prepararlos usted mismo. Todos los formularios del Consejo Judicial están publicados en el sitio web público de la corte de California, *www.courts.ca.gov*. Seleccione "Formularios" en la parte de arriba de la página de inicio del sitio, después seleccione el grupo del formulario en el menú desplegable en el centro de la página. Todos los formularios de tutela de adulto se recopilan en el grupo de formularios "Testamentos, Tutelas y tutelas de adulto". Están indicados con el prefijo "GC" seguido por un número de tres dígitos. Los formularios que aparecen en la lista desplegable con un asterisco son formularios obligatorios.

Los formularios se publican en el sitio web en versiones llenables y no llenables, como archivos en formato PDF. Las versiones no llenables están diseñadas para ser completadas a máquina o, en algunos casos, a mano. Los formularios llenables se pueden completar en línea y después imprimir listos para ser firmados y presentados en la corte, y también se pueden guardar en su computadora y llenarlos en distintas ocasiones. Vaya a la página de "Formularios e información" del sitio web del Centro de ayuda para obtener más información sobre cómo acceder a los formularios.

ACUSE DE RECIBO
de las Responsabilidades del tutor y del Manual del tutor
(Sección 1834 del Código Testamentario)

Reconozco que recibí esta declaración de las responsabilidades y obligaciones del cargo de tutor, las *Responsabilidades del tutor* (formulario GC-348) y el *Manual del tutor* adoptado por el Consejo Judicial.

Declaro bajo pena de perjurio conforme a las leyes del estado de California que lo anterior es verdadero y correcto.

Fecha:

_______________________ ▶ _______________________

(NOMBRE A MÁQUINA O EN LETRA DE MOLDE) (FIRMA DEL TUTOR (PROPUESTO))

Fecha:

_______________________ ▶ _______________________

(NOMBRE A MÁQUINA O EN LETRA DE MOLDE) (FIRMA DEL TUTOR (PROPUESTO))

Fecha:

_______________________ ▶ _______________________

(NOMBRE A MÁQUINA O EN LETRA DE MOLDE) (FIRMA DEL TUTOR (PROPUESTO))

AVISO

Esta declaración de responsabilidades y obligaciones es un resumen y no es una declaración completa de la ley. Sus acciones como tutor están regidos por la ley y no por este resumen ni por el *Manual del tutor* del Consejo Judicial. Cuando tenga una duda, consulte con su abogado.

ATTORNEY OR PARTY WITHOUT ATTORNEY STATE BAR NO.:	FOR COURT USE ONLY
NAME: Frank and Marv Doe FIRM NAME: STREET ADDRESS: 1234 Anv Street CITY: Monterev STATE: CA ZIP CODE: 93940 TELEPHONE NO.: (831) 123-4567 FAX NO.: E-MAIL ADDRESS: 2does@vahoo.com ATTORNEY FOR *(name)*: In pro per	
SUPERIOR COURT OF CALIFORNIA, COUNTY OF MONTEREY STREET ADDRESS: 1200 Aquaiito Road MAILING ADDRESS: 1200 Aquaiito Road CITY AND ZIP CODE: Monterev, CA 93940 BRANCH NAME: Monterev	
CONSERVATORSHIP OF *(name)*: JOHN DOE (PROPOSED) CONSERVATEE	
PETITION FOR APPOINTMENT OF ☐ SUCCESSOR **PROBATE CONSERVATOR OF THE ☒ PERSON ☐ ESTATE**	CASE NUMBER:
☒ **Limited Conservatorship**	HEARING DATE AND TIME: [Insert hrg date and time] DEPT.: [Dept]

1. **Petitioner *(name)*:** Frank and Marv Doe **requests that**

   a. *(Name):* FRANK DOE and MARY DOE *(Telephone):* (831) 123-4567
   (Address):
   1234 Any Street, Monterey, CA 93940

   be appointed ☐ successor ☐ conservator ☒ limited conservator
   of the PERSON of the (proposed) conservatee and Letters issue upon qualification.

   b. *(Name):* *(Telephone):*
   (Address):

   be appointed ☐ successor ☐ conservator ☐ limited conservator
   of the ESTATE of the (proposed) conservatee and Letters issue upon qualification.

   c. (1) ☒ bond not be required ☐ because the proposed ☐ successor conservator is a corporate fiduciary or an exempt government agency. ☒ for the reasons stated in Attachment 1c.

   (2) ☐ bond be fixed at: $ to be furnished by an authorized surety company or as otherwise provided by law. *(Specify reasons in Attachment 1c if the amount is different from the minimum required by Probate Code section 2320.)*

   (3) ☐ $ in deposits in a blocked account be allowed. Receipts will be filed.
   (Specify institution and location):

   d. ☐ orders authorizing independent exercise of powers under Probate Code section 2590 be granted. Granting the proposed ☐ successor conservator of the estate powers to be exercised independently under Probate Code section 2590 would be to the advantage and benefit and in the best interest of the conservatorship estate. *(Specify orders, powers, and reasons in Attachment 1d.)*

   e. ☐ orders relating to the capacity of the (proposed) conservatee under Probate Code section 1873 or 1901 be granted. *(Specify orders, facts, and reasons in Attachment 1e.)*

   f. ☐ orders relating to the powers and duties of the proposed ☐ successor conservator of the person under Probate Code sections 2351–2358 be granted. *(Specify orders, facts, and reasons in Attachment 1f.)*

   g. ☒ the (proposed) conservatee be adjudged to lack the capacity to give informed consent for medical treatment or healing by prayer and that the proposed ☐ successor conservator of the person be granted the powers specified in Probate Code section 2355. *(Complete item 9 on page 6.)*

Do NOT use this form for a temporary conservatorship.

CONSERVATORSHIP OF *(name):* (PROPOSED) CONSERVATEE	CASE NUMBER:

1. h. [x] *(for limited conservatorship only)* orders relating to the powers and duties of the proposed limited [ ] successor* conservator of the person under Probate Code section 2351.5 be granted. *(Specify orders, powers, and duties in Attachment 1h and complete item 1j.)*
   i. [ ] *(for limited conservatorship only)* orders relating to the powers and duties of the proposed limited [ ] successor* conservator of the estate under Probate Code section 1830(b) be granted. *(Specify orders, powers, and duties in Attachment 1i and complete item 1j.)*
   j. [x] *(for limited conservatorship only)* orders limiting the civil and legal rights of the (proposed) limited conservatee be granted. *(Specify limitations in Attachment 1j.)*
   k. [ ] orders authorizing placement or treatment for a major neurocognitive disorder (such as dementia) as specified in the *Attachment Requesting Special Orders Regarding a Major Neurocognitive Disorder* (form GC-313) under Probate Code section 2356.5 be granted. A *Capacity Declaration—Conservatorship* (form GC-335) and *Major Neurocognitive Disorder Attachment to Capacity Declaration—Conservatorship* (form GC-335A), executed by a licensed physician or by a licensed psychologist acting within the scope of his or her license with at least two years experience diagnosing major neurocognitive disorders (including dementia), [ ] are filed herewith. [ ] will be filed before the hearing.

      [ ] *(appointment of successor conservator only)* will not be filed because an order relating to placement or treatment for a major neurocognitive disorder (such as dementia) was filed on *(date):* . That order has neither expired by its terms nor been revoked.
   l. [ ] other orders be granted. *(Specify in Attachment 1l.)*

2. (Proposed) conservatee is *(name):* JOHN DOE *(Telephone):* (831) 123-4567
   (Current address):
   1234 Any Street, Monterey, CA 93940

3. a. [x] **Jurisdictional facts** *(initial appointment only)* The proposed conservatee has no conservator in California and is a
      (1) [x] resident of California and
         (a) [x] a resident of this county.
         (b) [ ] not a resident of this county, but commencement of the conservatorship in this county is in the best interests of the proposed conservatee for the reasons specified in Attachment 3a.
      (2) [ ] nonresident of California but
         (a) [ ] is temporarily living in this county, or
         (b) [ ] has property in this county, or
         (c) [ ] commencement of the conservatorship in this county is in the best interest of the proposed conservatee for the reasons specified in Attachment 3a.
   b. **Petitioner** *(answer items (1) and (2) and check all other items that apply)*
      (1) [ ] is [ ] is not a **creditor** or an agent of a creditor of the (proposed) conservatee.
      (2) [ ] is [ ] is not a **debtor** or an agent of a debtor of the (proposed) conservatee.
      (3) [x] is the proposed [ ] successor conservator.
      (4) [ ] is the (proposed) conservatee. *(If this item is* **not** *checked, you must also complete item 3f.)*
      (5) [ ] is the spouse of the (proposed) conservatee. *(You must also complete item 6.)*
      (6) [ ] is the domestic partner or former domestic partner of the (proposed) conservatee. *(You must also complete item 7.)*
      (7) [x] is a relative of the (proposed) conservatee as *(specify relationship):* Parents
      (8) [ ] is an interested person or friend of the (proposed) conservatee.
      (9) [ ] is a state or local public entity, officer, or employee.
      (10) [ ] is the guardian of the proposed conservatee.
      (11) [ ] is a bank [ ] is another entity authorized to conduct the business of a trust company.
      (12) [ ] is a professional fiduciary within the meaning of Business and Professions Code section 6501(f) who is licensed by the Professional Fiduciaries Bureau of the Department of Consumer Affairs. Petitioner's license number is provided in item 1 on page 1 of the attached Professional Fiduciary Attachment. *(Use form GC-210(A-PF)/GC-310(A-PF) for this attachment. You must also complete item 2 on page 2 of that form and item 3d below.)*

*** See item 5b on page 4.**

CONSERVATORSHIP OF (name): (PROPOSED) CONSERVATEE	CASE NUMBER:

3. c. **Proposed** ☐ **successor** **conservator** is *(check all that apply)*
   (1) ☐ a nominee. *(Affix nomination as Attachment 3c(1).)*
   (2) ☐ the spouse of the (proposed) conservatee. *(You must also complete item 6.)*
   (3) ☐ the domestic partner or former domestic partner of the (proposed) conservatee. *(You must also complete item 7.)*
   (4) ☒ a relative of the (proposed) conservatee as *(specify relationship):* Parents
   (5) ☐ a bank. ☐ another entity authorized to conduct the business of a trust company.
   (6) ☐ a nonprofit charitable corporation that meets the requirements of Probate Code section 2104.
   (7) ☐ a professional fiduciary, as defined in Business and Professions Code section 6501(f). His or her statement concerning licensure or exemption is provided in item 1 on page 1 of the attached *Professional Fiduciary Attachment. (Use form GC-210(A-PF)/GC-310(A-PF) for this attachment.)*
   (8) ☐ other *(specify):*

d. ☐ Engagement and prior relationship with petitioning professional fiduciary *(complete this item if petitioner is licensed by the Professional Fiduciaries Bureau.)*
   (1) ☐ Statements of who engaged petitioner, or how petitioner was engaged to file this petition, and a description of any prior relationship petitioner had with the (proposed) conservatee or his or her family or friends, are provided in item 2 on page 2 of the attached *Professional Fiduciary Attachment. (Use form GC-210(A-PF)/GC-310(A-PF) for this attachment.)*
   (2) ☐ A petition for appointment of a temporary conservator is filed with this petition. That petition contains statements of who engaged petitioner, how petitioner was engaged to file this petition, and a description of any prior relationship petitioner had with the (proposed) conservatee or his or her family and friends.

e. **Character and estimated value of the property of the estate** *(complete items (1) or (2) and (3), (4), and (5)):*
   (1) ☐ *(For appointment of successor conservator only, if complete Inventory and Appraisal filed by predecessor):*
   Personal property: $, per Inventory and Appraisal filed in this proceeding on *(specify dates of filing of all inventories and appraisals):*

   (2) ☐ Estimated value of personal property: $
   (3) Annual gross income from
      (a) real property: $
      (b) personal property: $
      (c) pensions: $
      (d) wages: $
      (e) public assistance benefits: $
      (f) other: $
   (4) **Total** of (1) or (2) and (3): $
   (5) Real property: $
      (a) ☐ per Inventory and Appraisal identified in item (1).
      (b) ☐ estimated value.

f. ☒ Due diligence *(complete this item if the (proposed) conservatee is not a petitioner):*
   (1) Efforts to find the (proposed) conservatee's relatives or reasons why it is not feasible to contact any of them are described on Attachment 3f(1).
   (2) Statements of the (proposed) conservatee's preferences concerning the appointment of any (successor) conservator and the appointment of the proposed (successor) conservator or reasons why it is not feasible to ascertain those preferences are contained on Attachment 3f(2).

CONSERVATORSHIP OF (name): (PROPOSED) CONSERVATEE	CASE NUMBER:

3. g. So far as known to petitioner, a conservatorship or equivalent proceeding concerning the proposed conservatee

☒ has not ☐ has been filed in another jurisdiction, including a court of a federally-recognized Indian tribe with jurisdiction (see Prob. Code, § 2031(b)).

(If you answered "has," identify the jurisdiction and state the date the case was filed):

4. **(Proposed) conservatee**

a. ☐ is ☒ is not a patient in or on leave of absence from a state institution under the jurisdiction of the California Department of State Hospitals or the California Department of Developmental Services *(specify state institution):*

b. ☐ is receiving or entitled to receive ☒ is neither receiving nor entitled to receive benefits from the U.S. Department of Veterans Affairs *(estimate amount of monthly benefit payable):*

c. ☐ is ☒ is not, so far as is known to petitioner, a member of a federally recognized Indian tribe.

(If you answered "is," complete items (1)–(4)):

(1) Name of tribe:

(2) Location of tribe *(if the tribe is located in more than one state, the state that is the tribe's principal location):*

(3) The proposed conservatee ☐ does ☐ does not reside on tribal land.*

(4) So far as known to petitioner, the proposed conservatee ☐ owns ☐ does not own property on tribal land.

5. a. ☒ Proposed conservatee *(initial appointment of conservator only)*

(1) ☐ is an adult.

(2) ☒ will be an adult on the effective date of the order *(date):* [Insert hearing date]

(3) ☐ is a married minor.

(4) ☐ is a minor whose marriage has been dissolved.

b. ☐ Vacancy in office of conservator *(appointment of successor conservator only. A petition for appointment of a limited conservator after the death of a predecessor is a petition for initial appointment. (Prob. Code, § 1860.5(a)(1).)*

There is a vacancy in the office of conservator of the ☐ person ☐ estate for the reasons

☐ specified in Attachment 5b. ☐ specified below.

*** "Tribal land" is land that is, with respect to a specific Indian tribe and the members of that tribe, "Indian country," as defined in 18 U.S.C. § 1151.**

CONSERVATORSHIP OF *(name):* (PROPOSED) CONSERVATEE	CASE NUMBER:

5. c. **(Proposed) conservatee** requires a conservator and is

(1) [x] unable to properly provide for his or her personal needs for physical health, food, clothing, or shelter.
Supporting facts are [ ] specified in Attachment 5c(1) [x] as follows:

The proposed conservatee is autistic with severe language development delays, having suffered a brain hemorrhage on delivery at birth. He helps out around the house with his chores that are limited. He can dress himself, feed himself, bathe himself, and toilet himself. He cannot communicate with others who do not understand his signals and vocalization. He cannot comprehend the complex nature of this conservatorship proceeding.

(2) [ ] substantially unable to manage his or her financial resources or to resist fraud or undue influence.
Supporting facts are [ ] specified in Attachment 5c(2) [ ] as follows:

CONSERVATORSHIP OF *(name):* (PROPOSED) CONSERVATEE	CASE NUMBER:

5\. d. ☐ (Proposed) conservatee voluntarily requests the appointment of a ☐ successor conservator. *(Specify facts showing good cause in Attachment 5(d).)*

e. ☒ *Confidential Supplemental Information* (form GC-312) is filed with this petition. *(Initial appointment of conservator only. All petitioners must file this form except banks and other entities authorized to do business as a trust company.)*

f. **(Proposed) conservatee** ☒ does ☐ does not have a developmental disability as defined in Probate Code section 1420. Petitioner is aware of the requirements of Probate Code section 1827.5. *(Specify the nature and degree of the alleged disability in Attachment 5f).*

6\. ☐ **Petitioner or proposed** ☐ **successor conservator is the spouse of the (proposed) conservatee.** *(If this statement is true, you must answer a or b.)*

a. ☐ The (proposed) conservatee's spouse is not a party to any action or proceeding against the (proposed) conservatee for legal separation, dissolution of marriage, annulment, or adjudication of nullity of their marriage.

b. ☐ Although the (proposed) conservatee's spouse is a party to an action or proceeding against the (proposed) conservatee for legal separation, dissolution, annulment, or adjudication of nullity of their marriage, or has obtained a judgment in one of these proceedings, it is in the best interest of the (proposed) conservatee that:

(1) ☐ a ☐ successor conservator be appointed.

(2) ☐ the spouse be appointed as the ☐ successor conservator.

(If you checked item 6b(1) or (2) or both, specify the facts and reasons in Attachment 6b.)

7\. ☐ **Petitioner or proposed** ☐ **successor conservator is the domestic partner or former domestic partner of the (proposed) conservatee.** *(If this statement is true, you must answer a or b.)*

a. ☐ The domestic partner of the (proposed) conservatee has not terminated and does not intend to terminate the domestic partnership.

b. ☐ Although the domestic partner or former domestic partner of the (proposed) conservatee intends to terminate or has terminated the domestic partnership, it is in the best interest of the (proposed) conservatee that

(1) ☐ a ☐ successor conservator be appointed.

(2) ☐ the domestic partner or former domestic partner be appointed as the ☐ successor conservator.

(If you checked item 7b(1) or (2) or both, specify the facts and reasons in Attachment 7b.)

8\. **(Proposed) conservatee** *(check all that apply)*

a. ☒ will attend the hearing AND ☐ is the petitioner ☒ is not the petitioner AND ☐ has ☒ has not nominated the proposed ☐ successor conservator.

b. ☐ *(initial appointment of conservator only)* is able but unwilling to attend the hearing AND ☐ does ☐ does not wish to contest the establishment of a conservatorship, ☐ does ☐ does not object to the proposed conservator, AND ☐ does ☐ does not prefer that another person act as conservator.

c. ☐ *(initial appointment of conservator only):* is unable to attend the hearing because of medical inability. A *Capacity Declaration—Conservatorship* (form GC-335), executed by a licensed medical practitioner or an accredited religious practitioner ☐ is filed with this petition. ☐ will be filed before the hearing.

d. ☐ *(initial appointment of conservator only)* is not the petitioner, is out of state, and will not attend the hearing.

e. ☐ *(appointment of successor conservator only)* will not attend the hearing.

9\. ☒ **Medical treatment of (proposed) conservatee**

a. There is no form of medical treatment for which the (proposed) conservatee has the capacity to give an informed consent.

b. A *Capacity Declaration—Conservatorship* (form GC-335) executed by a licensed physician or by a licensed psychologist acting within the scope of his or her licensure, stating that the (proposed) conservatee lacks the capacity to give informed consent for any form of medical treatment and giving reasons and the factual basis for this conclusion,

☐ is filed with this petition. ☒ will be filed before the hearing. ☐ will not be filed for the reason stated in c.

c. ☐ *(appointment of successor conservator only)* The conservatee's incapacity to consent to any form of medical treatment was determined by order filed in this matter on *(date):*

That order has neither expired by its terms nor been revoked.

d. (Proposed) conservatee ☐ is ☒ is not an adherent of a religion that relies on prayer alone for healing, as defined in Probate Code section 2355(b).

CONSERVATORSHIP OF (name): (PROPOSED) CONSERVATEE	CASE NUMBER:

10. [ ] **Temporary conservatorship**
Filed with this petition is a *Petition for Appointment of Temporary Conservator* (form GC-111).

11. **(Proposed) conservatee's relatives**

The names, residence addresses, and relationships of the spouse or registered domestic partner and the second-degree relatives of the (proposed) conservatee (his or her parents, grandparents, children, grandchildren, and brothers and sisters), so far as known to petitioner, are

a. [x] listed below.

b. [ ] not known, or no longer living, so the (proposed) conservatee's deemed relatives under Probate Code section 1821(b)(1)–(4) are listed below.

	Name and relationship to conservatee	Residence address
(1)	Frank and Mary Doe, parents	1234 Any Street Monterey, CA 93940
(2)	Brian Doe, brother	1234 Any Street Monterey, CA 93940
(3)	Susan Doe, sister	777 17th Street Collegetown, CA 95555
(4)	Stephen Doe, paternal grandfather (widowed)	3333 Wonder Avenue Disneyland, CA 93333
(5)	Amy Roe, maternal grandmother	4444 Gallant Drive Rich Haven, CN 01111
(6)	Arnold Roe, maternal grandfather	5555 Neighborhood Lane Friendly, FL 09999
(7)		
(8)		
(9)		
(10)		
(11)		
(12)		
(13)		
(14)		
(15)		
(16)		

[ ] Continued on Attachment 11.

CONSERVATORSHIP OF *(name)*: (PROPOSED) CONSERVATEE	CASE NUMBER:

12. [x] **Confidential conservator screening form**
    Submitted with this petition is a *Confidential Conservator Screening Form* (form GC-314) completed and signed by the proposed [ ] successor conservator. *(Required for all proposed conservators except banks and trust companies.)*

13. [x] **Court investigator**
    Filed with this petition is a proposed *Order Appointing Court Investigator* (form GC-330).

14. Number of pages attached: 2

Date:

________________________ ▶ ________________________

(TYPE OR PRINT NAME OF ATTORNEY FOR PETITIONER) (SIGNATURE OF ATTORNEY FOR PETITIONER)

(All petitioners must also sign (Prob. Code, § 1020; Cal. Rules of Court, rule 7.103).)

I declare under penalty of perjury under the laws of the State of California that the foregoing is true and correct.

Date: [Insert filing date]

FRANK DOE ▶ ________________________

(TYPE OR PRINT NAME OF PETITIONER) (SIGNATURE OF PETITIONER)

MARY DOE ▶ ________________________

(TYPE OR PRINT NAME OF PETITIONER) (SIGNATURE OF PETITIONER)

Limited Conservatorship of John Doe
Petition for Appointment of Limited Co-Conservators

Attachment 1c

No bond is required, as this is only a Limited Conservatorship for the Person, not for the Estate.

Attachment 1h

The proposed limited co-conservators request the following powers under Probate Code §2351.5(b):

(1) To fix the residence or specific dwelling of the limited conservatee.

The proposed co-conservators will work with San Andreas Regional Center to provide the least restricted living situation possible for the proposed conservatee.

(2) To access to the confidential records and papers of the limited conservatee.

The proposed co-conservators will be able to openly review and discuss the proposed conservatee's medical records with his care providers and the San Andreas Regional Center representatives.

(4) To limit the right of the limited conservatee to contract.

The proposed co-conservators appreciate that the proposed conservatee may be influenced to contract for any number of services, including cell phone services, and they would want to review any such contract as the issues arise.

(5) To give or withhold medical consent for the limited conservatee.

The proposed conservatee does not have the capacity to understand or appreciate the medical requests and inquiries of service providers.

(7) To make decisions concerning the education of the limited conservatee.

The proposed co-conservators will work with the proposed conservatee's social and health services providers to ensure the best educational opportunities possible for the proposed conservatee.

Attachment 1j

Petitioners request that the court grant an Order limiting the civil and legal rights of the proposed limited conservatee under Probate Code §2351.5, as follows:

(1) To limit the limited conservatee's right to choice of residence or specific dwelling.
(2) To limit the limited conservatee's sole access to his confidential records and papers.
(4) To limit the limited conservatee's right to contract.
(5) To limit the limited conservatee's right to consent or withhold consent to medical treatment.
(7) To limit the limited conservatee's right to make decisions concerning his education.

Attachment 3f(1)

All of the proposed conservatee's relatives to the second degree have been listed and are being notified of this conservatorship.

Attachment 3f(2)

The proposed conservatee is not capable of understanding the concept of limited conservatorship or of making his preferences for nomination known. He has lived with his parents and siblings all of his life.

Attachment 5f

The proposed conservatee is autistic with severe language developmental delays due to his having suffered a brain hemorrhage on delivery at birth, such that he is in need of supervision and care for most of his personal needs.

CONFIDENTIAL (DO NOT ATTACH TO PETITION)

GC-312

ATTORNEY OR PARTY WITHOUT ATTORNEY *(Name, state bar number, and address)*:	FOR COURT USE ONLY
Frank and Mary Doe 1234 Any Street Monterey, CA 93940 TELEPHONE NO.: (831) 123-4567 FAX NO. *(Optional)*: E-MAIL ADDRESS *(Optional)*: 2does@yahoo.com ATTORNEY FOR *(Name)*: In pro per	
SUPERIOR COURT OF CALIFORNIA, COUNTY OF MONTEREY STREET ADDRESS: 1200 Aguajito Road MAILING ADDRESS: 1200 Aguajito Road CITY AND ZIP CODE: Monterey, CA 93940 BRANCH NAME: Monterey	
CONSERVATORSHIP OF *(Name)*: JOHN DOE PROPOSED CONSERVATEE	
CONFIDENTIAL SUPPLEMENTAL INFORMATION **(Probate Conservatorship)** **Conservatorship of** ☑ **Person** ☐ **Estate** ☑ **Limited Conservatorship**	CASE NUMBER:
	HEARING DATE: [Insert hearing date]
	DEPT.: [Court Dept] TIME: [Hearing time]

1. a. **Proposed conservatee *(name)*:** JOHN DOE
   b. Date of birth: June 15, 2000
   c. Social security No.: 111-22-3333

2. ☑ UNABLE TO PROVIDE FOR PERSONAL NEEDS* The following facts support petitioner's allegation that the proposed conservatee is unable to provide properly for his or her needs for physical health, food, clothing, and shelter *(specify in detail, enlarging upon the reasons stated in the petition; provide specific examples from the proposed conservatee's daily life showing significant behavior patterns)*: ☐ Specified in Attachment 2.

The proposed conervatee is autistic with severe language developmental delays, having suffered a brain hemorrhage on delivery at birth. He is regularly seen by his treating physician, Dr. Doctor. He attends Oceanside High School, where he is enrolled in the Lifestudy Skills classes provided by Monterey County Special Education Local Plan Area. He helps out around the house with his chores that are limited. He can concentrate on a project for 10 minutes at a time and then needs re-direction of activity to stay on task. He is achieving in his ability to focus and complete two tasks on cue.

He has difficulty working in a group setting. He is easily distracted by others' activity, and he needs help with dressing, feeding, bathing, and toileting himself. He enjoys bowling with his family, riding horses at the local saddle ranch, and tossing balls at a basketball hoop.

Please see the most current IEP of the proposed conservatee, attached hereto and incorporated herein by this reference.

* If this item is not applicable, complete item 8.

(Continued on reverse)

CONSERVATORSHIP OF *(Name)*: JOHN DOE PROPOSED CONSERVATEE	CASE NUMBER:

3. ☐ UNABLE TO MANAGE FINANCIAL RESOURCES* The following facts support petitioner's allegation that the proposed conservatee is substantially unable to manage his or her financial resources or to resist fraud or undue influence *(specify in detail, enlarging upon the reasons stated in the petition; provide specific examples from the proposed conservatee's daily life showing significant behavior patterns)*: ☐ Specified in Attachment 3.

4. RESIDENCE *("Residence" means the place usually described as "home"; for example, owned real property or long-term rental.)*
   a. The proposed conservatee is **located** at *(street address, city, state)*:
      1234 Any Street
      Monterey, CA 93940
   b. The proposed conservatee's **residence** is* ☑ the address in item 4a ☐ other *(street address, city, state)*:

   c. **Ability to live in residence*** The proposed conservatee is
      (1) ☑ **living** in his or her residence and
         (a) ☑ will continue to live there unless circumstances change.
         (b) ☐ will need to be moved after a conservator is appointed *(specify supporting facts below in item 4c(3))*.
         (c) ☐ other *(specify and give supporting facts below in item 4c(3))*.

* If this item is not applicable, complete item 8.

(Continued on page three)

CONFIDENTIAL

CONSERVATORSHIP OF *(Name)*: JOHN DOE PROPOSED CONSERVATEE	CASE NUMBER:

4. c. *(continued)*

(2) ☐ **not living** in his or her residence and

(a) ☐ will return by *(date)*: *(specify supporting facts below in item 4c(3)).*

(b) ☐ will not return to live there *(specify supporting facts below in item 4c(3)).*

(c) ☐ other *(specify and give supporting facts below in item 4c(3)).*

(3) ☐ Supporting facts *(specify if required)*: ☐ Specified in Attachment 4c.

5. ALTERNATIVES TO CONSERVATORSHIP* Petitioner has considered the following alternatives to conservatorship and found them to be unsuitable or unavailable to the proposed conservatee *(specify the alternatives considered and the reason or reasons each is unsuitable or unavailable)*: ☐ Reasons specified in Attachment 5.

a. Voluntary acceptance of informal or formal assistance *(give reason this is unsuitable or unavailable)*:

The proposed conservatee cannot comprehend the need to ask for assistance with personal matters.

b. Special or limited power of attorney *(give reason this is unsuitable or unavailable)*:

See 5.a., above.

c. General power of attorney *(give reason this is unsuitable or unavailable)*:

See 5.a., above.

d. Durable power of attorney for ☐ health care ☐ estate management *(give reason this is unsuitable or unavailable)*:

See 5.a., above.

e. Trust *(give reason this is unsuitable or unavailable)*:

See 5.a., above.

f. Other alternatives considered *(specify and give reason each is unsuitable or unavailable)*:

See 5.a., above.

6. SERVICES PROVIDED* *(complete a or b, or both a and b)*

a. ☑ During the year before this petition was filed,

(1) **health services** ☑ were provided ☐ were not provided to the proposed conservatee *(explain)*:

☐ Explained in Attachment 6a(1).

The proposed conservatee is seen regularly by his treating physician, Dr. Doctor. He also sees his neurologist, Dr. Riddle, periodically, for maintenance of his seizure medication.

(2) **social services** ☑ were provided ☐ were not provided to the proposed conservatee *(explain)*:

☐ Explained in Attachment 6a(2).

The proposed conservatee's family is very active with him in providing social interactions. The proposed conservatee's school also provides various opportunities for social activities and community outings.

* If this item is not applicable, complete item 8.

(Continued on page four)

CONFIDENTIAL

CONSERVATORSHIP OF (*Name*): JOHN DOE PROPOSED CONSERVATEE	CASE NUMBER:

6. a. *(continued)*

(3) **estate management assistance** ☐ was provided ☑ was not provided to the proposed conservatee *(explain)*:

☐ Explained in Attachment 6a(3).

b. ☐ Petitioner has **no knowledge** of what ☐ social services ☐ health services ☐ estate management assistance was provided to the proposed conservatee during the year before this petition was filed. Petitioner has no reasonable means of determining what services were provided.

7. SUPPORTING FACTS (AFFIDAVITS) The information provided above is stated

a. Item 1: ☑ on petitioner's own knowledge ☐ in an affidavit (declaration) by another person attached as Attachment 1a.
b. Item 2: ☑ on petitioner's own knowledge ☐ in an affidavit (declaration) by another person attached as Attachment 2a.
c. Item 3: ☐ on petitioner's own knowledge ☐ in an affidavit (declaration) by another person attached as Attachment 3a.
d. Item 4: ☑ on petitioner's own knowledge ☐ in an affidavit (declaration) by another person attached as Attachment 4a.
e. Item 5: ☑ on petitioner's own knowledge ☐ in an affidavit (declaration) by another person attached as Attachment 5a.
f. Item 6: ☑ on petitioner's own knowledge ☐ in an affidavit (declaration) by another person attached as Attachment 6a.

8. ITEMS NOT APPLICABLE The following items on this form were not applicable to the proposed conservatee:
☐ 2 ☑ 3 ☐ 4b ☐ 4c ☐ 5 ☐ 6 *(specify reasons each item is not applicable)*:
☐ Reasons specified in Attachment 8.

9. Number of pages attached: _____

DECLARATION

I declare under penalty of perjury under the laws of the State of California that the foregoing is true and correct.

Date:

_______________________________ ▶ _______________________________
(TYPE OR PRINT NAME) (SIGNATURE OF PETITIONER)

ATTORNEY OR PARTY WITHOUT ATTORNEY *(Name, State Bar number, and address):*
Frank and Mary Doe
1234 Any Street, Monterey, CA 93940
TELEPHONE NO.: (831)123-4567 FAX NO. *(Optional):*
E-MAIL ADDRESS *(Optional):* 2does@yahoo.com
ATTORNEY FOR *(Name):* In pro per

FOR COURT USE ONLY

SUPERIOR COURT OF CALIFORNIA, COUNTY OF MONTEREY
STREET ADDRESS: 1200 Aguajito Road
MAILING ADDRESS: 1200 Aguajito Road
CITY AND ZIP CODE: Monterey, CA 93940
BRANCH NAME: Monterey

CONSERVATORSHIP OF THE ☑ PERSON ☐ ESTATE OF *(Name):*
JOHN DOE
☐ CONSERVATEE ☑ PROPOSED CONSERVATEE

CASE NUMBER

CAPACITY DECLARATION—CONSERVATORSHIP

TO PHYSICIAN, PSYCHOLOGIST, OR RELIGIOUS HEALING PRACTITIONER

The purpose of this form is to enable the court to determine whether the (proposed) conservatee *(check all that apply):*

A. ☑ is able to attend a court hearing to determine whether a conservator should be appointed to care for him or her. The court hearing is set for *(date):* [Insert date of hearing] . *(Complete item 5, sign, and file page 1 of this form.)*

B. ☑ has the capacity to give informed consent to medical treatment. *(Complete items 6 through 8, sign page 3, and file pages 1 through 3 of this form.)*

C. ☐ has dementia and, if so, (1) whether he or she needs to be placed in a secured-perimeter residential care facility for the elderly, and (2) whether he or she needs or would benefit from dementia medications. *(Complete items 6 and 8 of this form and form GC-335A; sign and attach form GC-335A. File pages 1 through 3 of this form and form GC-335A.)*

(If more than one item is checked above, sign the last applicable page of this form or form GC-335A if item C is checked. File page 1 through the last applicable page of this form; also file form GC-335A if item C is checked.)

COMPLETE ITEMS 1–4 OF THIS FORM IN ALL CASES.

GENERAL INFORMATION

1. *(Name):* Dr. Doctor, M.D.
2. *(Office address and telephone number):* 45 Professional Drive, Suite A, Monterey, CA 93940
   Telephone (831) 444-5555
3. I am
   a. ☑ a California licensed ☑ physician ☐ psychologist acting within the scope of my licensure
   ☐ with at least two years' experience in diagnosing dementia.
   b. ☐ an accredited practitioner of a religion whose tenets and practices call for reliance on prayer alone for healing, which religion is adhered to by the (proposed) conservatee. The (proposed) conservatee is under my treatment. *(Religious practitioner may make the determination under item 5 ONLY.)*
4. (Proposed) conservatee *(name):* JOHN DOE
   a. I last saw the (proposed) conservatee on *(date):* [Insert date of last visit]
   b. The (proposed) conservatee ☑ is ☐ is NOT a patient under my continuing treatment.

ABILITY TO ATTEND COURT HEARING

5. A court hearing on the petition for appointment of a conservator is set for the date indicated in item A above. *(Complete a or b.)*
   a. ☐ The proposed conservatee is able to attend the court hearing.
   b. ☐ Because of medical inability, the proposed conservatee is NOT able to attend the court hearing *(check all items below that apply)*
      (1) ☐ on the date set *(see date in box in item A above).*
      (2) ☐ for the foreseeable future.
      (3) ☐ until *(date):*
      (4) **Supporting facts** *(State facts in the space below or check this box* ☐ *and state the facts in Attachment 5):*

I declare under penalty of perjury under the laws of the State of California that the foregoing is true and correct.
Date:

Dr. Doctor, M.D.
(TYPE OR PRINT NAME) ▶ (SIGNATURE OF DECLARANT)

CONSERVATORSHIP OF THE ☑ PERSON ☐ ESTATE OF *(Name)*:	CASE NUMBER:
JOHN DOE	
☐ CONSERVATEE ☑ PROPOSED CONSERVATEE	

6. **EVALUATION OF (PROPOSED) CONSERVATEE'S MENTAL FUNCTIONS**

Note to practitioner: This form is ***not*** a rating scale. It is intended to assist you in recording your *impressions* of the (proposed) conservatee's mental abilities. Where appropriate, you may refer to scores on standardized rating instruments.
(Instructions for items 6A–6C): *Check the appropriate designation as follows:* ***a*** *= no apparent impairment;* ***b*** *= moderate impairment;* ***c*** *= major impairment;* ***d*** *= so impaired as to be incapable of being assessed;* ***e*** *= I have no opinion.)*

A. **Alertness and attention**

(1) Levels of arousal (lethargic, responds only to vigorous and persistent stimulation, stupor)
a ☐ b ☐ c ☐ d ☐ e ☐

(2) Orientation (types of orientation impaired)
a ☐ b ☐ c ☐ d ☐ e ☐ Person
a ☐ b ☐ c ☐ d ☐ e ☐ Time (day, date, month, season, year)
a ☐ b ☐ c ☐ d ☐ e ☐ Place (address, town, state)
a ☐ b ☐ c ☐ d ☐ e ☐ Situation ("Why am I here?")

(3) Ability to attend and concentrate (give detailed answers from memory, mental ability required to thread a needle)
a ☐ b ☐ c ☐ d ☐ e ☐

B. **Information processing.** Ability to:

(1) Remember (ability to remember a question before answering; to recall names, relatives, past presidents, and events of the past 24 hours)
i. Short-term memory a ☐ b ☐ c ☐ d ☐ e ☐
ii Long-term memory a ☐ b ☐ c ☐ d ☐ e ☐
iii Immediate recall a ☐ b ☐ c ☐ d ☐ e ☐

(2) Understand and communicate either verbally or otherwise (deficits reflected by inability to comprehend questions, follow instructions, use words correctly, or name objects; use of nonsense words)
a ☐ b ☐ c ☐ d ☐ e ☐

(3) Recognize familiar objects and persons (deficits reflected by inability to recognize familiar faces, objects, etc.)
a ☐ b ☐ c ☐ d ☐ e ☐

(4) Understand and appreciate quantities (deficits reflected by inability to perform simple calculations)
a ☐ b ☐ c ☐ d ☐ e ☐

(5) Reason using abstract concepts. (deficits reflected by inability to grasp abstract aspects of his or her situation or to interpret idiomatic expressions or proverbs)
a ☐ b ☐ c ☐ d ☐ e ☐

(6) Plan, organize, and carry out actions (assuming physical ability) in one's own rational self-interest (deficits reflected by inability to break complex tasks down into simple steps and carry them out)
a ☐ b ☐ c ☐ d ☐ e ☐

(7) Reason logically.
a ☐ b ☐ c ☐ d ☐ e ☐

C. **Thought disorders**

(1) Severely disorganized thinking (rambling thoughts; nonsensical, incoherent, or nonlinear thinking)
a ☐ b ☐ c ☐ d ☐ e ☐

(2) Hallucinations (auditory, visual, olfactory)
a ☐ b ☐ c ☐ d ☐ e ☐

(3) Delusions (demonstrably false belief maintained without or against reason or evidence)
a ☐ b ☐ c ☐ d ☐ e ☐

(4) Uncontrollable or intrusive thoughts (unwanted compulsive thoughts, compulsive behavior).
a ☐ b ☐ c ☐ d ☐ e ☐

(Continued on next page)

CONSERVATORSHIP OF THE [x] PERSON [ ] ESTATE OF *(Name)*: JOHN DOE [ ] CONSERVATEE [x] PROPOSED CONSERVATEE	CASE NUMBER:

6. *(continued)*

D. **Ability to modulate mood and affect.** The (proposed) conservatee [ ] has [ ] does NOT have a pervasive and persistent or recurrent emotional state that appears inappropriate in degree to his or her circumstances. *(If so, complete remainder of item 6D.)* [ ] I have no opinion.

(Instructions for item 6D):** Check the degree of impairment of each inappropriate mood state (if any) as follows:* ***a *= mildly inappropriate;* ***b*** *= moderately inappropriate;* ***c*** *= severely inappropriate.)*

Anger	a [ ]	b [ ]	c [ ]	Euphoria	a [ ]	b [ ]	c [ ]	Helplessness	a [ ]	b [ ]	c [ ]
Anxiety	a [ ]	b [ ]	c [ ]	Depression	a [ ]	b [ ]	c [ ]	Apathy	a [ ]	b [ ]	c [ ]
Fear	a [ ]	b [ ]	c [ ]	Hopelessness	a [ ]	b [ ]	c [ ]	Indifference	a [ ]	b [ ]	c [ ]
Panic	a [ ]	b [ ]	c [ ]	Despair	a [ ]	b [ ]	c [ ]				

E. The (proposed) conservatee's periods of impairment from the deficits indicated in items 6A–6D

(1) [ ] do NOT vary substantially in frequency, severity, or duration.

(2) [ ] do vary substantially in frequency, severity, or duration *(explain; continue on Attachment 6E if necessary)*:

F. [ ] *(Optional)* Other information regarding my evaluation of the (proposed) conservatee's mental function (e.g., diagnosis, symptomatology, and other impressions) is [ ] stated below [ ] stated in Attachment 6F.

ABILITY TO CONSENT TO MEDICAL TREATMENT

7. Based on the information above, it is my opinion that the (proposed) conservatee

a. [ ] has the capacity to give informed consent to any form of medical treatment. This opinion is limited to medical consent capacity.

b. [ ] lacks the capacity to give informed consent to any form of medical treatment because he or she is ***either*** (1) unable to respond knowingly and intelligently regarding medical treatment ***or*** (2) unable to participate in a treatment decision by means of a rational thought process, ***or both***. The deficits in the mental functions described in item 6 above significantly impair the (proposed) conservatee's ability to understand and appreciate the consequences of medical decisions. This opinion is limited to medical consent capacity.

(Declarant must initial here if item 7b applies:* ____________*.)

8. Number of pages attached: ______

I declare under penalty of perjury under the laws of the State of California that the foregoing is true and correct.

Date:

Dr. Doctor, M.D.
(TYPE OR PRINT NAME)   (SIGNATURE OF DECLARANT)

CONFIDENTIAL (DO NOT ATTACH TO PETITION)

GC-314

ATTORNEY OR PARTY WITHOUT ATTORNEY *(Name, State Bar number, and address):*
Frank and Mary Doe
1234 Any Street
Monterey, CA 93940

TELEPHONE NO.: (831) 123-4567 FAX NO. *(Optional):*
E-MAIL ADDRESS *(Optional):* 2does@yahoo.com
ATTORNEY FOR *(Name):* In pro per

FOR COURT USE ONLY

SUPERIOR COURT OF CALIFORNIA, COUNTY OF MONTEREY
STREET ADDRESS: 1200 Aguajito Road
MAILING ADDRESS: 1200 Aguajito Road
CITY AND ZIP CODE: Monterey, CA 93940
BRANCH NAME: Monterey

CONSERVATORSHIP OF
(Name): JOHN DOE
PROPOSED CONSERVATEE

CASE NUMBER:

CONFIDENTIAL CONSERVATOR SCREENING FORM
Conservatorship of ☑ **Person** ☐ **Estate** ☑ **Limited Conservatorship**

HEARING DATE AND TIME: [Insert date and time of hrg]
DEPT.: [Dept]

The proposed conservator must complete and sign this form. The person requesting appointment of a conservator must submit the completed and signed form to the court with the conservatorship petition.
This form must remain confidential.

How This Form Will Be Used

This form is **confidential** and will not be a part of the public file in this case. Each proposed conservator must complete and sign a separate copy of this form under rule 7.1050 of the California Rules of Court. The information provided in this form will be used by the court and by the persons and agencies designated by the court to assist the court in determining whether to appoint the proposed conservator as conservator. The proposed conservator **must** respond to each item.

1. a. **Proposed conservator *(name):*** Frank Doe
   b. Date of birth: 01/01/1963
   c. Social security number: 123-45-6789 d. Driver's license number: A00090000 State: CA
   e. Telephone numbers: Home: (831) 123-4567 Work: Other: cell: 610-0000

2. a. ☑ I am related to the proposed conservatee as *(specify relationship):* Father
   b. ☑ I have personally known the proposed conservatee for: 17 years, 10 months.

3. ☐ I was ☑ I was not nominated as conservator of the ☑ person ☐ estate of the proposed conservatee, by ☑ the proposed conservatee. ☐ the spouse or registered domestic partner of the proposed conservatee. ☐ a parent of the proposed conservatee. *(If you checked "I was," provide documentation in Attachment 3.)*

4. a. ☐ I am the spouse of the proposed conservatee. ☐ I have ☐ I have not filed for legal separation, dissolution of marriage, annulment, or adjudication of nullity of the marriage. *(If you checked "I have," explain in Attachment 4.)*
   b. ☑ I am not the spouse of the proposed conservatee.

5. a. ☐ I am the registered domestic partner of the proposed conservatee. ☐ I do not ☐ I do intend to terminate my domestic partnership with the proposed conservatee. *(If you checked "I do," explain in Attachment 5.)*
   b. ☐ I am a former domestic partner of the proposed conservatee. My domestic partnership with the proposed conservatee was terminated on *(date):* . *(Explain circumstances in Attachment 5.)*
   c. ☑ I am neither a current nor former domestic partner of the proposed conservatee.

6. a. ☐ I do ☑ I do not owe money or have a financial obligation to the proposed conservatee. *(If you checked "I do," explain in Attachment 6.)*
   b. The proposed conservatee ☐ does ☑ does not owe money or have a financial obligation to me. *(If you checked "does," explain in Attachment 6.)*
   c. ☐ I am ☑ I am not an agent for a creditor of the proposed conservatee. *If you checked "I am," explain in Attachment 6.)*

CONFIDENTIAL

CONSERVATORSHIP OF *(Name)*: JOHN DOE PROPOSED CONSERVATEE	CASE NUMBER:

7. ☐ I have ☑ I have not filed for bankruptcy protection within the last 10 years. *(If you checked "I have," explain in Attachment 7.)*
8. ☐ I have ☑ I have not been convicted of a felony or had a felony expunged from my record. *(If you checked "I have," explain in Attachment 8.)*
9. ☐ I have ☑ I have not been charged with, arrested for, or convicted of embezzlement, theft, or any other crime involving the taking of property. *(If you checked "I have," explain in Attachment 9.)*
10. ☐ I have ☑ I have not been charged with, arrested for, or convicted of a crime involving fraud, conspiracy, or misrepresentation of information. *(If you checked "I have," explain in Attachment 10.)*
11. ☐ I have ☑ I have not been charged with, arrested for, or convicted of any form of elder abuse or neglect. *(If you checked "I have," explain in Attachment 11.)*
12. ☐ I have ☑ I have not had a restraining order or protective order filed against me in the last 10 years. *(If you checked "I have," explain in Attachment 12.)*
13. ☐ I am ☑ I am not required to register as a sex offender under California Penal Code section 290. *(If you checked "I am," explain in Attachment 13.)*
14. ☐ I have ☑ I have not previously been appointed conservator, executor, or fiduciary in another proceeding. *(If you checked "I have," explain in Attachment 14.)*
15. ☐ I have ☑ I have not been removed or resigned as a conservator, guardian, executor, or fiduciary in any other case. *(If you checked "I have," explain in Attachment 15.)*
16. ☐ I have or may have ☑ I do not have an adverse interest that the court may consider to be a risk to, or to have an effect on, my ability to faithfully perform the duties of conservator. *(If you checked "I have or may have," explain in Attachment 16.)*
17. ☐ I am ☑ I am not a private professional fiduciary, as defined in Business and Professions Code section 6501(f). *(If you checked "I am," respond to item 18. If you checked "I am not," go to item 19.)*
18. ☐ I am ☐ I am not currently licensed by the Professional Fiduciaries Bureau of the Department of Consumer Affairs. My license status and information is stated in item 1 on page 1 of the Professional Fiduciary Attachment signed by me and attached to the petition that proposes my appointment as conservator in this matter. *(Complete and sign the Professional Fiduciary Attachment and attach it to the petition, or deliver it to the petitioner for attachment, before the petition is filed. See item 3c(7) of the petition. Use form GC-210(A-PF)/GC-310(A-PF) for this attachment.)*
19. ☐ I am ☑ I am not a responsible corporate officer authorized to act for *(name of corporation)*:

    a California nonprofit charitable corporation that meets the requirements for appointment as conservator of the proposed conservatee under Probate Code section 2104. I certify that the corporation's articles of incorporation specifically authorize it to accept appointments as conservator. *(If you checked "I am," explain the circumstances of the corporation's care of, counseling of, or financial assistance to the proposed conservatee in Attachment 19.)*
20. Do you, or does any other person living in your home, have a social worker or parole or probation officer assigned to him or her?
    ☐ Yes ☑ No *(If you checked "Yes," explain in Attachment 20 and provide the name, address, and telephone number of each social worker, parole officer, or probation officer.)*

DECLARATION

I declare under penalty of perjury under the laws of the State of California that the foregoing is true and correct.

Date: [Insert filing date]

FRANK DOE
(TYPE OR PRINT NAME OF PROPOSED CONSERVATOR)

▶ ______________________________
(SIGNATURE OF PROPOSED CONSERVATOR)*

*Each proposed conservator must fill out and file a separate screening form.

CONFIDENTIAL (DO NOT ATTACH TO PETITION)

GC-314

ATTORNEY OR PARTY WITHOUT ATTORNEY *(Name, State Bar number, and address):* Frank and Mary Doe 1234 Any Street Monterey, CA 93940 TELEPHONE NO.: (831) 123-4567 FAX NO. *(Optional):* E-MAIL ADDRESS *(Optional):* 2does@yahoo.com ATTORNEY FOR *(Name):* In pro per	*FOR COURT USE ONLY*
SUPERIOR COURT OF CALIFORNIA, COUNTY OF MONTEREY STREET ADDRESS: 1200 Aguajito Road MAILING ADDRESS: 1200 Aguajito Road CITY AND ZIP CODE: Monterey, CA 93940 BRANCH NAME: Monterey	
CONSERVATORSHIP OF *(Name):* JOHN DOE PROPOSED CONSERVATEE	CASE NUMBER:
CONFIDENTIAL CONSERVATOR SCREENING FORM **Conservatorship of** ☑ **Person** ☐ **Estate** ☑ **Limited Conservatorship**	HEARING DATE AND TIME: [Insert date and time of hrg] DEPT.: [Dept]

The proposed conservator must complete and sign this form. The person requesting appointment of a conservator must submit the completed and signed form to the court with the conservatorship petition.
This form must remain confidential.

How This Form Will Be Used

This form is **confidential** and will not be a part of the public file in this case. Each proposed conservator must complete and sign a separate copy of this form under rule 7.1050 of the California Rules of Court. The information provided in this form will be used by the court and by the persons and agencies designated by the court to assist the court in determining whether to appoint the proposed conservator as conservator. The proposed conservator **must** respond to each item.

1. a. **Proposed conservator *(name):*** Mary Doe
   b. Date of birth: 04/04/1963
   c. Social security number: 012-34-5678 d. Driver's license number: B00080000 State: CA
   e. Telephone numbers: Home: (831) 123-4567 Work: Other: cell: 610-0001

2. a. ☑ I am related to the proposed conservatee as *(specify relationship):* Mother
   b. ☑ I have personally known the proposed conservatee for: 17 years, 10 months.

3. ☐ I was ☑ I was not nominated as conservator of the ☑ person ☐ estate of the proposed conservatee, by ☑ the proposed conservatee. ☐ the spouse or registered domestic partner of the proposed conservatee. ☐ a parent of the proposed conservatee. *(If you checked "I was," provide documentation in Attachment 3.)*

4. a. ☐ I am the spouse of the proposed conservatee. ☐ I have ☐ I have not filed for legal separation, dissolution of marriage, annulment, or adjudication of nullity of the marriage. *(If you checked "I have," explain in Attachment 4.)*
   b. ☑ I am not the spouse of the proposed conservatee.

5. a. ☐ I am the registered domestic partner of the proposed conservatee. ☐ I do not ☐ I do intend to terminate my domestic partnership with the proposed conservatee. *(If you checked "I do," explain in Attachment 5.)*
   b. ☐ I am a former domestic partner of the proposed conservatee. My domestic partnership with the proposed conservatee was terminated on *(date):* . *(Explain circumstances in Attachment 5.)*
   c. ☑ I am neither a current nor former domestic partner of the proposed conservatee.

6. a. ☐ I do ☑ I do not owe money or have a financial obligation to the proposed conservatee. *(If you checked "I do," explain in Attachment 6.)*
   b. The proposed conservatee ☐ does ☑ does not owe money or have a financial obligation to me. *(If you checked "does," explain in Attachment 6.)*
   c. ☐ I am ☑ I am not an agent for a creditor of the proposed conservatee. *If you checked "I am," explain in Attachment 6.)*

CONSERVATORSHIP OF *(Name)*: JOHN DOE PROPOSED CONSERVATEE	CASE NUMBER:

7. ☐ I have ☑ I have not filed for bankruptcy protection within the last 10 years. *(If you checked "I have," explain in Attachment 7.)*
8. ☐ I have ☑ I have not been convicted of a felony or had a felony expunged from my record. *(If you checked "I have," explain in Attachment 8.)*
9. ☐ I have ☑ I have not been charged with, arrested for, or convicted of embezzlement, theft, or any other crime involving the taking of property. *(If you checked "I have," explain in Attachment 9.)*
10. ☐ I have ☑ I have not been charged with, arrested for, or convicted of a crime involving fraud, conspiracy, or misrepresentation of information. *(If you checked "I have," explain in Attachment 10.)*
11. ☐ I have ☑ I have not been charged with, arrested for, or convicted of any form of elder abuse or neglect. *(If you checked "I have," explain in Attachment 11.)*
12. ☐ I have ☑ I have not had a restraining order or protective order filed against me in the last 10 years. *(If you checked "I have," explain in Attachment 12.)*
13. ☐ I am ☑ I am not required to register as a sex offender under California Penal Code section 290. *(If you checked "I am," explain in Attachment 13.)*
14. ☐ I have ☑ I have not previously been appointed conservator, executor, or fiduciary in another proceeding. *(If you checked "I have," explain in Attachment 14.)*
15. ☐ I have ☑ I have not been removed or resigned as a conservator, guardian, executor, or fiduciary in any other case. *(If you checked "I have," explain in Attachment 15.)*
16. ☐ I have or may have ☑ I do not have an adverse interest that the court may consider to be a risk to, or to have an effect on, my ability to faithfully perform the duties of conservator. *(If you checked "I have or may have," explain in Attachment 16.)*
17. ☐ I am ☑ I am not a private professional fiduciary, as defined in Business and Professions Code section 6501(f). *(If you checked "I am," respond to item 18. If you checked "I am not," go to item 19.)*
18. ☐ I am ☐ I am not currently licensed by the Professional Fiduciaries Bureau of the Department of Consumer Affairs. My license status and information is stated in item 1 on page 1 of the Professional Fiduciary Attachment signed by me and attached to the petition that proposes my appointment as conservator in this matter. *(Complete and sign the Professional Fiduciary Attachment and attach it to the petition, or deliver it to the petitioner for attachment, before the petition is filed. See item 3c(7) of the petition. Use form GC-210(A-PF)/GC-310(A-PF) for this attachment.)*
19. ☐ I am ☑ I am not a responsible corporate officer authorized to act for *(name of corporation)*:

    a California nonprofit charitable corporation that meets the requirements for appointment as conservator of the proposed conservatee under Probate Code section 2104. I certify that the corporation's articles of incorporation specifically authorize it to accept appointments as conservator. *(If you checked "I am," explain the circumstances of the corporation's care of, counseling of, or financial assistance to the proposed conservatee in Attachment 19.)*
20. Do you, or does any other person living in your home, have a social worker or parole or probation officer assigned to him or her?
    ☐ Yes ☑ No *(If you checked "Yes," explain in Attachment 20 and provide the name, address, and telephone number of each social worker, parole officer, or probation officer.)*

DECLARATION

I declare under penalty of perjury under the laws of the State of California that the foregoing is true and correct.

Date: [Insert filing date]

MARY DOE
(TYPE OR PRINT NAME OF PROPOSED CONSERVATOR)

▶ ______________________
(SIGNATURE OF PROPOSED CONSERVATOR)*

*Each proposed conservator must fill out and file a separate screening form.

Frank and Mary Doe
1234 Any Street
Monterey, California 93940
Telephone: (831) 123-4567
Email: 2does@yahoo.com

Attorney for: In pro per

SUPERIOR COURT OF THE STATE OF CALIFORNIA

FOR THE COUNTY OF MONTEREY

In re the Limited Conservatorship of the Person of JOHN DOE, proposed conservatee. /	**Case No.** **EX PARTE PETITION FOR CONFIDENTIAL WRITTEN REPORT BY SAN ANDREAS REGIONAL CENTER**

Petitioners request an Order of the court pursuant to Probate Code §1827.5 requiring San Andreas [or your county named Center] Regional Center to file a confidential written report of its assessment of the proposed conservatee, with its findings and recommendations to the court in connection with the establishment of this limited conservatorship, in advance of the hearing on the petition, [Insert date of hearing].

Dated: ____________________

____
FRANK DOE and MARY DOE, Petitioners

Frank and Mary Doe
1234 Any Street
Monterey, California 93940
Telephone: (831) 123-4567
Email: 2does@yahoo.com

Attorney for: In pro per

SUPERIOR COURT OF THE STATE OF CALIFORNIA

FOR THE COUNTY OF MONTEREY

In re the Limited Conservatorship of the Person of JOHN DOE, proposed conservatee. /	**Case No.** **EX PARTE ORDER FOR CONFIDENTIAL WRITTEN REPORT BY SAN ANDREAS REGIONAL CENTER**

Good cause appearing,

IT IS HEREBY ORDERED that:

1. San Andreas Regional Center shall file herein a confidential written report, following its assessment of the proposed limited conservatee, stating its findings and recommendations regarding the establishment of this limited conservatorship.

2. Said report shall be filed on or before ________________, and served on the proposed limited conservatee, the attorney for the proposed limited conservatee, the attorney for the petitioner, and the court investigator.

Dated: ________________

____
JUDGE OF THE SUPERIOR COURT

Frank and Mary Doe
1234 Any Street
Monterey, California 93940
Telephone: (831) 123-4567
Email: 2does@yahoo.com

Attorney for: In pro per

SUPERIOR COURT OF THE STATE OF CALIFORNIA

FOR THE COUNTY OF MONTEREY

In re the Limited Conservatorship of the Person of JOHN DOE, proposed conservatee. _______________________________/	**Case No.** **EX PARTE APPLICATION FOR APPOINTMENT OF COUNSEL FOR PROPOSED LIMITED CONSERVATEE**

We, FRANK DOE and MARY DOE, hereby allege:

1. We are the parents of the proposed conservatee, JOHN DOE, a minor living with developmental disabilities.

2. We have filed concurrently with this Application a Petition for Appointment of Limited Conservator, stating grounds for the appointment of a limited probate conservator rather than a general probate conservator.

3. Probate Code §1417(c) requires that in a proceeding to establish a limited conservatorship, "The court shall immediately appoint the public defender or private counsel to represent the proposed limited conservatee" and that "The proposed limited conservatee shall pay the cost for such legal service if he or she is able."

4. We are informed and believe that the proposed conservatee has no funds to pay for such legal services and, therefore, request that the public defender be appointed to represent his interests at the hearing scheduled for [Insert date of hearing].

Dated: ____________________

____
FRANK DOE and MARY DOE, Petitioners

Frank and Mary Doe
1234 Any Street
Monterey, California 93940
Telephone: (831) 123-4567
Email: 2does@yahoo.com

Attorney for: In pro per

SUPERIOR COURT OF THE STATE OF CALIFORNIA

FOR THE COUNTY OF MONTEREY

In re the Limited Conservatorship of the Person of

JOHN DOE,

proposed conservatee.
_______________________________/

Case No.

ORDER APPOINTING COUNSEL FOR PROPOSED LIMITED CONSERVATEE

Good cause appearing,

IT IS HEREBY ORDERED that:

1. Counsel shall be appointed to represent the proposed limited conservatee at the hearing on [Insert date of hearing], for appointment of limited probate conservator.

2. _______________________________ shall serve as counsel for the proposed limited conservatee, effective immediately, and shall report to the court his or her recommendations concerning the appropriateness of the requested powers.

Dated: _______________

____
JUDGE OF THE SUPERIOR COURT

GC-330

ATTORNEY OR PARTY WITHOUT ATTORNEY: STATE BAR NO.:	FOR COURT USE ONLY
NAME: Frank and Mary Doe FIRM NAME: STREET ADDRESS: 1234 Any Street CITY: Monterey STATE: CA ZIP CODE: 93940 TELEPHONE NO.: (831) 123-4567 FAX NO.: E-MAIL ADDRESS: 2does@yahoo.com ATTORNEY FOR *(name)*: In pro per	
SUPERIOR COURT OF CALIFORNIA, COUNTY OF MONTEREY STREET ADDRESS: 1200 Aguajito Road MAILING ADDRESS: 1200 Aguajito Road CITY AND ZIP CODE: Monterey, CA 93940 BRANCH NAME: Monterey	
CONSERVATORSHIP OF THE [x] PERSON [ ] ESTATE of *(name)*: JOHN DOE [ ] CONSERVATEE [x] PROPOSED CONSERVATEE	
ORDER APPOINTING COURT INVESTIGATOR [ ] **Conservatorship** [x] **Limited Conservatorship**	CASE NUMBER:

To *(name)*: Court Investigation Unit

You are hereby appointed Court Investigator in the matter entitled above.

1. [x] **Before the appointment of a general conservator** YOU ARE DIRECTED TO:
   a. Conduct the interviews required by Probate Code section 1826(a)(1). Interview the proposed conservatee personally.
   b. Provide to the proposed conservatee the information required by Probate Code section 1826(a)(2).
   c. Determine whether it appears that the proposed conservatee is unable to attend the hearing and, if able to attend, whether he or she is willing to attend.
   d. Make the determinations required by Probate Code sections 1826(a)(4)–(7), and (9)–(10). In making those determinations, review the allegations of the *Petition for Appointment of Probate Conservator* (form GC-310) as to why the appointment of a conservator is required and refer to the *Confidential Supplemental Information* (form GC-312) submitted by the petitioner. Consider the facts shown in the latter form that address each of the categories specified in Probate Code section 1821(a)(1)–(5) and consider, to the extent practicable, whether you believe the proposed conservatee suffers from any of the mental function deficits listed in Probate Code section 811(a) that significantly impairs his or her ability to understand and appreciate the consequences of his or her actions in connection with any of the functions described in Probate Code section 1801(a) (if a conservator of the person is sought) or section 1801(b) (if a conservator of the estate is sought). If you believe the proposed conservatee suffers from one or more mental function deficits listed in Probate Code section 811(a), identify all observations that support your belief.
   e. A person is presumed competent to vote regardless of his or her conservatorship status. To determine whether this presumption is overcome, you must determine if the proposed conservatee is incapable of communicating, with or without reasonable accommodations, a desire to participate in the voting process, and therefore may be disqualified from voting pursuant to Section 2208 of the Elections Code. The proposed conservatee may not be disqualified from voting on the basis that he or she does, or would need to do, any of the following to complete an affidavit of voter registration: (1) signs the affidavit of voter registration with a mark or a cross (Elections Code section 2150(b)); (2) signs the affidavit of voter registration by means of a signature stamp (Elections Code section 354.5); (3) completes the affidavit of voter registration with the assistance of another person (Elections Code section 2150(d)); or (4) completes the affidavit of voter registration with reasonable accommodations.
   f. Report to the court in writing, at least five days before the hearing, concerning all of the foregoing, including the proposed conservatee's express communications concerning (1) representation by legal counsel; and (2) whether he or she is not willing to attend the hearing, does not wish to contest the establishment of the conservatorship, and does not object to the proposed conservator or prefers that another person act as conservator.
   g. Mail, at least five days before the date set for hearing, a copy of your report (1) to all persons listed in Probate Code section 1826(a)(12)
      [ ] **except** for the persons listed in attachment 1g(1) because the court has determined that mailing to those persons will result in harm to the proposed conservatee;
      [ ] **and** (2) to the other persons ordered by the court listed in Attachment 1g(2) *(specify names and addresses in the attachment)*.
   h. [ ] Comply with the other orders specified in Attachment 1h.

CONSERVATORSHIP OF THE of *(name)*: JOHN DOE	[✓] PERSON [ ] ESTATE [ ] CONSERVATEE [✓] PROPOSED CONSERVATEE	CASE NUMBER:

2. [ ] **On the filing of a *Petition for Appointment of Temporary Conservator*** YOU ARE DIRECTED TO:
   a. To the extent feasible, before the hearing on the petition or, if not feasible, within two court days after the hearing, conduct the interviews required by Probate Code section 2250.6(a)(1) (prehearing) or 2250.6(b)(1) (posthearing). Interview the temporary conservatee or proposed temporary conservatee personally.
   b. Provide to the temporary conservatee or proposed temporary conservatee the information required by Probate Code section 2250.6(a)(2) (prehearing) or 2250.6(b)(2) (posthearing).
   c. To the extent feasible, make the determinations required by Probate Code section 2250.6(a)(3)–(5) before the hearing on the petition.
   d. To the extent feasible, before the hearing on the petition, report to the court in writing concerning all of the matters stated in items 2a–c.
   e. If you do not visit the temporary conservatee until after the hearing at which a temporary conservator was appointed and the temporary conservatee objects to the appointment of the temporary conservator or requests an attorney, report this information to the court promptly and in no event more than three court days after the date of your interview with the temporary conservatee.
   f. If it appears to you that the temporary conservatorship is inappropriate, immediately, and in no event more than two court days after you make your determination, make a written report of your determination to the court.

3. [ ] **Before the court grants an order under Probate Code section 2253 authorizing the temporary conservator to change the residence of the temporary conservatee**
   a. [ ] YOU ARE DIRECTED TO:
      (1) Personally interview and inform the temporary conservatee of the contents of the request by the temporary conservator for authority to change the temporary conservatee's residence; of the nature, purpose, and effect of the proceedings; and of the right to oppose the request, attend the hearing, and be represented by legal counsel.
      (2) Make the determinations required by Probate Code section 2253(b)(3)–(7).
      (3) At least two days before the hearing on change of residence, report your findings concerning the foregoing in writing to the court, including in your report the temporary conservatee's express communications concerning representation by legal counsel and whether he or she is not willing to attend the hearing and does not wish to contest the petition.
      (4) [ ] Comply with the other orders specified in Attachment 3a(4) .
   b. [ ] Good cause appearing, YOU ARE DIRECTED NOT to conduct the investigation and NOT make the report described in Probate Code section 2253(b).
   c. [ ] Good cause appearing, YOU ARE DIRECTED as specified on Attachment 3c, INSTEAD of proceeding with the investigation and report described in Probate Code section 2253(b).

4. [x] **Before the court grants an order relating to medical consent under Probate Code section 1880.**

   The petition for an order determining that there is no form of medical treatment for which the conservatee or proposed conservatee has the capacity to give informed consent alleges that he or she is not willing to attend the hearing, or the court has received an affidavit or certificate attesting to the medical inability of the conservatee or proposed conservatee to attend the hearing.

   YOU ARE DIRECTED TO:
   a. Personally interview and inform the conservatee or proposed conservatee of the contents of the petition; of the nature, purpose, and effect of the proceedings; and of the right to oppose the petition, attend the hearing, and be represented by legal counsel.
   b. Make the determinations required by Probate Code section 1894(c)–(g).
   c. At least five days before the hearing on the petition, report your findings concerning the foregoing in writing to the court, including in your report the conservatee's express communications concerning representation by legal counsel and whether the conservatee is not willing to attend the hearing and does not wish to contest the petition.
   d. [ ] Comply with the other orders specified in Attachment 4d .

5. Number of pages attached:

Date:

____
JUDICIAL OFFICER

[ ] SIGNATURE FOLLOWS LAST ATTACHMENT

ORDER APPOINTING COURT INVESTIGATOR
(Probate—Guardianships and Conservatorships)

CI-123

ATTORNEY OR PARTY WITHOUT ATTORNEY	FOR COURT USE ONLY
NAME: Frank and Mary Doe STATE BAR NO: FIRM NAME: ADDRESS: 1234 Any Street CITY: Monterey STATE: CA ZIP CODE: 93940 E-MAIL ADDRESS (OPTIONAL): 2does@yahoo.com TELEPHONE NO: (831) 123-4567 ATTORNEY FOR (NAME): In pro per FAX NO. (OPTIONAL):	
SUPERIOR COURT OF CALIFORNIA, COUNTY OF MONTEREY Monterey Division 1200 Aguajito Road Monterey, California 93940	
☑ **Conservatorship** ☐ **Guardianship of** ☑ **Person** ☐ **Estate of** JOHN DOE	
REFERRAL TO COURT INVESTIGATOR — CONFIDENTIAL	CASE NUMBER:

Complete and file with initial petition, each accounting, and when any party changes residence.
Note: A fee may be assessed for Court Investigator Services – See Probate Code §1851.5

Hearing Date: [Insert hearing date]

This referral is being sent to the Probate Investigator's Office for an investigation regarding (check all that apply):

☑ Appointment ☐ Accounting/ Review ☐ Termination
☐ Medical Powers ☐ Dementia Powers ☐ Other: (Specify) ____________
☐ Sale of (former) Residence ☐ Substituted Judgment

Information about the (Proposed) CONSERVATEE:

(Proposed) Conservatee's CURRENT address:
Address: 1234 Any Street, Monterey, CA 93940
Phone number: (831) 123-4567

(Proposed) Conservatee's HOME address:
Address: same as above
Phone number: ____________

Birth Date: June 15, 2000
Social Security Number: 111-22-3333

Marital Status:
◉ Single/Divorced ○ Widowed ○ Married ○ Registered Domestic Partner

Special Needs (i.e. language)? ____________

Is (proposed) conservatee under an LPS Conservatorship now? ○ Yes ◉ No
If yes, LPS #: ____________

(Proposed) Conservatee's Attorney (name): Monterey County Public Defender
Address: 168 West Alisal Street, Salinas, CA 93901
Phone number: (831) 755-5058
Fax number: (831) 755-5873

(The reverse side may be used for additional information, if desired)

JOHN DOE	CASE NUMBER:

Information about the (Proposed) CONSERVATOR:

All proposed Conservators must complete the information on this page. If there is more than one proposed Conservator, attach a copy of this page for each person.

	Person	Estate
Name:	Frank Doe	
Address:	1234 Any Street	
	Monterey, CA 93940	
Daytime Phone:	(831) 123-4567	
Relationship to Conservatee/ward:	Father	
Date of Birth:	01/01/1963	
Social Security Number:	123-45-6789	
Driver's License Number:	A00090000	
Work Phone:		
Cell Phone:	(831) 610-0000	
Attorney:	In pro per	
Attorney's Address:		
Attorney's Phone:		
Attorney's Fax:		

I declare under penalty of perjury under the laws of the State of California that the foregoing is true and correct.

[Insert filing date]
Date:

Signature of Proposed Conservator

☑ Information sheet(s) for (number) 1 of (proposed) co-conservators is attached.

JOHN DOE	CASE NUMBER:

Information about the (Proposed) CONSERVATOR:

All proposed Conservators must complete the information on this page. If there is more than one proposed Conservator, attach a copy of this page for each person.

	Person	Estate
Name:	Mary Doe	
Address:	1234 Any Street	
	Monterey, CA 93940	
Daytime Phone:	(831) 123-4567	
Relationship to Conservatee/ward:	Mother	
Date of Birth:	04/04/1963	
Social Security Number:	012-34-5678	
Driver's License Number:	B00080000	
Work Phone:		
Cell Phone:	(831) 610-0001	
Attorney:	In pro per	
Attorney's Address:		
Attorney's Phone:		
Attorney's Fax:		

I declare under penalty of perjury under the laws of the State of California that the foregoing is true and correct.

[Insert filing date]
Date:

Signature of Proposed Conservator

☐ Information sheet(s) for (number)__________of (proposed) co-conservators is attached.

JOHN DOE	CASE NUMBER:

Information about the (Proposed) Conservatee's Relatives & Friends:

List the spouse or registered domestic partner, 1st and 2nd degree relatives (these are parents, children, brothers/sisters, grandparents and grandchildren), neighbors and close friends of the (proposed) conservatee.

Name: Brian Doe
Relationship to (proposed Conservatee: Brother
Home Address: 1234 Any Street, Monterey, CA 93940
Home Phone: (831) 123-4567 Work Phone: ______ Cell Phone: (831) 610-0002

Name: Susan Doe
Relationship to (proposed Conservatee: Sister
Home Address: 777 17th Street, Collegetown, CA 95555
Home Phone: (555) 666-7777 Work Phone: ______ Cell Phone: (831) 610-0004

Name: Stephen Doe
Relationship to (proposed Conservatee: Paternal Grandfather
Home Address: 3333 Wonder Avenue, Disneyland, CA 93333
Home Phone: (999) 222-3333 Work Phone: ______ Cell Phone: ______

Name: Amy Roe
Relationship to (proposed Conservatee: Maternal Grandmother
Home Address: 4444 Gallant Drive, Rich Haven CT 01111
Home Phone: (404) 505-6006 Work Phone: ______ Cell Phone: ______

Name: Arnold Roe
Relationship to (proposed Conservatee: Maternal Grandfather
Home Address: 5555 Neighborhood Lane, Friendly, FL 09999
Home Phone: (678) 234-5555 Work Phone: ______ Cell Phone: ______

Name: Jim and Judy Hitchings
Relationship to (proposed Conservatee: Family friends
Home Address: 1238 Any Street, Monterey, CA 93940
Home Phone: (831) 455-1789 Work Phone: ______ Cell Phone: ______

Name: ______
Relationship to (proposed Conservatee: ______
Home Address: ______
Home Phone: ______ Work Phone: ______ Cell Phone: ______

ATTORNEY OR PARTY WITHOUT ATTORNEY	FOR COURT USE ONLY
NAME: Frank and Mary Doe STATE BAR NO: FIRM NAME: ADDRESS: 1234 Any Street CITY: Monterey STATE: CA ZIP CODE: 93940 E-MAIL ADDRESS (OPTIONAL): 2does@yahoo.com TELEPHONE NO: (831) 123-4567 ATTORNEY FOR (NAME): In pro per FAX NO. (OPTIONAL):	
SUPERIOR COURT OF CALIFORNIA, COUNTY OF MONTEREY Monterey Division 1200 Aguajito Road Monterey, California 93940	
CONSERVATORSHIP OF: JOHN DOE	CASE NUMBER: [Insert case number]
CONSERVATOR VIEWING RECEIPT	

I acknowledge that I viewed "With Heart: Understanding Conservatorship" on [Insert date] (date) at:

- ☑ Online (http://www.courts.ca.gov/selfhelp-conservatorship.htm)
- ☐ Attorney's Office
- ☐ Self-Help Center
- ☐ Monterey Courthouse (fee)

Local Resource Information: http://www.co.monterey.ca.us/aaa/download/2016rg_eng.pdf

Información de Recursos Locales: http://www.co.monterey.ca.us/aaa/download/2016rg_sp.pdf

Conservatorship Handbook: http://www.courts.ca.gov/documents/handbook.pdf

I declare under penalty of perjury, under the laws of the State of California, the foregoing is true and correct.

____________________, at Monterey, California.
(Date Signed) (City)

Signature: ____________________

Print Name: FRANK DOE

**1 Receipt for each proposed conservator*

ATTORNEY OR PARTY WITHOUT ATTORNEY	FOR COURT USE ONLY
NAME: Frank and Mary Doe STATE BAR NO:	
FIRM NAME:	
ADDRESS: 1234 Any Street	
CITY: Monterey STATE: CA ZIP CODE: 93940	
E-MAIL ADDRESS (OPTIONAL): 2does@yahoo.com TELEPHONE NO: (831) 123-4567	
ATTORNEY FOR (NAME): In pro per FAX NO. (OPTIONAL):	
SUPERIOR COURT OF CALIFORNIA, COUNTY OF MONTEREY Monterey Division 1200 Aguajito Road Monterey, California 93940	
CONSERVATORSHIP OF: JOHN DOE	CASE NUMBER: [Insert case number]
CONSERVATOR VIEWING RECEIPT	

I acknowledge that I viewed "With Heart: Understanding Conservatorship" on [Insert date] (date) at:

- [x] Online (http://www.courts.ca.gov/selfhelp-conservatorship.htm)
- [ ] Attorney's Office
- [ ] Self-Help Center
- [ ] Monterey Courthouse (fee)

Local Resource Information: http://www.co.monterey.ca.us/aaa/download/2016rg_eng.pdf

Información de Recursos Locales: http://www.co.monterey.ca.us/aaa/download/2016rg_sp.pdf

Conservatorship Handbook: http://www.courts.ca.gov/documents/handbook.pdf

I declare under penalty of perjury, under the laws of the State of California, the foregoing is true and correct.

______________________, at Monterey ______________________, California.
(Date Signed) (City)

Signature: ______________________

Print Name: MARY DOE

**1 Receipt for each proposed conservator*

ATTORNEY OR PARTY WITHOUT ATTORNEY *(Name, State Bar number, and address):*	FOR COURT USE ONLY
Frank and Mary Doe 1234 Any Street Monterey, CA 93940 TELEPHONE NO.: (831) 123-4567 FAX NO. *(Optional):* E-MAIL ADDRESS *(Optional):* 2does@yahoo.com ATTORNEY FOR *(Name):* In pro per	
SUPERIOR COURT OF CALIFORNIA, COUNTY OF MONTEREY STREET ADDRESS: 1200 Aguajito Road MAILING ADDRESS: 1200 Aguajito Road CITY AND ZIP CODE: Monterey, CA 93940 BRANCH NAME: Monterey	
TEMPORARY CONSERVATORSHIP OF *(Name):* JOHN DOE CONSERVATEE	CASE NUMBER:
PETITION FOR APPOINTMENT OF TEMPORARY CONSERVATOR ☑ **Person** ☐ **Estate** ☐ **Person and Estate**	HEARING DATE: [For temp hrg] DEPT.: [Dept] TIME: [Time]

1. **Petitioner** *(name each):*
Frank and Mary Doe **requests that**
   a. *(Name):* FRANK DOE and MARY DOE
   (Address and telephone number): 1234 Any Street, Monterey, CA 93940 Telephone (831) 123-4567
   be appointed temporary conservator of the PERSON of the proposed conservatee and Letters issue upon qualification.
   b. *(Name):*
   (Address and telephone number):
   be appointed temporary conservator of the ESTATE of the proposed conservatee and Letters issue upon qualification.
   c. (1) ☑ bond not be required because petition is for a temporary conservatorship of the person only.
   (2) ☐ bond not be required for the reasons stated in attachment 1c.
   (3) ☐ $ bond be fixed. It will be furnished by an admitted surety insurer or as otherwise provided by law. *(Specify reasons in attachment 1c if the amount is different from maximum required by Probate Code section 2320 and Cal. Rules of Court, rule 7.207(c).)*
   (4) ☐ $ in deposits in a blocked account be allowed. Receipts will be filed. *(Specify institution and location):*
   d. ☐ a request for an exception to notice of the hearing on this petition for good cause is filed with this petition.
   e. ☑ the powers specified in Attachment 1e be granted in addition to the powers provided by law.
   f. ☐ other orders be granted *(specify in attachment 1f).*
2. **The proposed conservatee is** *(name):* JOHN DOE
Current address: 1234 Any Street, Monterey, CA 93940
Current telephone no.: (831) 123-4567
3. **The proposed conservatee requires a temporary conservator** to ☑ provide for temporary care, maintenance, and support ☐ protect property from loss or injury because *(facts are* ☑ *specified in attachment 3* ☐ *as follows):*

PETITION FOR APPOINTMENT OF TEMPORARY CONSERVATOR
(Probate—Guardianships and Conservatorships)

Probate Code, § 2250;
Cal. Rules of Court, rules 7.101, 7.1062
www.courtinfo.ca.gov

TEMPORARY CONSERVATORSHIP OF (Name): JOHN DOE CONSERVATEE	CASE NUMBER:

4. **Temporary conservatorship is required**
   a. [x] pending the hearing on the petition for appointment of a general conservator.
   b. [ ] pending the appeal under Probate Code section 1301.
   c. [ ] during the suspension of powers of the conservator.

5. [ ] **Character and estimated value of the property of the estate** *(complete if a temporary conservatorship of the estate or the person and estate is requested):*
   a. Personal property: $
   b. Annual gross income from all sources, including real and personal property, wages, pensions, and public benefits: $
   c. Additional amount for cost of recovery on the bond, calculated as required under Cal. Rules of Court, rule 7.207(c): $ ______
   d. **Total:** $ ______

6. [ ] **Petitioner requests authority to change the proposed conservatee's residence during the temporary conservatorship**
   a. [ ] Petitioner proposes to change the residence of the proposed conservatee to *(address):*

   The proposed conservatee will suffer irreparable harm if his or her residence is not changed as requested and no means less restrictive of the proposed conservatee's liberty will suffice to prevent the harm because *(reasons are* [ ] *specified in attachment 6a* [ ] *as follows):*

   b. [ ] The proposed conservatee must be removed from the State of California to permit the performance of the following nonpsychiatric medical treatment essential to the proposed conservatee's physical survival. The proposed conservatee consents to this medical treatment. *(Facts and place of treatment are* [ ] *specified in attachment 6b* [ ] *as follows):*

7. [ ] **Petitioner is a professional fiduciary**
   a. Petitioner holds license no. *(specify):* from the Professional Fiduciaries Bureau of the Department of Consumer Affairs issued or last renewed on *(specify later date of initial issuance or renewal):* .
   b. Petitioner was requested to file this petition by *(name):* .
   c. The circumstances leading to petitioner's engagement to file this petition are described in attachment 7c.
   d. Petitioner had: (1) [ ] No relationship to the proposed conservatee, his or her family, or his or her friends before engagement to file this petition.
      (2) [ ] A relationship to the proposed conservatee, his or her family, or his or her friends before engagement to file this petition. That relationship is described in [ ] attachment 7d. [ ] the *Petition for Appointment of Probate Conservator (form GC-310)* filed with this petition or an attachment to that petition *(specify attachment to general petition):*

TEMPORARY CONSERVATORSHIP OF *(Name):* JOHN DOE CONSERVATEE	CASE NUMBER:

8. **Petitioner's contact with persons named in *Petition for Appointment of Probate Conservator***
   a. ☐ Petitioner is the proposed conservatee. *(If this item is selected, go to item 9.)*
   b. ☑ Petitioner is not the proposed conservatee. All persons other than the proposed conservatee named in the *Petition for Appointment of Probate Conservator* filed with this petition:
      (1) ☑ Have been found and contacted. All will be given notice of the hearing on this petition.
      (2) ☐ Have not been found or have not been contacted. Efforts to find the persons who have not been found and the reasons why any person cannot be contacted are described in one or more declarations under penalty of perjury attached to this petition as attachment 8b. *(Attachment 8b is not a request for a good cause exception to notice. See Prob. Code, § 2250(e) and rule 7.1062 of the Cal. Rules of Court.)*
   c. ☐ Petitioner is not the proposed conservatee. Facts showing the preferences of the proposed conservatee concerning the appointment of any temporary conservator, and the appointment of the temporary conservator proposed in this petition, or why it was not feasible to ascertain those preferences, are specified in one or more declarations attached to this petition as attachment 8c.
9. **Petitioner is informed and believes that the proposed conservatee**
   a. ☐ will attend the hearing.
   b. ☐ is able but unwilling to attend the hearing, does not wish to contest the establishment of a conservatorship, does not object to the proposed conservator, and does not prefer that another person act as conservator.
   c. ☑ is unable to attend the hearing because of medical inability. An affidavit or certificate of a licensed medical practitioner or an accredited religious practitioner is affixed as attachment 9c.
   d. ☐ is not the petitioner, is out of state, and will not attend the hearing.
10. ☑ Filed with this petition is a proposed *Order Appointing Court Investigator* (form GC-330).
11. All attachments to this form are incorporated by this reference as though placed here in this form. There are 1 pages attached to this form.

Date:

▶ ______________________________
(SIGNATURE OF ATTORNEY*)

* **(Signature of all petitioners also required (Prob. Code, § 1020).)**

I declare under penalty of perjury under the laws of the State of California that the foregoing is true and correct.

Date: [Insert filing date]

FRANK DOE
(TYPE OR PRINT NAME)

▶ ______________________________
(SIGNATURE OF PETITIONER)

MARY DOE
(TYPE OR PRINT NAME)

▶ ______________________________
(SIGNATURE OF PETITIONER)

Temporary Limited Conservatorship of John Doe
Petition for Appointment of Temporary Limited Co-Conservators

Attachment 1e

The proposed limited co-conservators request the following powers under Probate Code §2351.5(b):

(1) To fix the residence or specific dwelling of the limited conservatee.

(2) To access to the confidential records and papers of the limited conservatee.

(4) To limit the right of the limited conservatee to contract.

(5) To give or withhold medical consent for the limited conservatee.

(7) To make decisions concerning the education of the limited conservatee.

Attachment 3

The proposed conservatee will be 18 years old in two weeks, and he is presently admitted to the Stanford Medical Clinic for observation following a petit mal seizure last week. It is imperative that petitioners be appointed temporary limited co-conservators before the hearing date on the general petition. The proposed limited conservatee cannot make decisions regarding his medical needs, and someone must be given the legal powers to make those decisions for him in the interim.

ATTORNEY OR PARTY WITHOUT ATTORNEY *(Name, State Bar number, and address)*:	FOR COURT USE ONLY
Frank and Mary Doe 1234 Any Street Monterey, CA 93940 TELEPHONE NO.: (831) 123-4567 FAX NO. *(Optional)*: E-MAIL ADDRESS *(Optional)*: 2does@yahoo.com ATTORNEY FOR *(Name)*: In pro per	
SUPERIOR COURT OF CALIFORNIA, COUNTY OF MONTEREY STREET ADDRESS: 1200 Aguajito Road MAILING ADDRESS: 1200 Aguajito Road CITY AND ZIP CODE: Monterey, CA 93940 BRANCH NAME: Monterey	
☐ GUARDIANSHIP ☑ CONSERVATORSHIP OF THE ☑ PERSON ☐ ESTATE OF *(Name)*: JOHN DOE ☐ MINOR ☑ (PROPOSED) CONSERVATEE	
NOTICE OF HEARING—GUARDIANSHIP OR CONSERVATORSHIP	CASE NUMBER:

This notice is required by law.
This notice does not require you to appear in court, but you may attend the hearing if you wish.

1. NOTICE is given that *(name)*: FRANK DOE and MARY DOE
   (representative capacity, if any):
   has filed *(specify)*:

   PETITION FOR APPOINTMENT OF TEMPORARY LIMITED CONSERVATORS OF THE PERSON

2. You may refer to documents on file in this proceeding for more information. *(Some documents filed with the court are confidential. Under some circumstances you or your attorney may be able to see or receive copies of confidential documents if you file papers in the proceeding or apply to the court.)*

3. ☐ The petition includes an application for the independent exercise of powers by a guardian or conservator under
   ☐ Probate Code section 2108 ☐ Probate Code section 2590.
   Powers requested are ☐ specified below ☐ specified in Attachment 3.

4. A HEARING on the matter will be held as follows:

   a. Date: [Temp hrg date] Time: [Time] ☑ Dept.: [Dept] ☐ Room:

   b. Address of court ☑ same as noted above ☐ is *(specify)*:

Assistive listening systems, computer-assisted real-time captioning, or sign language interpreter services are available upon request if at least 5 days notice is provided. Contact the clerk's office for *Request for Accommodations by Persons with Disabilities and Order* (form MC-410). (Civil Code section 54.8.)

☐ GUARDIANSHIP ☑ CONSERVATORSHIP OF THE ☑ PERSON ☐ ESTATE OF (Name): JOHN DOE ☐ MINOR ☑ (PROPOSED) CONSERVATEE	CASE NUMBER:

NOTE: *

A copy of this *Notice of Hearing—Guardianship or Conservatorship* ("Notice") must be "served" on—delivered to—each person who has the right under the law to be notified of the date, time, place, and purpose of a court hearing in a guardianship or conservatorship. Copies of this Notice may be served by mail in most situations. In a guardianship, however, copies of this Notice must sometimes be personally served on certain persons; and copies of this Notice may be personally served instead of served by mail in both guardianships and conservatorships. The petitioner (the person who requested the court hearing) **may not personally perform either service by mail or personal service**, but must show the court that copies of this Notice have been served in a way the law allows. The petitioner does this by arranging for someone else to perform the service and complete and sign a proof of service, which the petitioner then files with the original Notice.

This page contains a proof of service that may be used only to show service by mail. To show personal service, each person who performs the service must complete and sign a proof of personal service, and each signed copy of that proof of service must be attached to this Notice when it is filed with the court.. You may use form GC-020(P) to show personal service of this Notice.

* *(This Note replaces the clerk's certificate of posting on prior versions of this form. If notice by posting is desired, attach a copy of form GC-020(C),* Clerk's Certificate of Posting Notice of Hearing—Guardianship or Conservatorship. *(See Prob. Code, § 2543(c).)*

PROOF OF SERVICE BY MAIL

1. I am over the age of 18 and not a party to this cause. I am a resident of or employed in the county where the mailing occurred.
2. My residence or business address is *(specify):*
   [Insert independent person's physical address]
3. I served the foregoing *Notice of Hearing—Guardianship or Conservatorship* on each person named below by enclosing a copy in an envelope addressed as shown below AND
   a. ☑ **depositing** the sealed envelope with the United States Postal Service on the date and at the place shown in item 4 with the postage fully prepaid.
   b. ☐ **placing** the envelope for collection and mailing on the date and at the place shown in item 4 following our ordinary business practices. I am readily familiar with this business's practice for collecting and processing correspondence for mailing. On the same day that correspondence is placed for collection and mailing, it is deposited in the ordinary course of business with the United States Postal Service in a sealed envelope with postage fully prepaid.
4. a. Date mailed: [Date of mailing] b. Place mailed *(city, state):* Monterey, California
5. ☑ I served with the *Notice of Hearing—Guardianship or Conservatorship* a copy of the petition or other document referred to in the Notice.

I declare under penalty of perjury under the laws of the State of California that the foregoing is true and correct.

Date: [Insert date signed]

Independent person's printed name ▶ ______________________

(TYPE OR PRINT NAME OF PERSON COMPLETING THIS FORM) (SIGNATURE OF PERSON COMPLETING THIS FORM)

NAME AND ADDRESS OF EACH PERSON TO WHOM NOTICE WAS MAILED

	Name of person served	Address *(number, street, city, state, and zip code)*
1.	(See attached Mailing List)	
2.		
3.		
4.		

☑ Continued on an attachment. *(You may use form DE-120(MA)/GC-020(MA) to show additional persons served.)*

☐ ESTATE ☐ GUARDIANSHIP ☑ CONSERVATORSHIP ☐ MATTER OF *(Name):* JOHN DOE	CASE NUMBER:

ATTACHMENT TO NOTICE OF HEARING PROOF OF SERVICE BY MAIL

(This Attachment is for use with forms DE-120 and GC-020.)

NAME AND ADDRESS OF EACH PERSON TO WHOM NOTICE WAS MAILED

No.	Name of person served	Address *(number, street, city, state, and zip code)*
1	Brian Doe	1234 Any Street Monterey, CA 93940
2	Susan Doe	777 17th Street Collegetown, CA 95555
3	Stephen Doe	3333 Wonder Avenue Disneyland, CA 93333
4	Amy Roe	4444 Gallant Drive Rich Haven, CT 01111
5	Arnold Roe	5555 Neighborhood Lane Friendly, FL 09999
6	Court Investigation Unit	1200 Aguajito Road Monterey, CA 93940
7	Monterey County Public Defender	168 West Alisal Street Salinas, CA 93901

☐ GUARDIANSHIP ☑ CONSERVATORSHIP OF THE ☑ PERSON ☐ ESTATE	CASE NUMBER:
OF (Name): JOHN DOE	
☐ MINOR ☑ (PROPOSED) CONSERVATEE	

PROOF OF PERSONAL SERVICE OF NOTICE OF HEARING—GUARDIANSHIP OR CONSERVATORSHIP

(Attach a separate completed and signed copy of this form or other proof of personal service to Notice of Hearing—Guardianship or Conservatorship *for each person who personally served a copy of the Notice.)*

1. I am over the age of 18 and not a party to this cause.
2. I served the attached *Notice of Hearing—Guardianship or Conservatorship* by personally delivering a copy to each person listed below at the address and on the date and time indicated below.
3. ☑ I served with the attached *Notice of Hearing—Guardianship or Conservatorship* a copy of the petition or other document referred to in the Notice.
4. ☐ I served with the attached *Notice of Hearing—Guardianship or Conservatorship* copies of the following documents *(specify)*:

   ☐ Continued on Attachment 4.

5. I am *(check all that apply)*:
   a. ☑ not a registered California process server.
   b. ☐ a California sheriff or marshal.
   c. ☐ a registered California process server.
   d. ☐ an employee or independent contractor of a registered California process server.
   e. ☐ exempt from registration (Bus. & Prof. Code, § 22350(b)).
6. My name, address, telephone number, and, if applicable, county of registration and number, are *(specify)*:
   Jim Hitchings Telephone (831) 455-1789
   1238 Any Street
   Monterey, CA 93940

NAME OF EACH PERSON PERSONALLY SERVED, ADDRESS WHERE SERVED, AND DATE AND TIME SERVICE WAS MADE

	Name	Address where served *(number, street, city, and state)*	Date and time service made
1.	John Doe	4545 Sand Hill Road Palo Alto, CA 90909	Date: [Date served] Time: [Time served]
2.			Date: Time:
3.			Date: Time:
4.			Date: Time:

☐ List of names and addresses of persons personally served by the undersigned continued on an attachment. *(You may use* Attachment to Notice of Hearing Proof of Personal Service, *form DE-120(PA)/GC-020(PA), for this purpose.)*

I declare under penalty of perjury under the laws of the State of California that the foregoing is true and correct.

Date: [Date signed]

▶ ______________________________
(SIGNATURE)

(For California sheriff or marshal use only)
I certify that the foregoing is true and correct

Date:

▶ ______________________________
(SIGNATURE)

PROOF OF PERSONAL SERVICE OF NOTICE OF HEARING—GUARDIANSHIP OR CONSERVATORSHIP
(Probate—Guardianships and Conservatorships)

ATTORNEY OR PARTY WITHOUT ATTORNEY *(Name, State Bar number, and address)*:	FOR COURT USE ONLY
Frank and Mary Doe 1234 Any Street Monterey, CA 93940 TELEPHONE NO.: (831) 123-4567 FAX NO. *(Optional)*: E-MAIL ADDRESS *(Optional)*: 2does@yahoo.com ATTORNEY FOR *(Name)*: In pro per	
SUPERIOR COURT OF CALIFORNIA, COUNTY OF MONTEREY STREET ADDRESS: 1200 Aguajito Road MAILING ADDRESS: 1200 Aguajito Road CITY AND ZIP CODE: Monterey, CA 93940 BRANCH NAME: Monterey	
TEMPORARY CONSERVATORSHIP OF THE ☑ PERSON ☐ ESTATE OF *(Name)*: JOHN DOE CONSERVATEE	
ORDER APPOINTING TEMPORARY CONSERVATOR	CASE NUMBER:

WARNING: THIS APPOINTMENT IS NOT EFFECTIVE UNTIL LETTERS HAVE ISSUED.

1. The petition for appointment of a temporary conservator came on for hearing as follows *(check boxes c–j to indicate personal presence)*:
   a. Judicial officer *(name)*: The Honorable Judy Judge
   b. Hearing date: June 1, 2018 Time: 8:30 a.m. ☑ Dept.: 13 ☐ Room:
   c. ☑ Petitioner *(name)*: Frank Doe and Mary Doe
   d. ☐ Attorney for petitioner *(name)*:
   e. ☐ Conservatee *(name)*:
   f. ☑ Attorney for conservatee *(name)*: Monterey County Public Defender
   g. ☐ Conservatee's spouse or registered domestic partner, and relatives *(names and relationships)*:
   h. ☐ Attorneys for persons listed in item g *(names and persons represented)*:
   i. ☐ Public Guardian *(name)*:
   j. ☐ Attorney for Public Guardian *(name)*:

THE COURT FINDS

2. a. ☑ Notice of time and place of hearing has been given as required by law.
   b. ☐ Notice of time and place of hearing has been modified or dispensed with under *Order on Ex Parte Application for Good Cause Exception to Notice on Petition for Appointment of Temporary Conservator* filed on *(date)*:
3. ☑ It is necessary that a temporary conservator be appointed to ☑ provide for temporary care, maintenance, and support
   ☐ protect property from loss or injury
   a. ☑ pending the hearing on the petition for appointment of a general conservator.
   b. ☐ pending an appeal under Probate Code section 1301.
   c. ☐ during the suspension of powers of the conservator.
4. ☐ To prevent irreparable harm, the residence of the conservatee must be changed. No means less restrictive of the conservatee's liberty will prevent irreparable harm.

TEMPORARY CONSERVATORSHIP OF *(Name):* JOHN DOE CONSERVATEE	CASE NUMBER:

5. ☐ The conservatee must be removed from the State of California to permit the performance of nonpsychiatric medical treatment essential to the conservatee's physical survival. The conservatee consents to this medical treatment.
6. ☑ The conservatee need not attend the hearing.

THE COURT ORDERS

7. a. ☑ *(Name):* FRANK DOE and MARY DOE
(Address): 1234 Any Street, Monterey, CA 93940 *(Telephone):* (831) 123-4567
is appointed temporary conservator of the PERSON of *(name):* JOHN DOE
and Letters shall issue upon qualification.
b. ☐ *(Name):*
(Address): *(Telephone):*
is appointed temporary conservator of the ESTATE of *(name):*
and Letters shall issue upon qualification.

8. a. ☑ Bond is not required.
b. ☐ Bond is fixed at: $ to be furnished by an authorized surety company or as otherwise provided by law.
c. ☐ Deposits of: $ are ordered to be placed in a blocked account at *(specify institution and location):*
and receipts shall be filed. No withdrawals shall be made without a court order. ☐ Additional orders in attachment 8c.
d. ☐ The temporary conservator is not authorized to take possession of money or any other property without a specific court order.

9. ☐ The temporary conservator is authorized to change the residence of the conservatee to *(address):*

10. ☐ The temporary conservator is authorized to remove the conservatee from the State of California to the following address to permit the performance of nonpsychiatric medical treatment essential to the conservatee's physical survival *(address):*

11. ☑ The conservatee need not attend the hearing.
12. ☑ In addition to the powers granted by law, the temporary conservator is granted other powers. These powers are specified ☑ in attachment 12 ☐ below *(specify):*

13. ☐ Other orders as specified in attachment 13 are granted.
14. ☑ Unless modified by further order of the court, this order expires on *(date):* [General hrg date]
15. Number of boxes checked in items 7–14: 6
16. Number of pages attached: 1

Date:

JUDICIAL OFFICER

☑ SIGNATURE FOLLOWS LAST ATTACHMENT

Temporary Limited Conservatorship of John Doe
Order Appointing Temporary Limited Co-Conservators

Attachment 12

The proposed limited co-conservators are granted the following powers under Probate Code §2351.5(b):

(1) To fix the residence or specific dwelling of the limited conservatee.

(2) To access to the confidential records and papers of the limited conservatee.

(4) To limit the right of the limited conservatee to contract.

(5) To give or withhold medical consent for the limited conservatee.

(7) To make decisions concerning the education of the limited conservatee.

Date: ____________________ ____
JUDGE OF THE SUPERIOR COURT

GC-150

ATTORNEY OR PARTY WITHOUT ATTORNEY *(name, address, and State Bar number)*:
After recording, return to:
Frank and Mary Doe
1234 Any Street
Monterey, CA 93940

TEL NO.: (831) 123-4567 FAX NO. *(optional)*:
E-MAIL ADDRESS *(optional)*: 2does@yahoo.com
ATTORNEY FOR *(name)*: In pro per

SUPERIOR COURT OF CALIFORNIA, COUNTY OF MONTEREY
STREET ADDRESS: 1200 Aguajito Road
MAILING ADDRESS: 1200 Aguajito Road
CITY AND ZIP CODE: Monterey, CA 93940
BRANCH NAME: Monterey

FOR RECORDER'S USE ONLY

TEMPORARY [ ] GUARDIANSHIP [x] CONSERVATORSHIP
OF *(name)*: JOHN DOE
[ ] MINOR [x] CONSERVATEE

CASE NUMBER:
[Insert case number here]

LETTERS OF TEMPORARY [ ] GUARDIANSHIP [x] CONSERVATORSHIP
[x] Person [ ] Estate

FOR COURT USE ONLY

LETTERS

1. *(Name)*: FRANK DOE and MARY DOE
is appointed temporary [ ] guardian [x] conservator of the [x] person
[ ] estate of *(name)*:
JOHN DOE

2. [x] Other powers that have been granted or restrictions imposed on the temporary
[ ] guardian [x] conservator are [x] specified in Attachment 2.
[ ] specified below:

3. These Letters shall expire
a. [x] on *(date)*: [Gen Hrg date] or upon earlier issuance of Letters to a general guardian or conservator.
b. [ ] on other date *(specify)*:

4. [ ] The temporary [ ] guardian [ ] conservator is not authorized to take possession of money or any other property without a specific court order.

5. Number of pages attached: 1

WITNESS, clerk of the court, with seal of the court affixed.

(SEAL)

Date:

Clerk, by ______________________________, Deputy

This form may be recorded as notice of the establishment of a temporary conservatorship of the estate as provided in Probate Code section 1875.

Form Adopted for Mandatory Use
Judicial Council of California
GC-150 [Rev. January 1, 2015]

LETTERS OF TEMPORARY GUARDIANSHIP OR CONSERVATORSHIP
(Probate—Guardianships and Conservatorships)

Probate Code, §§ 2250 et seq., 2890–2893;
Code of Civil Procedure, § 2015.6
www.courts.ca.gov

TEMPORARY ☐ GUARDIANSHIP ☑ CONSERVATORSHIP OF (name): JOHN DOE ☐ MINOR ☑ CONSERVATEE	CASE NUMBER: [Insert case number here]

NOTICE TO INSTITUTIONS AND FINANCIAL INSTITUTIONS
(Probate Code sections 2890–2893)

When these *Letters of Temporary Guardianship* or *Letters of Temporary Conservatorship* (Letters) are delivered to you as an employee or other representative of an *institution* or *financial institution* (described below) in order for the temporary guardian or temporary conservator of the estate (1) to take possession or control of an asset of the minor or conservatee named above held by your institution (including changing title, withdrawing all or any portion of the asset, or transferring all or any portion of the asset) or (2) to open or change the name of an account or a safe-deposit box in your financial institution to reflect the guardianship or conservatorship, you must fill out Judicial Council form GC-050 (for an institution) or form GC-051 (for a financial institution). An officer authorized by your institution or financial institution must date and sign the form, and you must file the completed form with the court.

There is no filing fee for filing the form. You may either arrange for personal delivery of the form or mail it to the court for filing at the address given for the court on page 1 of these Letters.

The temporary guardian or temporary conservator should deliver a blank copy of the appropriate form to you with these Letters, but it is your institution's or financial institution's responsibility to complete the correct form, have an authorized officer sign it, and file the completed form with the court. If the correct form is not delivered with these Letters or is unavailable for any other reason, blank copies of the forms may be obtained from the court. The forms may also be accessed from the judicial branch's public Web site free of charge. The Internet address (URL) is *www.courts.ca.gov/forms/.* Select the form group *Probate—Guardianships and Conservatorships* and scroll down to form GC-050 for an institution or form GC-051 for a financial institution. The forms may be printed out as blank forms and filled in by typewriter, or may be filled out online and printed out ready for signature and filing.

An *institution* under California Probate Code section 2890(c) is an insurance company, insurance broker, insurance agent, investment company, investment bank, securities broker-dealer, investment advisor, financial planner, financial advisor, or any other person who takes, holds, or controls an asset subject to a conservatorship or guardianship other than a financial institution. Institutions must file a *Notice of Taking Possession or Control of an Asset of Minor or Conservatee* (form GC-050) for an asset of the minor or conservatee held by the institution. A single form may be filed for all affected assets held by the institution.

A *financial institution* under California Probate Code section 2892(b) is a bank, trust (including a Totten trust account but excluding other trust arrangements described in Probate Code section 82(b)), savings and loan association, savings bank, industrial bank, or credit union. Financial institutions must file a *Notice of Opening or Changing a Guardianship or Conservatorship Account or Safe-Deposit Box* (form GC-051) for an account or a safe deposit box held by the financial institution. A single form may be filed for all affected accounts or safe deposit boxes held by the financial institution.

LETTERS OF TEMPORARY ☐ GUARDIANSHIP ☒ CONSERVATORSHIP
AFFIRMATION

I solemnly affirm that I will perform according to law the duties of temporary ☐ guardian. ☒ conservator.

Executed on *(date)*: [Date of filing] , at *(place)*: [Place signed]

FRANK DOE and MARY DOE ▶ ______________________

(TYPE OR PRINT NAME) (SIGNATURE OF APPOINTEE)

CERTIFICATION

I certify that this document, including any attachments, is a correct copy of the original on file in my office and that the Letters issued to the person appointed above have not been revoked, annulled, or set aside and are still in full force and effect.

(SEAL)

Date:

Clerk, by ______________________, Deputy

Temporary Limited Conservatorship of John Doe
Letters of Temporary Limited Co-Conservators

Attachment 2

The proposed limited co-conservators are granted the following powers under Probate Code §2351.5(b):

(1) To fix the residence or specific dwelling of the limited conservatee.

(2) To access to the confidential records and papers of the limited conservatee.

(4) To limit the right of the limited conservatee to contract.

(5) To give or withhold medical consent for the limited conservatee.

(7) To make decisions concerning the education of the limited conservatee.

Date: ____________________

____
JUDGE OF THE SUPERIOR COURT

What is Proof of Service in a Limited Conservatorship?
(Adapted from Judicial Council form GC-510 for Guardianships)

What is "service"?

- When you are involved in a court case, you are responsible for delivery ("service") of copies of important papers you file with the court to other people involved in the case.
- If you file a petition for appointment of conservator of an adult with developmental disabilities, you are a **petitioner**. At the beginning of the case, the petitioner must arrange for personal service of copies of the petition and other papers on certain people, must see that these papers are served on certain other people by mail, and then must show the court that this has been done (called "proving service," or "proof of service").
- This form explains what papers must be served at the beginning of a limited conservatorship, who must be served with these papers, how and when service must be made, and how and when you, as a conservatorship petitioner, must prove to the court that service has been made.

What papers must be personally served at the beginning of a limited conservatorship case?

- A filled-in copy of the *Petition for Appointment of a Conservator* (the "*Petition*"). In a limited conservatorship of the person, this document is Form GC-310. Copies of all papers attached to the *Petition* must also be served with it.
- A filled-in copy of Form GC-320, *Citation for Conservatorship*, showing the date, time, and place of the hearing on the *Petition*, including the unsigned proof of service on the back page.

Who and what must be personally served?

- The adult who lives with developmental disabilities (or minor who will soon be an adult) who needs a limited conservatorship must be personally served with a copy of the *Petition* and a copy of the *Citation for Conservatorship*.

How do I arrange for personal service?

Someone-not you or anyone else who signed the *Petition* - must personally serve (hand-deliver copies of the *Citation* and *Petition* to the person who lives with developmental disabilities. Service lets this person know:

- That you are asking the court to appoint a limited conservator for the adult (or soon to be adult) named in the *Petition*.
- The person you want the court to appoint as limited conservator for the adult (or soon to be adult) named in the *Petition*.
- The date and time when, and the place where, the court will hear your request.

Who can serve?

- The server must be at least 18 years old.
- The server may be a registered process server in the business of delivering court forms for a cost. Look in a telephone directory under "Process Serving".
- The server may be a deputy sheriff you can locate in the civil division office at the courthouse. You will also have to pay for its services.

How does the server personally serve the *Citation* and the *Petition*?

- Walk up to the person to be served and make sure he or she is the right person.
- Hand the person copies of the court-stamped *Citation* and *Petition*.
- Fill out and sign the back page of the original *Citation* (with blue stamp from the court), *Proof of Personal Service*. Only the server can sign the form.
- Give you the filled-out and signed original *Citation* for e-filing.

Who else must be served at the beginning of a limited conservatorship case?

- The developmentally disabled person's
    - ☐ Parents (if they are not the petitioners)
    - ☐ Paternal Grandmother (father's mother)
    - ☐ Paternal Grandfather (father's father)
    - ☐ Maternal Grandmother (mother's mother)
    - ☐ Maternal Grandfather (mother's father)
    - ☐ Children (if any)
    - ☐ Spouse or domestic partner (if any)
    - ☐ Siblings (including half-sisters and half-brothers) if 12 years of age or older
    - ☐ Parents or guardians of siblings under the age of 12 years
    - ☐ Regional Center for your area

What documents must be served on these persons?

- A court-stamped copy of the *Petition* e-filed with the court.

- A court-stamped copy of Form GC-020, *Notice of Hearing*, showing the date, time, and place of the hearing on the *Petition*, including (unsigned) copies of all attachments showing proof of service.

How are these persons served?

Someone - not you or anyone else who signed the *Petition* - must mail copies of the *Notice of Hearing* and the *Petition* to the persons listed above. Service is designed to let each person know:

- That you are asking the court to appoint a limited conservator for the adult (or soon to be adult) named in the *Petition*.
- The person you want the court to appoint as limited conservator of the adult (or soon to be adult) named in the *Petition*.
- The date and time when, and the place where, the court will hear your request.

Does anyone get copies of more than those two documents?

The following persons are entitled to copies of every document e-filed in the court case:

- ☐ The attorney appointed by the court to represent the adult (or soon to be adult) living with developmental disabilities.
- ☐ The court's conservatorship investigation unit.

How is service given?

To prove you have served everyone required by law, you will e-file with the court:

- A filled-in *Notice of Hearing* showing who, when, and how someone other than the petitioner mailed copies of the required documents to everyone entitled to notice in this case, and
- The filled-in *Citation for Conservatorship* showing who, when, and where someone other than the petitioner personally served the adult (or soon to be adult) living with developmental disabilities;

making 3 copies of the court-stamped documents returned to petitioner for

1. The petitioner,
2. The court-appointed attorney for the proposed conservatee, and
3. The court investigator.

The documents must be e-filed with the court at least 15 days before the hearing on the *Petition for Appointment of Limited Conservator*.

GC-510 S ¿Qué es la "prueba de entrega" en una tutela?

¿Qué es la "entrega"?

- Cuando usted participa en un caso de la corte, es responsable por la entrega (**"aviso legal"**) de copias de los papeles importantes que presenta en la corte a otras personas que tienen que ver con el caso. Dependiendo de las circunstancias, esos papeles se deben entregar personalmente (llamado **"entrega personal"**) o se pueden entregar por correo (llamado "**entrega por correo**").
- Si presenta una petición para el nombramiento de un tutor para un niño, usted es el **solicitante**. Al principio del caso el solicitante debe hacer arreglos para la entrega personal de copias de la petición y de otros papeles a ciertas personas, tiene que verificar que esos papeles se entregan a ciertas personas por correo o por entrega personal (a opción del solicitante), y después tiene que demostrar a la corte que eso se hizo (llamado **"probar la entrega"** o **"prueba de entrega"**).
- Este formulario explica qué papeles se tienen que entregar al principio de una tutela, a quiénes se tienen que entregar esos papeles, cómo y cuándo se tiene que hacer la entrega y cómo y cuándo usted, como solicitante de una tutela, debe probar a la corte que se hizo la entrega. Puede averiguar más sobre los papeles que tiene que presentar en un formulario disponible en la corte, el **Formulario GC-505**, *Los formularios que necesita pedir a la corte para nombrar a un tutor de un menor de edad.*

¿Qué papeles se tienen que entregar al principio de un caso de tutela?

- **Una copia llenada de la petición de nombramiento de un tutor (la *"Petición"*).**
  En la tutela de un menor de edad, eso puede ser el **Formulario GC-210(P),** *Petición para nombrar al tutor de un menor de edad* o el **Formulario GC-210**, *Petición de tutela de un menor de edad.* También hay que entregar al mismo tiempo copias de todos los papeles adjuntos a la *Petición.*
- **Una copia llenada del Formulario GC-020,** *Aviso de audiencia de tutela de un menor o adulto,* (el *"Aviso de audiencia"*) con la fecha, la hora y el lugar de la audiencia en la *Petición,* incluyendo copias (no firmadas) de todos los anexos que demuestren que se entregaron los papeles.

¿A quiénes hay que entregar los papeles personalmente?

(Puede usar este formulario como una lista de control. Marque todo lo que corresponda a su caso.)

¡No entregue éstos por correo!

- ☐ Al niño que necesita tutor, pero sólo si tiene al menos 12 años de edad.
- ☐ A los padres del niño.
- ☐ A cualquier persona que tenga custodia legal del niño o que esté sirviendo como tutor nombrado por la corte de los bienes del niño (el **"patrimonio"** del niño).
- ☐ A todas las personas nombradas como tutores del niño por uno de los padres del niño, o por ambos padres (si su petición no pide a la corte que nombre a esa persona como tutor).
- ☐ A todas las personas nombradas como tutores del patrimonio del niño para bienes que recibió el niño de la persona que hace el nombramiento.

¿Cómo se hace la entrega personal?

Alguien, no usted ni ninguna persona que firmó la *Petición,* tiene que entregar personalmente (en mano) copias del *Aviso de audiencia* y de la *Petición* a las personas nombradas arriba. La entrega informa a esas personas:

- Que usted está pidiendo a la corte que nombre a un tutor para el niño nombrado en la *Petición.*
- Qué persona desea que la corte nombre como tutor (usted o alguna otra persona).
- La fecha, la hora y el lugar en que la corte escucha su pedido.

¿Quiénes pueden entregar los papeles?

Pídale a alguien que conozca, a un profesional de entrega registrado o a un representante de la división civil de los alguaciles del condado que entregue personalmente copias de los formularios a las personas nombradas arriba. Los formularios ***no*** se pueden enviar por correo a esas personas.

- El que entrega los papeles tiene que tener al menos 18 años de edad.
- Un profesional de entrega registrado es una empresa a la que usted paga para que entregue los papeles de la corte. Busque en el directorio telefónico bajo "Process Serving".
- La división civil de los alguaciles a menudo tiene una oficina en el tribunal. También tendrá que pagar por sus servicios.

¿Cómo se hace la entrega del *Aviso de Audiencia* y la *Petición?*

Pida a la persona que entregue los papeles que:

- Se acerque a persona a quien se tiene que entregar los papeles y que verifique que sea la persona correcta.
- Entregue en mano a cada persona copias llenadas del *Aviso de audiencia* y de la *Petición.*
- Llene y firme el **Formulario GC-020(P)**, *Prueba de entrega personal del Aviso de audiencia.* Si la persona que entrega papeles tiene que entregar a más personas que las que se puedan escribir en este formulario, pida al entregador que añada los nombres de las demás personas a las que entregó los papeles en una o más copias del **Formulario DE-120(PA)/GC-20(PA)**, *Anexo de la prueba de entrega personal del Aviso de audiencia.*
- Entregue a usted el **Formulario GC-020(P)** llenado y firmado y las páginas adjuntas, si las hay.

¿Qué pasa si la persona a la que se le entregan los papeles no los acepta o los rompe?

La persona que entrega tiene que intentar entregarlos personalmente (**¡pero de manera pacífica!**) incluso si la persona no quiere aceptar los papeles. No importa si la persona los rompe o los tira después de que se le entregan. **(Un profesional de entrega registrado o un alguacil sabrán cómo efectuar la entrega. Si le parece que alguien a quien se tenga que entregar papeles tratará de evitar que se los entreguen, conviene emplear uno de estos profesionales para que entreguen papeles a esa persona.)**

¿Quién firma la Prueba de entrega personal?

- Sólo la persona que entrega el *Aviso de audiencia* y la *Petición* puede firmar el **Formulario GC-020(P). Ni usted, ni ningún otro solicitante, ni la persona a la que le entregaron los papeles pueden firmar este formulario.**
- Si más de una persona entrega papeles personalmente, cada entregador tiene que llenar y firmar su propio **Formulario GC-020(P)** separado mostrando los nombres de las personas a las que entregó papeles.

¿A quiénes se les pueden entregar los papeles por correo?

(Puede usar este formulario como lista de control. Marque todo lo que corresponda a su caso.)

☐ A los parientes del niño que figuren en el **Formulario GC-210(CA)**, *Petición de tutela—Anexo de información sobre el niño,* adjunto a la *Petición.*

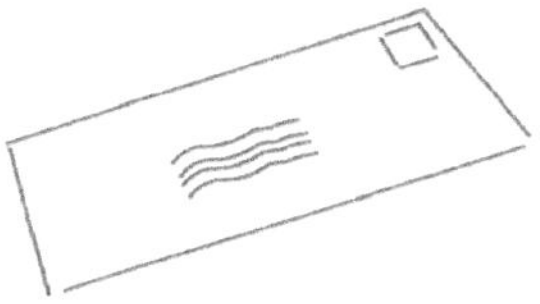

¡A estas personas se les pueden entregar los papeles por correo!

- ☐ Al abuelo (padre del padre)
- ☐ A la abuela (madre del padre)
- ☐ Al abuelo (padre de la madre)
- ☐ A la abuela (madre de la madre)
- ☐ Al/los hermano(s) (incluyendo los medios hermanos) (si tienen 12 años de edad o más)
- ☐ A la/las hermana(s) (incluyendo las medias hermanas) (si tienen 12 años de edad o más)

☐ **Si el niño tiene un hermano o hermana menores de 12 años de edad, hay que enviar copias por correo del *Aviso de audiencia* y de la *Petición* a una de las siguientes personas en su nombre, en lugar de enviarlas al hermano/a menor:**

- ☐ al padre o a la madre del hermano/a,
- ☐ al tutor del hermano/a nombrado por la corte, o
- ☐ a la persona con custodia legal del hermano o de la hermana que vive con ese hermano/a.

(Si un padre, tutor o custodio de un hermano o hermana del niño involucrado en el caso es solicitante, no es necesario entregar la notificación a esa persona en nombre del hermano o de la hermana.)

☐ Toda persona que tenga el cuidado físico del niño, pero que no tenga la custodia legal del niño.

☐ **Si su petición solicita el nombramiento de un tutor de un menor de edad que no es pariente del niño,** al: Director of the Department of Social Services, Children's Services Operations and Evaluation Branch, 744 P Street MS 3-34, Sacramento, CA 95814.

☐ **Es posible que su corte requiera que entregue papeles por correo a otras personas u organizaciones.** Averigüe cuáles son las reglas y las prácticas locales de su corte para determinar si esto le corresponde.

¿A quiénes se les pueden entregar los papeles por correo? (continuación)

- ☐ **Si el niño es un paciente de, o está de licencia de**, un hospital estatal administrado por los Departamentos del Estado de Salud Mental o de Discapacidades del Desarrollo, al director de ese departamento. La dirección del director de Salud Mental es Director of Mental Health, 1600 Ninth Street, Room 151, Sacramento, CA 95814. La dirección del director de Discapacidades del Desarrollo es Director of Developmental Disabilities, 1600 Ninth Street, Room 240, Sacramento, CA 95814, Attn.: Office of Legal Affairs.
- ☐ **Si el niño tiene discapacidades del desarrollo** y la persona que usted desea que se nombre como tutor: (1) no es uno de los padres naturales del niño; (2) es un proveedor de servicios a personas con discapacidades del desarrollo o el cónyuge o un empleado de un proveedor y (3) no es una entidad pública, al director del Centro Regional para Discapacitados del Desarrollo en el condado del niño. (Pero vea **¿Cuándo hay que entregar el *Aviso de audiencia* y la *Petición?***, en la página 4 de este formulario, para información sobre un requisito especial aplicable al envío de papeles por correo a un director de un Centro Regional.)
- ☐ **Si el niño es o puede ser un indígena norteamericano o es de ascendencia indígena norteamericano,** hay envíos por correo y otros requisitos que pueden ser aplicables a su caso. Esos requisios no se mencionan en este formulario. Si puede entrar en Internet, puede ir al sitio web del Centro de Ayuda de la Cortes de California para obtener información sobre los requisitos especiales para la tutela de un niño indígena norteamericano. La dirección del sitio web es *www.courtinfo.ca.gov/selfhelp/family/guardianship* (inglés) o *www.courtinfo.ca.gov/selfhelp/espanol/familia/tutela* (español).

¿A quiénes no es necesario entregar papeles (a menos que la corte indique lo contrario)?

A menos que la corte ordene que se les entreguen papeles, no necesita hacer arreglos para entregar papeles a los padres o a otros parientes de un niño que haya sido cedido a una agencia de adopción autorizada o a los padres de un niño que una corte haya declarado que está libre de la custodia y el control de sus padres.

¿Cómo hago los arreglos para la entrega por correo?

Alguien—no usted ni ninguna otra persona que haya firmado la *Petición*—tiene que hacer el envío por correo a las personas y organizaciones nombradas arriba que tengan que ver con su caso. "Hacer el envío por correo" significa poner los papeles en los sobres y entregar los sobres sellados a la posesión del Servicio Postal de EE UU. Alguna otra persona puede escribir la dirección en los sobres y añadir el franqueo, pero la persona que firma la prueba de entrega (vea abajo) puede poder decir que puso los papeles en los sobres y que entregó los sobres sellados al Servicio Postal de EE UU en una cierta fecha y en un lugar específico (ciudad y estado) y que las direcciones en los sobres eran como figuran en la prueba de entrega.

¿Quién puede hacer la entrega por correo?

- La persona que hace la entrega tiene que tener al menos 18 años de edad.
- No puede ser el solicitante ni un tutor propuesto en su caso.
- Tiene que vivir o estar empleada en el condado en que se hace el envío por correo (depositarlo en el Servicio Postal de EE UU).

¿Cómo se entrega por correo el *Aviso de audiencia* y la *Petición?*

Pida a la persona que entregue los papeles que:

- Deposite en el Servicio Postal de EE UU, con franqueo prepagado de primera clase, sobres sellados (se recomiendan sobres Manila de 9" x 12" o de 10" x 13") dirigidos a las personas u organizaciones que figuran arriba aplicables a su caso. Los sobres deben contener copias llenadas del **Formulario GC-020,** *Aviso de audiencia—Tutela de un menor o adulto* y de la *Petición*, incluyendo todas las páginas adjuntas mencionadas en ella.
- Verifique que las direcciones en los sobres para los parientes coincidan con las direcciones que aparezcan para esos parientes en el **Formulario GC-210(CA)** *Petición de tutela—Anexo de información sobre el niño* de cada niño.

¿Cómo se entrega el *Aviso de audiencia* y la *Petición* por correo? (continuación)

Pida a la persona que entregue los papeles que *(continuación):*

- Llene el formulario, feche y firme la *Prueba de entrega* en la segunda página del original del original del **Formulario GC-020. No firme ese formulario usted mismo.**
- Si hay más de cuatro personas a quienes se les entregarán documentos por correo, continúe la lista de personas a quienes se les entregará por correo en una o más copias del **Formulario DE-120(MA)/GC-020(MA)**, *Anexo del Aviso de audiencia—Prueba de entrega por correo.*
- Entregue a usted la *Prueba de entrega* original llenada y firmada y todas las páginas adjuntas que llenó.

¿Cuándo se tienen que entregar el *Aviso de audiencia* y la *Petición?*

- Cuando usted presente su *Petición*, el secretario de la corte la dará una fecha, hora y una sala o un departamento de la corte en que el juez oirá su pedido de nombramiento de tutor.
- Cuando tenga la fecha, la hora y el lugar de la audiencia, tiene que poner esa información en el **Formulario GC-020**, *Aviso de audiencia—Tutela de un menor o adulto*, y ese formulario y la *Petición*, con todas las páginas adjuntas a él, se deben entregar personalmente o entregar por correo a las personas y organizaciones mencionadas arriba que sean aplicables a su caso.
- Con la excepción señalada abajo, **la entrega personal y la entrega por correo se deben completar al menos 15 días antes de la fecha de la audiencia.**
- Si la entrega se tiene que hacer al Director del Centro Regional para los Discapacitados del Desarrollo del condado del niño, **la entrega se debe completar al menos 30 días antes de la audiencia.** Si el niño en su caso tiene una discapacidad del desarrollo y le parece que tendrá que entregar papeles de la corte al director del Centro Regional, es recomendable que cuando presente su Petición le pida al secretario una fecha de audiencia dentro de más tiempo, porque necesitará más tiempo que lo habitual para entregar el *Aviso de audiencia* y la *Petición.*

¿Qué pasa si los papeles no se entregan a tiempo?

Si el *Aviso de audiencia* y la *Petición* no se entregan a tiempo, la corte continuará (aplazará) la fecha de la audiencia en su Petición. Eso causará una demora del nombramiento de un tutor para el/los niño(s) involucrado(s) en este caso.

¿Qué hago con el *Aviso de audiencia* y las pruebas adjuntas de entrega personal y de entrega por correo?

- Presente en la corte al menos 5 días antes de la fechas de su audiencia el **Formulario GC-020,** *Aviso de audiencia—Tutela de un menor o adulto* original, con la Prueba de entrega llenada y firmada en la segunda página, el **Formulario GC-020(P)**, *Prueba de entrega personal del Aviso de audiencia—Tutela de un menor o adulto* llenado y firmado y todas las páginas adjuntas que muestren personas adicionales a las que se entregaron papeles de la corte. Presente esos papeles en la corte lo antes posible. El período de 5 días mencionado anteriormente es un período de tiempo mínimo.
- Cuando presente el **Formulario GC-020**, lleve consigo una copia adicional a la corte para que lo sellen, mostrando que el formulario original fue presentado en esa fecha.
- Lleve esa copia a la audiencia.

Frank and Mary Doe
1234 Any Street
Monterey, California 93940
Telephone: (831) 123-4567
Email: 2does@yahoo.com

Attorney for: In pro per

SUPERIOR COURT OF THE STATE OF CALIFORNIA

FOR THE COUNTY OF MONTEREY

In re the Limited Conservatorship of the Person of

JOHN DOE,

proposed conservatee.
_________________________________/

Case No.

PROOF OF SERVICE

Date: [Date of hearing]
Time: [Time of hearing]
Dept: [Court Department]

I, the undersigned say:

That I am now and at all times herein mentioned a citizen of the United States, over the age of eighteen years, a resident of __________ County, California, and not a party to the within action or cause; that my address is ____________________________; that on ___________, I served a copy of the following document(s):

EX PARTE ORDER REQUIRING REGIONAL CENTER TO PREPARE AN ASSESSMENT REPORT

PETITION FOR APPOINTMENT OF LIMITED CO-CONSERVATORS OF THE PERSON

NOTICE OF HEARING

on the following person(s) addressed as follows:

Evelyn Executive Director
SAN ANDREAS REGIONAL CENTER
33 Salinas Street, Suite 3
Salinas, CA 93901

by depositing the sealed envelope with the United States Postal Service at ______________, California, with the postage fully prepaid.

I declare under penalty of perjury under the laws of the State of California that the foregoing is true and correct. Executed on _________________, at _____________, California.

____
PRINTED NAME OF SERVER (not petitioner)

ATTORNEY OR PARTY WITHOUT ATTORNEY *(Name, State Bar number, and address):*	FOR COURT USE ONLY
Frank and Mary Doe 1234 Any Street Monterey, CA 93940 TELEPHONE NO.: (831) 123-4567 FAX NO. *(Optional):* E-MAIL ADDRESS *(Optional):* 2does@yahoo.com ATTORNEY FOR *(Name):* In pro per	
SUPERIOR COURT OF CALIFORNIA, COUNTY OF MONTEREY STREET ADDRESS: 1200 Aguajito Road MAILING ADDRESS: 1200 Aguajito Road CITY AND ZIP CODE: Monterey, CA 93940 BRANCH NAME: Monterey	
☐ GUARDIANSHIP ☑ CONSERVATORSHIP OF THE ☑ PERSON ☐ ESTATE OF *(Name):* JOHN DOE ☐ MINOR ☑ (PROPOSED) CONSERVATEE	
NOTICE OF HEARING—GUARDIANSHIP OR CONSERVATORSHIP	CASE NUMBER:

This notice is required by law.
This notice does not require you to appear in court, but you may attend the hearing if you wish.

1. NOTICE is given that *(name):* FRANK DOE and MARY DOE
(representative capacity, if any):
has filed *(specify):*

PETITION FOR APPOINTMENT OF LIMITED CONSERVATORSHIP OF THE PERSON

2. You may refer to documents on file in this proceeding for more information. *(Some documents filed with the court are confidential. Under some circumstances you or your attorney may be able to see or receive copies of confidential documents if you file papers in the proceeding or apply to the court.)*

3. ☐ The petition includes an application for the independent exercise of powers by a guardian or conservator under
☐ Probate Code section 2108 ☐ Probate Code section 2590.
Powers requested are ☐ specified below ☐ specified in Attachment 3.

4. A HEARING on the matter will be held as follows:

a. Date: [Insert hrg date] Time: [Insert time] ☑ Dept.: [Court dept] ☐ Room:

b. Address of court ☑ same as noted above ☐ is *(specify):*

Assistive listening systems, computer-assisted real-time captioning, or sign language interpreter services are available upon request if at least 5 days notice is provided. Contact the clerk's office for *Request for Accommodations by Persons with Disabilities and Order* (form MC-410). (Civil Code section 54.8.)

☐ GUARDIANSHIP ☑ CONSERVATORSHIP OF THE ☑ PERSON ☐ ESTATE	CASE NUMBER:
OF *(Name)*: JOHN DOE ☐ MINOR ☑ (PROPOSED) CONSERVATEE	

NOTE: *

A copy of this *Notice of Hearing—Guardianship or Conservatorship* ("Notice") must be "served" on—delivered to—each person who has the right under the law to be notified of the date, time, place, and purpose of a court hearing in a guardianship or conservatorship. Copies of this Notice may be served by mail in most situations. In a guardianship, however, copies of this Notice must sometimes be personally served on certain persons; and copies of this Notice may be personally served instead of served by mail in both guardianships and conservatorships. The petitioner (the person who requested the court hearing) **may not personally perform either service by mail or personal service**, but must show the court that copies of this Notice have been served in a way the law allows. The petitioner does this by arranging for someone else to perform the service and complete and sign a proof of service, which the petitioner then files with the original Notice.

This page contains a proof of service that may be used only to show service by mail. To show personal service, each person who performs the service must complete and sign a proof of personal service, and each signed copy of that proof of service must be attached to this Notice when it is filed with the court.. You may use form GC-020(P) to show personal service of this Notice.

* *(This Note replaces the clerk's certificate of posting on prior versions of this form. If notice by posting is desired, attach a copy of form GC-020(C),* Clerk's Certificate of Posting Notice of Hearing—Guardianship or Conservatorship. *(See Prob. Code, § 2543(c).)*

PROOF OF SERVICE BY MAIL

1. I am over the age of 18 and not a party to this cause. I am a resident of or employed in the county where the mailing occurred.
2. My residence or business address is *(specify)*:
   [Insert independent person's physical address]
3. I served the foregoing *Notice of Hearing—Guardianship or Conservatorship* on each person named below by enclosing a copy in an envelope addressed as shown below AND
   a. ☑ **depositing** the sealed envelope with the United States Postal Service on the date and at the place shown in item 4 with the postage fully prepaid.
   b. ☐ **placing** the envelope for collection and mailing on the date and at the place shown in item 4 following our ordinary business practices. I am readily familiar with this business's practice for collecting and processing correspondence for mailing. On the same day that correspondence is placed for collection and mailing, it is deposited in the ordinary course of business with the United States Postal Service in a sealed envelope with postage fully prepaid.
4. a. Date mailed: [Insert date mailed] b. Place mailed *(city, state)*: Monterey, California
5. ☑ I served with the *Notice of Hearing—Guardianship or Conservatorship* a copy of the petition or other document referred to in the Notice.

I declare under penalty of perjury under the laws of the State of California that the foregoing is true and correct.

Date: [Insert date signed]

Printed name of independent person ▶ ______________________

(TYPE OR PRINT NAME OF PERSON COMPLETING THIS FORM) (SIGNATURE OF PERSON COMPLETING THIS FORM)

NAME AND ADDRESS OF EACH PERSON TO WHOM NOTICE WAS MAILED

	Name of person served	Address *(number, street, city, state, and zip code)*
1.	Brian Doe	1234 Any Street Monterey, CA 93940
2.	Susan Doe	777 17th Street Collegetown, CA 95555
3.	Stephen Doe	3333 Wonder Avenue Disneyland, CA 93333
4.	Amy Roe	4444 Gallant Drive Rich Haven, CT 01111

☑ Continued on an attachment. *(You may use form DE-120(MA)/GC-020(MA) to show additional persons served.)*

☐ ESTATE ☐ GUARDIANSHIP ☑ CONSERVATORSHIP ☐ MATTER OF *(Name):* JOHN DOE	CASE NUMBER:

ATTACHMENT TO NOTICE OF HEARING PROOF OF SERVICE BY MAIL

(This Attachment is for use with forms DE-120 and GC-020.)

NAME AND ADDRESS OF EACH PERSON TO WHOM NOTICE WAS MAILED

No.	Name of person served	Address *(number, street, city, state, and zip code)*
5	Arnold Roe	5555 Neighborhood Lane Friendly, FL 09999
6	Court Investigation Unit	1200 Aguajito Road Monterey, CA 93940
7	Monterey County Public Defender	168 West Alisal Street Salinas, CA 93901

ATTORNEY OR PARTY WITHOUT ATTORNEY: STATE BAR NO.:	FOR COURT USE ONLY
NAME: Frank and Mary Doe FIRM NAME: STREET ADDRESS: 1234 Any Street CITY: Monterey STATE: CA ZIP CODE: 93940 TELEPHONE NO.: (831) 123-4567 FAX NO.: E-MAIL ADDRESS: 2does@yahoo.com ATTORNEY FOR (*name*): In pro per	
SUPERIOR COURT OF CALIFORNIA, COUNTY OF MONTEREY STREET ADDRESS: 1200 Aguajito Road MAILING ADDRESS: 1200 Aguajito Road CITY AND ZIP CODE: Monterey, CA 93940 BRANCH NAME: Monterey	
CONSERVATORSHIP OF THE [x] PERSON [ ] ESTATE of (*name*): JOHN DOE PROPOSED CONSERVATEE	
CITATION FOR CONSERVATORSHIP [ ] **Limited Conservatorship**	CASE NUMBER:

THE PEOPLE OF THE STATE OF CALIFORNIA,

To (*name*): JOHN DOE

1. **You are hereby cited and required to appear at a hearing in this court on**

   a. Date: [Insert hearing date] Time: [Insert time] [x] Dept.: [Court dept] [ ] Room:

   b. Address of court: [x] same as noted above [ ] other (*specify*):

   and to give any legal reason why, according to the verified petition filed with this court, you should not be found to be [x] unable to provide for your personal needs [ ] unable to manage your financial resources and by reason thereof, why the following person should not be appointed [ ] conservator [x] limited conservator of your [x] person [ ] estate (*name*): FRANK DOE and MARY DOE

2. A conservatorship of the person may be created for a person who is unable properly to provide for his or her personal needs for physical health, food, clothing, or shelter. A conservatorship of the property (estate) may be created for a person who is unable to resist fraud or undue influence, or who is substantially unable to manage his or her own financial resources. "Substantial inability" may not be proved solely by isolated incidents of negligence or improvidence.

3. At the hearing a conservator may be appointed for your [x] person [ ] estate.
   The appointment may affect or transfer to the conservator your right to contract, to manage and control your property, to give informed consent for medical treatment, to fix your place of residence, and to marry.

4. You may be disqualified from voting if you are found to be incapable of communicating, with or without reasonable accommodations, a desire to participate in the voting process. You will not be disqualified from voting on the basis that you do, or would need to do, any of the following to complete an affidavit of voter registration:
   a. Sign the affidavit of voter registration with a mark or a cross, pursuant to Section 2150(b) of the Elections Code;
   b. Sign the affidavit of voter registration by means of a signature stamp pursuant to Section 354.5 of the Elections Code;
   c. Complete the affidavit of voter registration with the assistance of another person pursuant to Section 2150(d) of the Elections Code; or
   d. Complete the affidavit of voter registration with reasonable accommodations.

5. The judge or the court investigator will explain to you the nature, purpose, and effect of the proceedings and answer questions concerning the explanation.

CONTINUED ON PAGE 2. THE CLERK'S SEAL IS ALSO ON THAT PAGE.

CONSERVATORSHIP OF THE ☐ PERSON ☐ ESTATE of *(name)*: PROPOSED CONSERVATEE	CASE NUMBER:

6. You have the right to appear at the hearing and oppose the petition. You have the right to hire an attorney of your choice to represent you. The court will appoint an attorney to represent you if you are unable to retain one. You must pay the cost of that attorney if you are able. You have the right to a jury trial if you wish.

7. *(For limited conservatorship only)* In addition to the rights stated in item 6 above, you have the right to oppose the petition in part by objecting to any or all of the requested duties or powers of the limited conservator.

Date: Clerk, by ______________________________, Deputy

(SEAL)

Assistive listening systems, computer-assisted real-time captioning, or sign language interpreter services are available upon request if at least 5 days notice is provided. Contact the clerk's office for *Request for Accommodations by Persons With Disabilities and Order* (form MC-410). (Civil Code section 54.8.)

CONSERVATORSHIP OF THE [✓] PERSON [ ] ESTATE of (name): JOHN DOE PROPOSED CONSERVATEE	CASE NUMBER:

PROOF OF SERVICE

1. At the time of service I was at least 18 years of age and not a party to this proceeding. **I served copies** of the *Citation for Conservatorship* and the *Petition for Appointment of Probate Conservator* (form GC-310) as follows:

2. a. Person cited *(name)*: JOHN DOE
   b. Person served: (1) [X] person in item 2a
   (2) [ ] other *(specify name and title or relationship to the person named in item 2a)*:
   c. Address *(specify)*: 1234 Any Street
   Monterey, CA 93940

3. I served the person named in item 2
   a. [X] **by personally delivering** the copies (1) on *(date)*: [Date served] (2) at *(time)*: [Time served]
   b. [ ] **by mailing** the copies to the person served, addressed as shown in item 2c, by first-class mail, postage prepaid,
   (1) on *(date)*: (2) from *(city)*:
   (3) [ ] with two copies of the *Notice and Acknowledgment of Receipt—Civil* and a postage-paid return envelope addressed to me. *(Attach completed* Notice and Acknowledgment of Receipt—Civil *(form POS-015).)*
   (4) [ ] to an address outside California with return receipt requested. *(Attach completed return receipt.)*
   c. [ ] **other** *(specify other manner of service, and the authorizing code section and order of the court)*:

4. a. Person serving *(name, address, and telephone number)*:
   Sally Service
   333 You From Me Road
   Monterey, CA 93940
   (831) 444-6666
   b. [ ] Fee for service: $
   c. [X] Not a registered California process server.
   d. [ ] Exempt from registration under Business and Professions Code section 22350(b).
   e. [ ] Registered California process server.
   (1) [ ] Employee or independent contractor.
   (2) Registration no. *(specify)*:
   (3) County *(specify)*:
   (4) Expiration *(date)*:

5. [X] **I declare** under penalty of perjury under the laws of the State of California that the foregoing is true and correct.
6. [ ] **I am a California sheriff or marshal** and I certify that the foregoing is true and correct.

Date: [Insert date signed]

▶ ______________________________
(SIGNATURE OF PERSON SERVING)

ATTORNEY OR PARTY WITHOUT ATTORNEY: STATE BAR NO.:	FOR COURT USE ONLY
NAME: Frank and Mary Doe FIRM NAME: STREET ADDRESS: 1234 Any Street CITY: Monterey STATE: CA ZIP CODE: 93940 TELEPHONE NO.: (831) 123-4567 FAX NO.: E-MAIL ADDRESS: 2does@yahoo.com ATTORNEY FOR *(name)*: In pro per	
SUPERIOR COURT OF CALIFORNIA, COUNTY OF MONTEREY STREET ADDRESS: 1200 Aguajito Road MAILING ADDRESS: 1200 Aguajito Road CITY AND ZIP CODE: Monterey, CA 93940 BRANCH NAME: Monterey	
CONSERVATORSHIP OF *(name)*: JOHN DOE CONSERVATEE	
ORDER APPOINTING ☐ SUCCESSOR **PROBATE CONSERVATOR OF THE ☒ PERSON ☐ ESTATE** **☒ Limited Conservatorship**	CASE NUMBER:

WARNING: THIS APPOINTMENT IS NOT EFFECTIVE UNTIL LETTERS HAVE ISSUED.

1. The petition for appointment of ☐ successor conservator came on for hearing as follows *(check boxes c, d, e, and f or g to indicate personal presence)*:
   a. Judicial officer *(name)*: The Honorable Judy Judge
   b. Hearing date: [Insert date] Time: [Insert time] ☒ Dept.: [Ct Dept] ☐ Room:
   c. ☒ Petitioner *(name)*: FRANK DOE and MARY DOE
   d. ☐ Attorney for petitioner *(name)*:
   e. ☒ Attorney for ☒ person cited ☐ the conservatee on petition to appoint successor conservator:
   (Name): Monterey County Public Defender *(Telephone)*: (831) 755-5058
   (Address): 168 West Alisal Street
   Salinas, CA 93901
   f. ☒ Person cited was ☒ present. ☐ unable to attend. ☐ able but unwilling to attend. ☐ out of state.
   g. ☐ The conservatee on petition to appoint successor conservator was ☐ present. ☐ not present.

THE COURT FINDS

2. All notices required by law have been given.
3. Granting the conservatorship is the least restrictive alternative needed for the protection of the conservatee.
4. *(Name)*: JOHN DOE
   a. ☒ is unable properly to provide for his or her personal needs for physical health, food, clothing, or shelter.
   b. ☐ is substantially unable to manage his or her financial resources or to resist fraud or undue influence.
   c. ☐ has voluntarily requested appointment of a conservator and good cause has been shown for the appointment.
5. The conservatee
   a. ☐ is an adult.
   b. ☒ will be an adult on the effective date of this order.
   c. ☐ is a married minor.
   d. ☐ is a minor whose marriage has been dissolved.
6. ☒ There is no form of medical treatment for which the conservatee has the capacity to give an informed consent.
   ☐ The conservatee is an adherent of a religion defined in Probate Code section 2355(b).
7. ☐ Granting the ☐ successor conservator powers to be exercised independently under Probate Code section 2590 is to the advantage and benefit and in the best interest of the conservatorship estate.
8. ☒ The conservatee cannot communicate, with or without reasonable accommodations, a desire to participate in the voting process.

Do NOT use this form for a temporary conservatorship.

CONSERVATORSHIP OF *(name)*: CONSERVATEE	CASE NUMBER:

9. [ ] The conservatee has dementia as defined in Probate Code section 2356.5, and the court finds all other facts required to make the orders specified in item 28.
10. [x] Attorney *(name)*: Monterey County Public Defender has been appointed by the court as legal counsel to represent the conservatee in these proceedings. The cost for representation is: $
The conservatee has the ability to pay [ ] all [x] none [ ] a portion of this sum *(specify)*: $
11. [ ] The conservatee need not attend the hearing.
12. [x] The appointed court investigator is *(name)*: Court Investigation Unit
(Address and telephone): 1200 Aguajito Road, Monterey, CA 93940 Telephone (831) 010-2002
13. [x] *(For limited conservatorship only)* The limited conservatee is developmentally disabled as defined in Probate Code section 1420.
14. [ ] The [ ] successor conservator is a professional fiduciary as defined by Business and Professions Code section 6501(f).
15. [ ] The [ ] successor conservator holds a valid, unexpired, unsuspended license as a professional fiduciary issued by the Professional Fiduciaries Bureau of the California Department of Consumer Affairs under chapter 6 (commencing with section 6500) of division 3 of the Business and Professions Code.
License no.: Issuance or last renewal date: Expiration date:
16. *(Either a, b, or c must be checked)*:
a. [x] The [ ] successor conservator is not the spouse of the conservatee.
b. [ ] The [ ] successor conservator is the spouse of the conservatee and is not a party to an action or proceeding against the conservatee for legal separation, dissolution, annulment, or adjudication of nullity of their marriage.
c. [ ] The [ ] successor conservator is the spouse of the conservatee and is a party to an action or proceeding against the conservatee for legal separation, dissolution, annulment, or adjudication of nullity of their marriage.
It is in the best interest of the conservatee to appoint the spouse as [ ] successor conservator.
17. *(Either a, b, or c must be checked)*:
a. [x] The [ ] successor conservator is not the domestic partner or former domestic partner of the conservatee.
b. [ ] The [ ] successor conservator is the domestic partner of the conservatee and has neither terminated nor intends to terminate their domestic partnership.
c. [ ] The [ ] successor conservator is the domestic partner or former domestic partner of the conservatee and intends to terminate or has terminated their domestic partnership. It is in the best interest of the conservatee to appoint the domestic partner or former domestic partner as [ ] successor conservator.

THE COURT ORDERS

18. a. *(Name)*: FRANK DOE and MARY DOE *(Telephone)*: (831) 123-4567
(Address): 1234 Any Street, Monterey, CA 93940

is appointed [ ] successor [ ] conservator [x] limited conservator of the PERSON of *(name)*:
JOHN DOE and *Letters of Conservatorship* shall issue upon qualification.

b. *(Name)*: *(Telephone)*:
(Address):

is appointed [ ] successor [ ] conservator [ ] limited conservator of the ESTATE of *(name)*:
and *Letters of Conservatorship* shall issue upon qualification.

19. [ ] The conservatee need not attend the hearing.
20. a. [x] Bond is not required.
b. [ ] Bond is fixed at: $ to be furnished by an authorized surety company or as otherwise provided by law.
c. [ ] Deposits of: $ are ordered to be placed in a blocked account at *(specify institution and location)*:

and receipts shall be filed. No withdrawals shall be made without a court order.
[ ] Additional orders in attachment 20c.

CONSERVATORSHIP OF (name): JOHN DOE CONSERVATEE	CASE NUMBER:

20. *(cont.)*
   d. ☐ The ☐ successor conservator is not authorized to take possession of money or any other property without a specific court order.

21. ☐ For legal services rendered, ☐ conservatee ☐ conservatee's estate shall pay the sum of: $
to *(name)*:
☐ forthwith ☐ as follows *(specify terms, including any combination of payors)*:

☐ Continued in attachment 21.

22. ☒ The conservatee is disqualified from voting.

23. ☒ The conservatee lacks the capacity to give informed consent for medical treatment and the ☐ successor conservator of the person is granted the powers specified in Probate Code section 2355.
   ☐ The treatment shall be performed by an accredited practitioner of a religion as defined in Probate Code section 2355(b).

24. ☐ The ☐ successor conservator of the estate is granted authorization under Probate Code section 2590 to exercise independently the powers specified in attachment 24 ☐ subject to the conditions provided.

25. ☐ Orders relating to the capacity of the conservatee under Probate Code sections 1873 or 1901 as specified in attachment 25 are granted.

26. ☐ Orders relating to the powers and duties of the ☐ successor conservator of the person under Probate Code sections 2351–2358 as specified in attachment 26 are granted. (*Do not include orders under Probate Code section 2356.5 relating to dementia.)*

27. ☐ Orders relating to the conditions imposed under Probate Code section 2402 on the ☐ successor conservator of the estate as specified in attachment 27 are granted.

28. ☐ a. ☐ The ☐ successor conservator of the person is granted authority to place the conservatee in a care or nursing facility described in Probate Code section 2356.5(b).
   b. ☐ The ☐ successor conservator of the person is granted authority to authorize the administration of medications appropriate for the care and treatment of dementia described in Probate Code section 2356.5(c).

29. ☐ Other orders as specified in attachment 29 are granted.

30. ☐ The probate referee appointed is *(name and address)*:

31. ☒ *(For limited conservatorship only)* Orders relating to the powers and duties of the ☐ successor limited conservator of the person under Probate Code section 2351.5 as specified in attachment 31 are granted.

32. ☐ *(For limited conservatorship only)* Orders relating to the powers and duties of the ☐ successor limited conservator of the estate under Probate Code section 1830(b) as specified in attachment 32 are granted.

33. ☒ *(For limited conservatorship only)* Orders limiting the civil and legal rights of the limited conservatee as specified in attachment 33 are granted.

34. ☒ This order is effective on the ☐ date signed ☒ date minor attains majority *(specify)*: June 15, 2018

35. Number of boxes checked in items 18–34: 8

36. Number of pages attached: 1

Date:

JUDICIAL OFFICER

☑ SIGNATURE FOLLOWS LAST ATTACHMENT

Limited Conservatorship of John Doe
Order Appointing Limited Co-Conservators

Attachment 31

The limited co-conservators are granted the following powers under Probate Code §2351.5(b):

(1) To fix the residence or specific dwelling of the limited conservatee.
(2) To access to the confidential records and papers of the limited conservatee.
(4) To limit the right of the limited conservatee to contract.
(5) To give or withhold medical consent for the limited conservatee.
(7) To make decisions concerning the education of the limited conservatee.

Attachment 33

The limited co-conservators are granted the authority to limit conservatee's civil and legal rights as follows:

(1) To limit the limited conservatee's right to choice of residence or specific dwelling.
(2) To limit the limited conservatee's sole access to his confidential records and papers.
(4) To limit the limited conservatee's right to contract.
(5) To limit the limited conservatee's right to consent or withhold consent to medical treatment.
(7) To limit the limited conservatee's right to make decisions concerning his education.

Date: ________________________

____
JUDGE OF THE SUPERIOR COURT

Approved as to form and content:

____
DEPUTY PUBLIC DEFENDER

GC-350

ATTORNEY OR PARTY WITHOUT ATTORNEY *(name, address, and State Bar number)*:
After recording return to:

Frank and Mary Doe
1234 Any Street
Monterey, CA 93940

TEL NO.: (831) 123-4567 FAX NO. *(optional)*:
E-MAIL ADDRESS *(optional)*: 2does@yahoo.com
ATTORNEY FOR *(name)*: In pro per

SUPERIOR COURT OF CALIFORNIA, COUNTY OF MONTEREY
STREET ADDRESS: 1200 Aguajito Road
MAILING ADDRESS: 1200 Aguajito Road
CITY AND ZIP CODE: Monterey, CA 93940
BRANCH NAME: Monterey

FOR RECORDER'S USE ONLY

CONSERVATORSHIP OF *(name)*:
JOHN DOE
CONSERVATEE

CASE NUMBER:
[Court will insert case number]

FOR COURT USE ONLY

LETTERS OF CONSERVATORSHIP

[x] **Person** [ ] **Estate** [x] **Limited Conservatorship**

1. [x] *(Name):* FRANK DOE and MARY DOE is the appointed
[ ] conservator [x] limited conservator of the [x] person [ ] estate
of *(name):* JOHN DOE
2. [ ] *(For conservatorship that was on December 31, 1980, a guardianship of an adult or of the person of a married minor) (Name):*
was appointed the guardian of the [ ] person [ ] estate by order dated *(specify)*: and is now the conservator of the [ ] person [ ] estate of *(name):*
3. [x] Other powers have been granted or conditions imposed as follows:
   a. [x] Exclusive authority to give consent for and to require the conservatee to receive medical treatment that the conservator in good faith based on medical advice determines to be necessary even if the conservatee objects, subject to the limitations stated in Probate Code section 2356.
      (1) [ ] This treatment shall be performed by an accredited practitioner of the religion whose tenets and practices call for reliance on prayer alone for healing of which the conservatee was an adherent prior to the establishment of the conservatorship.
      (2) [ ] *(If court order limits duration)* This medical authority terminates on *(date)*:
   b. [ ] Authority to place the conservatee in a care or nursing facility described in Probate Code section 2356.5(b).
   c. [ ] Authority to authorize the administration of medications appropriate for the care and treatment of dementia described in Probate Code section 2356.5(c).
   d. [ ] Powers to be exercised independently under Probate Code section 2590 are specified in Attachment 3d *(specify powers, restrictions, conditions, and limitations)*.
   e. [ ] Conditions relating to the care and custody of property under Probate Code section 2402 are specified in Attachment 3e.
   f. [ ] Conditions relating to the care, treatment, education, and welfare of the conservatee under Probate Code section 2358 are specified in Attachment 3f.
   g. [x] *(For limited conservatorship only)* Powers of the limited conservator of the person under Probate Code section 2351.5 are specified in Attachment 3g.
   h. [ ] *(For limited conservatorship only)* Powers of the limited conservator of the estate under Probate Code section 1830(b) are specified in Attachment 3h.
   i. [x] Other powers granted or conditions imposed are specified in Attachment 3i.

(SEAL)

4. [ ] The conservator is **not** authorized to take possession of money or any other property without a specific court order.

5. Number of pages attached:

WITNESS, clerk of the court, with seal of the court affixed.
Date:

Clerk, by ______________________________, Deputy

This form may be recorded as notice of the establishment of a conservatorship of the estate as provided in Probate Code § 1875.

CONSERVATORSHIP OF *(name):* CONSERVATEE	CASE NUMBER:

NOTICE TO INSTITUTIONS AND FINANCIAL INSTITUTIONS
(Probate Code sections 2890–2893)

When these *Letters of Conservatorship* (Letters) are delivered to you as an employee or other representative of an *institution* or *financial institution* (described below) in order for the conservator of the estate (1) to take possession or control of an asset of the conservatee named above held by your institution (including changing title, withdrawing all or any portion of the asset, or transferring all or any portion of the asset) or (2) to open or change the name of an account or a safe-deposit box in your financial institution to reflect the conservatorship, you must fill out Judicial Council form GC-050 (for an institution) or form GC-051 (for a financial institution). An officer authorized by your institution or financial institution must date and sign the form, and you must file the completed form with the court.

There is no filing fee for filing the form. You may either arrange for personal delivery of the form or mail it to the court for filing at the address given for the court on page 1 of these Letters.

The conservator should deliver a blank copy of the appropriate form to you with these Letters, but it is your institution's or financial institution's responsibility to complete the correct form, have an authorized officer sign it, and file the completed form with the court. If the correct form is not delivered with these Letters or is unavailable for any other reason, blank copies of the forms may be obtained from the court. The forms may also be accessed from the judicial branch's public Web site free of charge. The Internet address (URL) is *www.courts.ca.gov/forms/.* Select the form group *Probate—Guardianships and Conservatorships* and scroll down to form GC-050 for an institution or form GC-051 for a financial institution. The forms may be printed out as blank forms and filled in by typewriter or may be filled out online and printed out ready for signature and filing.

An *institution* under California Probate Code section 2890(c) is an insurance company, agent, or broker; an investment company; an investment bank; a securities broker-dealer; an investment advisor; a financial planner; a financial advisor; or any other person who takes, holds, or controls an asset subject to a conservatorship or guardianship other than a financial institution. Institutions must file a *Notice of Taking Possession or Control of an Asset of Minor or Conservatee* (form GC-050) for an asset of the conservatee held by the institution. A single form may be filed for all affected assets held by the institution.

A *financial institution* under California Probate Code section 2892(b) is a bank, a trust, a savings and loan association, a savings bank, an industrial bank, or a credit union. Financial institutions must file a *Notice of Opening or Changing a Guardianship or Conservatorship Account or Safe-Deposit Box* (form GC-051) for an account or a safe-deposit box held by the financial institution. A single form may be filed for all affected accounts or safe-deposit boxes held by the financial institution.

LETTERS OF CONSERVATORSHIP

AFFIRMATION

I solemnly affirm that I will perform according to law the duties of ☐ conservator ☒ limited conservator.

Executed on *(date):* [Insert filing date] , at *(place):* [Insert city and state where signed]

FRANK DOE and MARY DOE
(TYPE OR PRINT NAME)

▶ ______________________________
(SIGNATURE OF APPOINTEE)

CERTIFICATION

I certify that this document, including any attachments, is a correct copy of the original on file in my office, and that the Letters issued to the person appointed above have not been revoked, annulled, or set aside, and are still in full force and effect.

(SEAL)

Date:

Clerk, by ______________________________, Deputy

Limited Conservatorship of John Doe
Letters of Co-Conservatorship

Attachment 3g

The limited co-conservators are granted the following powers under Probate Code §2351.5(b):

(1) To fix the residence or specific dwelling of the limited conservatee.
(2) To access to the confidential records and papers of the limited conservatee.
(4) To limit the right of the limited conservatee to contract.
(5) To give or withhold medical consent for the limited conservatee.
(7) To make decisions concerning the education of the limited conservatee.

Attachment 3i

The limited co-conservators are granted the authority to limit conservatee's civil and legal rights as follows:

(1) To limit the limited conservatee's right to choice of residence or specific dwelling.
(2) To limit the limited conservatee's sole access to his confidential records and papers.
(4) To limit the limited conservatee's right to contract.
(5) To limit the limited conservatee's right to consent or withhold consent to medical treatment.
(7) To limit the limited conservatee's right to make decisions concerning his education.

ATTORNEY OR PARTY WITHOUT ATTORNEY (Name, State Bar number, and address):	FOR COURT USE ONLY
Frank and Mary Doe 1234 Any Street Monterey, CA 93940 TELEPHONE NO.: (831) 123-4567 FAX NO. (Optional): E-MAIL ADDRESS (Optional): 2does@yahoo.com ATTORNEY FOR (Name): In pro per	
SUPERIOR COURT OF CALIFORNIA, COUNTY OF MONTEREY STREET ADDRESS: 1200 Aguajito Road MAILING ADDRESS: 1200 Aguajito Road CITY AND ZIP CODE: Monterey, CA 93940 BRANCH NAME: Monterey	
CONSERVATORSHIP OF THE ☑ PERSON ☐ ESTATE OF (Name): JOHN DOE CONSERVATEE	
NOTICE OF CONSERVATEE'S RIGHTS	CASE NUMBER: [Insert case number here]

When a person becomes a conservatee, he or she does not necessarily lose the right to take part in important decisions affecting his or her property and way of life. Every conservatee has the right to be treated with understanding and respect and to have his or her wishes considered. Every conservatee has all basic human rights and the right to be well cared for by his or her conservator.

The conservatee has the right to ask questions and to express concerns and complaints about the conservatorship and the actions of his or her conservator. The conservatee may ask the court to review the conservator's management of the conservatorship if disputes cannot be worked out between them. Even if the conservatee does not take direct action, the court will periodically send a person, called a **court investigator**, to visit the conservatee, to inquire about his or her circumstances and desires, and to advise the conservatee of his or her rights. The court also may appoint a lawyer to represent the conservatee.

The conservatee will be allowed the greatest degree of freedom and privacy possible consistent with the underlying reasons for the conservatorship. The conservator should give as much regard to the wishes of the conservatee as possible under the circumstances so that the conservatee may function at the highest level his or her ability permits. The conservator must give due regard to the preferences of the conservatee and to encourage the conservatee's participation in decision-making.

THE CONSERVATEE'S RIGHTS

After appointment of a conservator, the conservatee keeps the right to:

- Be represented by a lawyer;
- Ask a judge to replace the conservator;
- Ask a judge to end the conservatorship;
- Make or change his or her will;
- Directly receive and control his or her salary; and
- Control an allowance (an allowance is personal spending money the court has authorized the conservator to pay directly to the conservatee).

(Conservatee's rights continued on next page)

CONSERVATORSHIP OF THE ☑ PERSON ☐ ESTATE OF (*Name*): JOHN DOE CONSERVATEE	CASE NUMBER: [Insert case number here]

THE CONSERVATEE'S RIGHTS (continued)

Unless the court has limited or taken the right away, the conservatee also keeps the right to:

- Receive personal mail;
- Vote;
- Marry or enter into a registered domestic partnership;
- Receive visits from family and friends;
- Make his or her own medical decisions;
- Enter into transactions, to the extent reasonable to (1) provide the necessaries of life to the conservatee and his or her minor children, and (2) provide the necessaries of life to his or her spouse or basic living expenses to his or her registered domestic partner;
- Engage in other activities the court expressly allows him or her to do, at the time of the conservator's appointment, or a later time following a court hearing on a request for authority to engage in the activity; and
- If the conservatee is a **limited conservatee**, to engage in any activity that the court has not expressly reserved to his or her **limited conservator.**

(Proof of mailing on page 3)
(Instructions for mailing on page 4)

CONSERVATORSHIP OF THE ☑ PERSON ☐ ESTATE OF (Name): JOHN DOE — CONSERVATEE	CASE NUMBER: [Insert case number here]

PROOF OF MAILING

1. I am over the age of 18. I am the appointed conservator of the above-named conservatee, the conservator's attorney, or an employee of the conservator's attorney. I am a resident of or employed in the county where the mailing occurred.
2. My residence or business address is *(specify)*:
   [Insert independent person's physical address]
3. I mailed the foregoing *Notice of Conservatee's Rights* to each person named below by enclosing a copy in an envelope addressed as shown below AND
   a. ☑ **depositing** the sealed envelope on the date and at the place shown in item 4 with the United States Postal Service with the postage fully prepaid.
   b. ☐ **placing** the envelope for collection and mailing on the date and at the place shown in item 4 following our ordinary business practices. I am readily familiar with this business's practice for collecting and processing correspondence for mailing. On the same day that correspondence is placed for collection and mailing, it is deposited in the ordinary course of business with the United States Postal Service in a sealed envelope with postage fully prepaid.
4. a. Date mailed: [Insert date] b. Place mailed *(city, state)*: Monterey, California
5. Each copy of the *Notice of Conservatee's Rights* was mailed with an attached conformed copy, showing the date of its filing and the judicial officer's signature, of the *Order Appointing Probate Conservator* filed in this matter on *(date)*: [Date order signed] .

I declare under penalty of perjury under the laws of the State of California that the foregoing is true and correct.

Date: [Insert date mailed]

Printed name of independent person
(TYPE OR PRINT NAME OF PERSON COMPLETING THIS FORM)

▶ ______________________________
(SIGNATURE OF PERSON COMPLETING THIS FORM)

NAME AND ADDRESS OF EACH PERSON TO WHOM NOTICE WAS MAILED

	Name and relationship to conservatee	Address *(number, street, city, state, and zip code)*
1.	John Doe Conservatee	1234 Any Street Monterey, CA 93940
2.	Monterey County Public Defender Attorney for conservatee	168 West Alisal Street Salinas, CA 93901
3.	Spouse or registered domestic partner	
4.	Brian Doe Relationship: Brother	1234 Any Street Monterey, CA 93940
5.	Susan Doe Relationship: Sister	777 17th Street Collegetown, CA 95555

☑ Continued on an attachment. *(You may use form GC-341(MA) to show additional addressees.)*

CONSERVATORSHIP OF THE [✔] PERSON [ ] ESTATE OF (Name): JOHN DOE CONSERVATEE	CASE NUMBER: [Insert case number here]

INSTRUCTIONS FOR MAILING COPIES OF *NOTICE OF CONSERVATEE'S RIGHTS* AND *ORDER APPOINTING PROBATE CONSERVATOR*

1. **What to mail:** The conservator, the conservator's attorney, or the attorney's employee must mail a copy of this *Notice of Conservatee's Rights*, **with an attached copy of the *Order Appointing Probate Conservator* showing the judicial officer's signature and the date of filing,** to each person identified in item 2 below.
2. **Who must receive the mailing:** The persons to whom copies of this *Notice of Conservatee's Rights* and the *Order Appointing Probate Conservator* must be mailed are:
   a. The conservatee;
   b. The conservatee's attorney, if any;
   c. The following relatives of the conservatee named in Probate Code section 1821(b) (spouse or registered domestic partner and second-degree relatives required to be named in the *Petition for Appointment of Probate Conservator*):
      (1) Spouse or registered domestic partner;
      (2) Parents;
      (3) Children at least 12 years old (see item e below if there are children under the age of 12);
      (4) Grandparents;
      (5) Grandchildren at least 12 years old (see item e below if there are grandchildren under the age of 12); and
      (6) Brothers and sisters, including half-brothers and half-sisters.
   d. If the conservator knows of no spouse or registered domestic partner or second-degree relative of the conservatee, copies of this *Notice of Conservatee's Rights* and the *Order Appointing Probate Conservator* must be mailed to the following persons:
      (1) Spouse or registered domestic partner of a predeceased parent of the conservatee;
      (2) Children of a predeceased spouse or predeceased registered domestic partner of the conservatee at least 12 years old (see item e below if there are children under the age of 12);
      (3) Brothers and sisters of the conservatee's parents (conservatee's aunts and uncles), if any, or, if none, to their natural and adoptive children at least 12 years old (see item e below if there are children under the age of 12); and
      (4) The natural and adoptive children of the conservatee's brothers and sisters at least 12 years old (see item e below if there are children under the age of 12).
   e. If a person named above is under the age of 12, a parent, guardian, or other person having legal custody of the person entitled to notice, with whom the person entitled to notice resides.
3. **When the mailing must be completed:** The mailing described in item 1 must be completed on or before the 30th day following the filing date of the *Order Appointing Probate Conservator.*
4. **Fill out Proof of Mailing:** The conservator or his or her attorney of record must fill out the Proof of Mailing on page 3 of this form, including the correct addresses of the persons to receive the mailing, identified in item 2 above, before making the copies to be mailed. If the Proof of Mailing does not have enough space for the names and addresses of all persons who will receive the mailing, the names and addresses not shown on the Proof of Mailing must be shown on one or more additional pages attached to this form. One or more copies of *Attachment to Notice of Conservatee's Rights* (form GC-341(MA)) may be used for this purpose.
   After the mailing described in item 5 below, the conservator or his or her attorney must date and sign the Proof of Mailing on page 3 of this form.
5. **How to mail:** The conservator, the conservator's attorney of record, or an employee of the attorney, must do the following:
   a. Place copies of this *Notice of Conservatee's Rights*, with attached conformed copies of the *Order Appointing Probate Conservator* in sealed envelopes, addressed to each person at the address shown for that person on the Proof of Mailing on page 3 of this form, or on attached additional pages, with postage fully prepaid.
   b. Deposit (mail) the sealed envelope(s) with the United States Postal Service on the date and from the place (city and state) shown in item 4 of the Proof of Mailing on page 3 of this form.
6. **Filing Notice of Conservatee's Rights:** The conservator, or his or her attorney of record, must file with the court the original *Notice of Conservatee's Rights*, with a signed and dated Proof of Mailing and all attached additional address pages.
   Do not attach a copy of the *Order Appointing Probate Conservator* to the original *Notice of Conservatee's Rights* filed with the court.

CONSERVATORSHIP OF THE ☑ PERSON ☐ ESTATE OF (Name): JOHN DOE — CONSERVATEE	CASE NUMBER: [Insert case number here]

ATTACHMENT TO NOTICE OF CONSERVATEE'S RIGHTS

(This attachment is for use with Form GC-341.)

NAME AND ADDRESS OF EACH PERSON TO WHOM NOTICE WAS MAILED

	Name and relationship to conservatee	Address *(number, street, city, state, and zip code)*
6	Stephen Doe Relationship: Paternal Grandfather	3333 Wonder Avenue Disneyland, CA 93333
7	Amy Roe Relationship: Maternal Grandmother	4444 Gallant Drive Rich Haven, CT 01111
8	Arnold Roe Relationship: Maternal Grandfather	5555 Neighborhood Lane Friendly, FL 09999
9	Court Investigation Unit Relationship: Court Investigator	1200 Aguajito Road Monterey, CA 93940
	Relationship:	
	Relationship:	
	Relationship:	
	Relationship:	
	Relationship:	

Form Approved for Optional Use
Judicial Council of California
GC-341(MA) [New January 1, 2008]

ABOGADO o PARTE SIN ABOGADO: *(Nombre, Núm. del colegio de abogados estatal y dirección):* TELÉFONO: FAX: EMAIL: ABOGADO DE (nombre):	SOLO PARA USO DE LA CORTE ***Solo para Información*** ***No entregue a la corte***
CORTE SUPERIOR DE CALIFORNIA, CONDADO DE DIRECCIÓN (calle y número): DIRECCIÓN POSTAL: CIUDAD Y CÓDIGO POSTAL: NOMBRE DE LA SUCURSAL:	
TUTELA DE ADULTO ☐ DE LA PERSONA ☐ DEL PATRIMONIO DE *(Nombre):* PUPILO	
AVISO DE DERECHOS DEL PUPILO	NÚMERO DE CASO:

Si una persona se convierte en pupilo, no necesariamente perderá el derecho a participar en las decisiones importantes que afectan su vida o sus bienes. Todo pupilo tiene el derecho a ser tratado con comprensión y respeto, y a que se tengan en cuenta sus deseos. También cuenta con todos los derechos humanos básicos y al derecho a a un buen cuidado por parte del tutor.

También tiene el derecho de hacer preguntas y expresar sus dudas y quejas sobre la tutela y sobre las acciones del tutor. Si el pupilo tiene una disputa con su tutor y no la puede resolver, puede pedirle a la corte que revise la manera en que el tutor está administrando la tutela. Incluso si el pupilo no toma ninguna acción directa para pedirle a la corte que revise las acciones del tutor, la corte puede enviar periódicamente a una persona, llamada "**investigador de la corte**", para que lo vea, le pregunte sobre su situación y deseos, y lo informe sobre sus derechos. La corte también puede nombrar a un abogado para que lo represente.

El pupilo tendrá la máxima libertad y privacidad posibles en vista de los motivos que hayan generado la tutela. El tutor debe tomar en cuenta los deseos del pupilo en la mayor medida de lo posible según las circunstancias, de manera que el pupilo pueda desempeñarse al mayor nivel posible según su capacidad. El tutor debe prestar debida atención a las preferencias del pupilo y alentar la participación del pupilo en la toma de decisiones.

DERECHOS DEL PUPILO

Después de la designación de un tutor, el pupilo conserva los siguientes derechos:

- Tener un abogado;
- Pedir al juez que cambie el tutor;
- Pedir al juez que dé por terminada la tutela;
- Hacer o cambiar su testamento;
- Recibir y controlar directamente su propio salario; y
- Controlar su dinero para gastos personales (esto sería dinero que la corte haya autorizado al tutor pagarle directamente al pupilo)

(Los derechos del pupilo continúan en la página siguiente)

TUTELA DE ADULTO ☐ DE LA PERSONA ☐ DEL PATRIMONIO DE *(Nombre)*: ***Solo para información*** PUPILO	NÚMERO DE CASO: ***No entregue a la corte***

DERECHOS DEL PUPILO (continuación)

El pupilo también conserva los siguientes derechos, a menos que la corte los haya limitado o quitado:

- Recibir correspondencia;
- Votar;
- Casarse o tener una pareja de hecho;
- Recibir visitas de familiares y amigos;
- Tomar sus propias decisiones sobre atención de la salud;
- Realizar, en la medida de lo razonable, transacciones financieras para (1) suplir las necesidades básicas del pupilo y de sus hijos menores, y (2) suplir las necesidades básicas de su cónyuge o gastos básicos de su pareja de hecho registrada;
- Participar en otras actividades expresamente permitidas por la corte cuando nombre al tutor, o más adelante después de una audiencia para considerar una solicitud de participar en la actividad; y
- Si el pupilo es un **pupilo limitado**, participar de todas las actividades que la corte no haya reservado expresamente a su **tutor limitado**.

(Prueba de envío por correo, en la página 3)
(Instrucciones para el envío por correo, en la página 4)

TUTELA DE ADULTO ☐ DE LA PERSONA ☐ DEL PATRIMONIO DE *(Nombre)*: ***Solo para información*** PUPILO	NÚMERO DE CASO: ***No entregue a la corte***

PRUEBA DE ENVÍO POR CORREO

1. Soy mayor de 18 años. Soy el tutor nombrado del pupilo mencionado, el abogado del tutor o un empleado del abogado del tutor. Soy residente de o trabajo en el condado dónde se realizó el envío por correo.
2. La dirección de mi domicillio o trabajo es *(especificar)*.
3. Envié por correo el *Aviso de derechos del pupilo* a cada persona mencionada más adelante adjuntando una copia en un sobre con la dirección según lo indicado más adelante Y
   a. ☐ **depositando** el sobre cerrado en la fecha y en el lugar indicados en el punto 4 en el Correo de los Estados Unidos con franqueo prepagado.
   b. ☐ **colocando** el sobre para que fuera recogido y enviado por correo en la fecha y en el lugar que se indican en el punto 4 según nuestras prácticas comerciales habituales. Estoy bien familiarizado con la práctica comercial de recolectar y procesar correspondencia para su envío por correo. El mismo día en que se deja la correspondencia para su recolección y envío por correo, se deposita, según los trámites habituales, en el Servicio Postal de los Estados Unidos en un sobre cerrado con franqueo prepago.
4. a. Fecha de envío: b. Lugar de envío *(ciudad, estado)*:
5. Cada copia del *Aviso de derechos del pupilo* fue enviada con una copia conforme adjunta, que muestra la fecha de presentación y la firma del funcionario judicial, de la *Orden de nombramiento de un tutor testamentario* presentada en este caso el (*fecha*).

Declaro bajo pena de perjurio conforme a las leyes del estado de California que lo anterior es verdadero y correcto.

Fecha:

(NOMBRE DE LA PERSONA QUE LLENA EL FORMULARIO ESCRITO A MÁQUINA O EN LETRA DE MOLDE)	▶ (FIRMA DE LA PERSONA QUE LLENA EL FORMULARIO)

NOMBRE Y DIRECCIÓN DE CADA UNA DE LAS PERSONAS A LAS QUE SE LES ENVIÓ EL AVISO

	Nombre y relación con el pupilo	Dirección *(número, calle, ciudad, estado y código postal)*
1.	Pupilo	
2.	Abogado del pupilo	
3.	Cónyuge o pareja de hecho registrada	
4.	Relación:	
5.	Relación:	

☐ Sigue en el adjunto. *(Puede usar el formulario GC-341(MA) para incluir más direcciones.)*

TUTELA DE ADULTO ☐ DE LA PERSONA ☐ DEL PATRIMONIO DE *(Nombre)*: ***Solo para información*** PUPILO	NÚMERO DE CASO: ***No entregue a la corte***

INSTRUCCIONES PARA ENVIAR POR CORREO COPIAS DEL *AVISO DE DERECHOS DEL PUPILO* Y DE LA *ORDEN DE NOMBRAMIENTO DE UN TUTOR TESTAMENTARIO*

1. **Qué hay que enviar:** El tutor, el abogado del tutor o el empleado del abogado tienen que enviar por correo una copia de este *Aviso de derechos del pupilo,* **con una copia adjunta de la *Orden de nombramiento de un tutor testamentario* con la firma del funcionario judicial y la fecha de presentación,** a cada una de las personas indicadas en el punto 2 siguiente.

2. **Quién tiene que recibir el envío:** Las personas a las que hay que enviar por correo el *Aviso de derechos del pupilo* y la *Orden de nombramiento de un tutor testamentario* son:
   a. El pupilo;
   b. El abogado del pupilo, si lo tuviera;
   c. Los siguientes familiares del pupilo mencionados en la sección 1821(b) del Código Testamentario (cónyuge o pareja de hecho registrada y familiares en el segundo grado que tengan que ser mencionados en la *Solicitud de nombramiento de tutor de un adulto)*:
      (1) Cónyuge o pareja de hecho registrada;
      (2) Padres;
      (3) Hijos de 12 años o más (ver el punto "e" a continuación si hay hijos menores de 12 años);
      (4) Abuelos;
      (5) Nietos de 12 años o más (ver el punto "e" a continuación si hay nietos menores de 12 años); y
      (6) Hermanos y hermanas, incluidos los medio hermanos y las medio hermanas.
   d. Si el tutor no sabe de la existencia de un cónyuge o pareja de hecho registrada o de familiares en el segundo grado del pupilo, hay que enviar copias de este *Aviso de derechos del pupilo* y de la *Orden de nombramiento de un tutor testamentario* a las siguientes personas:
      (1) Cónyuge o pareja de hecho registrada de un padre que ya haya fallecido del pupilo;
      (2) Hijos de 12 años o más de un cónyuge o pareja de hecho registrada que ya haya fallecido del pupilo (ver el punto "e" a continuación si hay hijos menores de 12 años);
      (3) Hermanos y hermanas de los padres del pupilo (tíos y tías del pupilo), si los hubiera, o, si no hubiera, sus hijos biológicos y adoptivos de 12 años o más (ver el punto "e" a continuación si hay hijos menores de 12 años); e
      (4) Hijos biológicos y adoptivos de los hermanos y hermanas del pupilo de 12 años o más (ver el punto "e" a continuación si hay hijos menores de 12 años).
   e. Si una de las personas mencionadas anteriormente tiene menos de 12 años, uno de los padres, el tutor u otra persona que tenga la custodia legal de la persona con derecho a recibir el aviso, con quien viva la persona con derecho a recibir el aviso.

3. **Cuándo hay que realizar el envío:** El envío por correo explicado en el punto 1 debe haber terminado a más tardar 30 días después de la fecha de presentación de la *Orden de nombramiento de un tutor testamentario.*

4. **Completar la prueba de envío por correo:** El tutor o su abogado tienen que completar la Prueba de envío por correo de la página 3 de este formulario, incluyendo la dirección correcta de las personas que tienen que recibir el correo, mencionadas en el punto 2 anterior, antes de hacer las copias que se enviarán. Si la Prueba de envío por correo no tiene suficiente espacio para los nombres y las direcciones de todas las personas que recibirán el correo, los nombres y las direcciones que no quepan en la Prueba de envío por correo tienen que incluirse en una o más páginas adicionales adjuntas a este formulario. Se pueden usar una o más copias del *Adjunto al Aviso de derechos del pupilo* (formulario GC-341(MA)) para esos fines.
   Después de hacer el envío por correo mencionado en el punto 5 siguiente, el tutor o su abogado tiene que fechar y firmar la Prueba de envío por correo de la página 3 de este formulario.

5. **Cómo hacer el envío por correo:** El tutor, el abogado del tutor o un empleado del abogado tiene que hacer lo siguiente:
   a. Poner las copias de este *Aviso de derechos del pupilo,* con las copias conformes adjuntas de la *Orden de nombramiento de un tutor testamentario,* en sobres cerrados, dirigidos a la dirección de cada persona indicada en la Prueba de envío por correo de la página 3 de este formulario o en hojas adicionales adjuntas, con franqueo prepagado.
   b. Depositar (enviar por correo) el/los sobre/s cerrado/s en el Servicio Postal de los Estados Unidos, en la fecha y desde el lugar (ciudad y estado) indicados en el punto 4 de la Prueba de envío por correo de la página 3 de este formulario.

6. **Presentación del Aviso de derechos del pupilo:** El tutor o su abogado tiene que presentar en la corte el *Aviso de derechos del pupilo* original, con una Prueba de envío por correo firmada y fechada y todas las páginas de direcciones adicionales adjuntas.
   No adjunte una copia de la *Orden de nombramiento de un tutor testamentario* al *Aviso de derechos del pupilo* original presentado en la corte.

ATTORNEY OR PARTY WITHOUT ATTORNEY *(Name, State Bar number, and address):*	FOR COURT USE ONLY
Frank and Mary Doe 1234 Any Street Monterey, CA 93940 TELEPHONE NO.: (831) 123-4567 FAX NO. *(Optional):* E-MAIL ADDRESS *(Optional):* 2does@yahoo.com ATTORNEY FOR *(Name):* In pro per	
SUPERIOR COURT OF CALIFORNIA, COUNTY OF MONTEREY STREET ADDRESS: 1200 Aguajito Road MAILING ADDRESS: 1200 Aguajito Road CITY AND ZIP CODE: Monterey, CA 93940 BRANCH NAME: Monterey	
CONSERVATORSHIP OF THE PERSON ☐ AND ESTATE OF *(Name):* JOHN DOE CONSERVATEE	
DETERMINATION OF CONSERVATEE'S APPROPRIATE LEVEL OF CARE	CASE NUMBER: [Insert case number here]

Notice to Conservator of the Person

You must prepare a written determination of the conservatee's appropriate level of care, sign it under penalty of perjury, and file it with the court within 60 days of the date of the court's order appointing you as conservator. You must use this form for that purpose. Your determination must include an evaluation of the conservatee's level of care on the date the conservatorship proceeding was started (the date the petition for the appointment of a conservator was filed with the court or, if more than one petition was filed, the date the first petition was filed), and the measures that would be necessary to keep the conservatee in his or her **personal residence.** If the conservatee was not living in that residence on the date the proceeding was started, your determination must include either a plan to return the conservatee to that residence or an explanation of the reasons why the conservatee cannot return to that residence in the foreseeable future. **This determination is in addition to, not a replacement for, any written care or placement plan the court may require. Check the court's local rules to see if a care or placement plan must also be filed.**

The conservatee's **personal residence** is the residence he or she understood or believed, or appeared to understand or believe, was his or her permanent residence on the date the conservatorship proceeding was started, whether or not he or she was living there on that date. If the conservatee could not then form or communicate an understanding or belief about his or her permanent residence, the conservatee's personal residence is the residence he or she last previously understood or appeared to understand was his or her permanent residence. (See Cal. Rules of Court, rule 7.1063.)

(Name): FRANK DOE and MARY DOE , declares as follows:

1. I am conservator of the person of the above-named conservatee. I am determining the conservatee's appropriate level of care as of *(date):* [Date order signed] , the date of the order appointing me as conservator.

2. a. On the date stated in item 1, the conservatee was living at the following residence or facility *(address and name of facility, if any):*
   Family's residence

   1234 Any Street
   Monterey, CA 93940

   Telephone: (831) 123-4567

   b. The conservatee has been living in the above residence or facility since *(date):* 05/12/2005 .

CONSERVATORSHIP OF (*Name*): JOHN DOE CONSERVATEE	CASE NUMBER: [Insert case number here]

2. c. The residence or facility identified in item 2a is described as follows *(select all that apply)*:

[✓] Conservatee's single family home, condominium, or apartment
[ ] Relative's or friend's single family home, condominium, or apartment
[ ] Acute care hospital [ ] Acute psychiatric hospital [ ] Intermediate-care facility [ ] Skilled nursing facility
[ ] Licensed residential care facility [ ] Assisted living facility (7 or more beds)
[ ] Board and care home (6 or fewer beds) [ ] Continuing-care retirement community [ ] Secured perimeter
[ ] Congregate living health facility—terminal or life-threatening illness type (hospice)
[ ] Other *(describe)*:

3. a. The conservatee's care requirements as of the date given in item 1 are as follows *(select all that apply; you may provide additional information concerning any items selected below under "other assistance required")*:

[✓] No assistance is needed at this time. [ ] Light housekeeping help required, ____ hours per week.
[ ] Personal caregivers required, ____ hours per week: [ ] 24-hour care [ ] Part-time, ____ hours per day.
[ ] Assistance with daily living skills, ____ hours per week.
[ ] Nursing care required, ____ hours per week. [ ] Meal preparation assistance required, ____ hours per week.
[ ] Assistance with medication required, ____ hours per week: [ ] Dispensing [ ] Set-up only
[ ] Assistance with ambulation: [ ] Maximum [ ] Standby [ ] In-home hospice services.
[✓] Other assistance required, 5 hours per week *(describe)*:

Travel to and from educational facility weekdays is provided by MPUSD.

Parents and siblings provide assistance with activities of daily living as needed.

[ ] Continued on Attachment 3a.

b. [ ] A professional assessment of the conservatee's care needs has been made. A copy of the assessment, including a statement of the professional's qualifications, is provided on Attachment 3b. *(A professional assessment of the conservatee's care needs is not required, but is recommended if the conservatee's circumstances and condition warrant it and the conservatee can afford the expense. Include any written assessment performed by a professional fiduciary proposed for appointment or appointed as conservator.)*

CONSERVATORSHIP OF (Name): JOHN DOE CONSERVATEE	CASE NUMBER: [Insert case number here]

4. *(Complete item 4a if the residence identified in item 2 is the conservatee's* personal residence *as defined in Cal. Rules of Court, rule 7.1063. Complete item 4b if the residence identified in item 2 is not the conservatee's* personal residence.*)*

a. [✓] **Conservatee living in personal residence**
The residence or facility described in item 2 is the conservatee's **personal residence** within the meaning of Cal. Rules of Court, rule 7.1063. The following measures are necessary to keep the conservatee in that residence:

Conservatee lives with his parents. There is no plan to move conservatee to another residential facility for the foreseeable future.

San Andreas Regional Center reporting psychologists stated in their report filed on April 26, 2018, that "John's mother is a teacher, and [John] has been home schooled since kindergarten...John's parents appear to have his best interests at heart."

The court investigator stated in his report filed on April 26, 2018, that "the continuing placement with the proposed conservatee's family appears to be the least restrictive and appropriate setting."

[ ] Continued on Attachment 4a.

b. [ ] **Conservatee not living in personal residence**
The residence or facility described in item 2 **is not** the conservatee's **personal residence** within the meaning of Cal. Rules of Court, rule 7.1063. The conservatee's **personal residence** is *(address and name of facility, if any):*

(Complete either item 4b(1) below or item 4b(2) on page 4. Complete item 4b(1) if you believe the conservatee can be returned to his or her personal residence *in the foreseeable future. Complete item 4b(2) if you believe the conservatee cannot be returned to his or her* personal residence *in the foreseeable future.)*

(1) [ ] The conservator's plan to restore the conservatee to his or her **personal residence** is as follows:

[ ] Continued on Attachment 4b(1).

CONSERVATORSHIP OF (Name): JOHN DOE CONSERVATEE	CASE NUMBER: [Insert case number here]

4. b. (2) ☐ The limitations or restrictions on the conservatee's return to his or her **personal residence** in the foreseeable future are as follows:

☐ Continued on Attachment 4b(2).

5. Number of pages attached: _____

I declare under penalty of perjury under the laws of the State of California that the foregoing is true and correct.

Date: [Insert date signed]

FRANK DOE and MARY DOE ▶ ______________________

(TYPE OR PRINT NAME OF CONSERVATOR OF THE PERSON) (SIGNATURE OF CONSERVATOR OF THE PERSON)

Appendix B
Timelines

Timeline for Temporary Conservatorships:

Five (5) days are required for service to all interested parties before the Temporary hearing can be set. In Monterey County, hearings are scheduled on Thursdays at 10:00 a.m. in Department 13.

Call the Conservatorship Investigation Unit and let them know you will be filing a Temporary Conservatorship.	Day 1
E-file paperwork necessary for the Temporary Conservatorship (Petition, Notice of Hearing, Capacity Declaration, together with all paperwork for the permanent hearing date).	Day 1
Submit executed Temporary Letters (dated same date as filing) to the court clerk.	Day 1
Serve the Temporary Petition and Notice of Hearing on all relatives to the 2nd degree, the proposed conservatee, the Court-appointed Attorney for the proposed conservatee, and the Court Investigator by personal service once you have confirmed the date with the court clerk.	Day 1
Sign the Proof of Service on the back of the Notice of Hearing, and E-file the Notice of Hearing for Temporary Conservatorship showing all were served 5 days before the hearing, not counting the date of service.	Day 2

Timeline for Permanent Conservatorships:

In Monterey County, you should set the hearing date forty-five (45) days from the date you file the paperwork.

E-file paperwork for Conservatorship (see list of documents in Exercise #10).	Day 1
Submit the executed Letters (dated same date as filing date) to the court clerk.	Day 1
Serve all filed documents on the Court Investigation Unit and the Court-appointed Attorney for the proposed conservatee.	Day 2
Serve the Notice of Hearing and Petition on all interested persons, sign the Proof of Service on the back of the Notice of Hearing, and e-file the Notice of Hearing with the court.	At least 15 days before the hearing date
Serve the Citation and a copy of the Petition on the proposed conservatee, sign the Proof of Personal Service on the back of the Citation, and e-file the Citation with the court, serving a copy on the Court Investigation Unit and the Court-appointed Attorney for the proposed conservatee.	At least 15 days before the hearing date

Timeline After Appointment of Conservator:

Serve the Notice of Conservatee's Rights (with a copy of the Order) on the conservatee, all relatives to the 2nd degree, the Court Investigator, and the Court-appointed Attorney.	Within 30 days of appointment
Sign the Proof of Service on page 3 of the Notice of Conservatee's Rights, and e-file it with the court (without an attached copy of the Order).	Within 30 days of appointment
Complete and e-file the Determination of Conservatee's Appropriate Level of Care with Proof of Service showing copies were served on the Court Investigator and the Court-appointed Attorney for the conservatee.	Within 60 days of appointment

Acknowledgments

The book has been a remarkable journey, due to the encouragement and assistance of many individuals, which is a story in itself. I want to thank Tony Robbins for helping me discover this calling in my life, Brendon Burchard for honing my entrepreneurial skills, Julie Cavassa for her mentoring and coaching, Holly Craig for her tenacity and perseverance, Charlotte Ophaug for her edits and suggestions, Judge Kay T. Kingsley and Judge Elisabeth K. Mineta for their reviews and encouragement, Nate Danielson, Jeni.Leah Bullock, Joaquin Gonzalez, Tammy Nunez, and Eamon Winston for their participation in the workshops and enlightening dialogs over bagels and fruit, and my unfailingly supportive husband and best friend Miguel Mejía, together with dozens of colleagues and friends who walked this journey with us all.

Soli Deo Gloria,

Barbara Mejía

Meet the Author

Barbara Mejía is a California licensed attorney with over 27 years of experience in legal matters affecting persons who are parties to conservatorship proceedings. She has represented conservators, conservatees, parents, grandparents, children, and siblings. Prior to her legal career, she taught high school English for 14 years in Salinas, California.

Ms. Mejía designed this Workbook to supplement her practice in conservatorship law. She recognizes that every person has unique gifts to share with the world. Protecting the legal rights of those living with developmental disabilities is an opportunity to structure the setting for continuing growth and opportunities. Parents using this Workbook have changed their blueprints of life to make a space that works best for their children, that opens for them so that all of their potential as human beings can blossom. They want to watch and pray and be there to encourage their children to color their worlds, to make their imprint on the worlds that are uniquely theirs. They know what dreams their children have dreamed and the challenges they have faced. And they have seen what incredible work ethic their children have brought to every new adventure as they have grown up from their youth to this time. The conservatorship process is just the next step.

Barbara is married to a former school counselor/teacher. She is a step-mother, grandmother, and great grandmother.

She is passionate about educating and equipping individuals to understand and take control of their unique family needs for the protection of their persons and estates.

She welcomes readers' feedback at her website: www.barbaramejia.com.

Made in the USA
Middletown, DE
05 November 2026

36599694R00117